PEER INTERACTION AND SECOND LANGUAGE LEARNING

Peer Interaction and Second Language Learning synthesizes the existing body of research on the role of peer interaction in second language learning in one comprehensive volume. In spite of the many hours that language learners spend interacting with peers in the classroom, there is a tendency to evaluate the usefulness of this time by comparison to whole class interaction with the teacher. Yet teachers are teachers and peers are peers—as partners in interaction, they are likely to offer very different kinds of learning opportunities. This book encourages researchers and instructors alike to take a new look at the potential of peer interaction to foster second language development. Acknowledging the context of peer interaction as highly dynamic and complex, the book considers the strengths and limitations of peer work from a range of theoretical perspectives. In doing so, *Peer Interaction and Second Language Learning* clarifies features of effective peer interaction for second language learning across a range of educational contexts, age spans, proficiency levels, and classroom tasks and settings.

Jenefer Philp works in the Department of Linguistics and English Language at Lancaster University and is a research associate of the University of Auckland.

Rebecca Adams is the associate director of the Center for Faculty Excellence at Northcentral University and is a research associate of the University of Auckland.

Noriko Iwashita is a senior lecturer in applied linguistics at The University of Queensland.

Second Language Acquisition Research Series: Theoretical and Methodological Issues

Susan M. Gass and Alison Mackey, Editors

Monographs on Theoretical Issues:

Schachter/Gass Second Language Classroom Research: Issues and Opportunities (1996)

Birdsong Second Language Acquisition and the Critical Period Hypotheses (1999)

Ohta Second Language Acquisition Processes in the Classroom: Learning Japanese (2001)

Major Foreign Accent: Ontogeny and Phylogeny of Second Language Phonology (2001)

VanPatten Processing Instruction: Theory, Research, and Commentary (2003)

VanPatten/Williams/Rott/Overstreet Form-Meaning Connections in Second Language Acquisition (2004)

Bardovi-Harlig/Hartford Interlanguage Pragmatics: Exploring Institutional Talk (2005)

Dörnyei The Psychology of the Language Learner: Individual Differences in Second Language Acquisition (2005)

Long Problems in SLA (2007)

VanPatten/Williams Theories in Second Language Acquisition (2007)

Ortega/Byrnes The Longitudinal Study of Advanced L2 Capacities (2008)

Liceras/Zobl/Goodluck The Role of Formal Features in Second Language Acquisition (2008)

Philp/Adams/Iwashita Peer Interaction and Second Language Learning (2013)

Monographs on Research Methodology:

Tarone/Gass/Cohen Research Methodology in Second Language Acquisition (1994)

Yule Referential Communication Tasks (1997)

Gass/Mackey Stimulated Recall Methodology in Second Language Research (2000)

Markee Conversation Analysis (2000)

Gass/Mackey Data Elicitation for Second and Foreign Language Research (2007)

Duff Case Study Research in Applied Linguistics (2007)

McDonough/Trofimovich Using Priming Methods in Second Language Research (2008)

Larson-Hall A Guide to Doing Statistics in Second Language Research Using SPSS (2009)

Dörnyei/Taguchi Questionnaires in Second Language Research: Construction, Administration, and Processing, Second Edition (2009)

Bowles The Think-Aloud Controversy in Second Language Research (2010)

Jiang Conducting Reaction Time Research for Second Language Studies (2011)

Barkhuizen/Benson/Chik Narrative Inquiry in Language Teaching and Learning Research (2013)

Of Related Interest:

Gass Input, Interaction, and the Second Language Learner (1997)

Gass/Sorace/Selinker Second Language Learning Data Analysis, Second Edition (1998)

Mackey/Gass Second Language Research: Methodology and Design (2005)

Gass/Selinker Second Language Acquisition: An Introductory Course, Third Edition (2008)

PEER INTERACTION AND SECOND LANGUAGE LEARNING

Jenefer Philp, Rebecca Adams, and Noriko Iwashita

Lancaster University, Northcentral University, and
The University of Queensland, Brisbane

 Routledge
Taylor & Francis Group

NEW YORK AND LONDON

First published 2014
by Routledge
711 Third Avenue, New York, NY 10017

Published in the UK
by Routledge
2 Park Square, Milton Park, Abingdon, Oxon OX14 4RN

Routledge is an imprint of the Taylor & Francis Group,
an informa business

Library of Congress Cataloging-in-Publication Data

Philp, Jenefer.
Peer interaction and second language learning / By Jenefer Philp,
    Rebecca Adams, and Noriko Iwashita ; Lancaster University,
    Northcentral University, and The University of Queensland, Brisbane.
        pages cm. — (Second Language Acquisition Research Series)
    Includes bibliographical references.
    1. Language and languages—Study and teaching. 2. Interaction
analysis in education. 3. Conversation analysis. I. Adams, Rebecca
Jane. II. Iwashita, Noriko. III. Title.
    P53.447.P55 2014
    418.0071—dc23
    2013016247

ISBN: 978-0-415-89571-2 (hbk)
ISBN: 978-0-415-89572-9 (pbk)
ISBN: 978-0-203-55134-9 (ebk)

Typeset in Bembo
by Apex CoVantage LLC

Editor: Leah Babb-Rosenfeld

Editorial Assistant: Elysse Preposi

Production Manager: Sioned Jones

Marketing Manager: Deb Donnelly Robinson

Project Manager: Kimberly Cleary

Copy Editor: Heather F. Brashear

Proofreader: Kay Mariea

Cover Design: John Maloney

Printed and bound in the United States of America by
Edwards Brothers Malloy

CONTENTS

SECTION III
The Purpose and Mode of Peer Interaction   **121**

ACKNOWLEDGMENTS

We are grateful to our series editors, Alison Mackey and Sue Gass, for their encouragement to write this book, and their support and feedback along the way. We acknowledge with heartfelt thanks our colleagues, friends, and family who supported us in the writing of this book. Rob Batstone, Sue Duchesne, Marije Michel, and Anne Philp kindly read earlier drafts of chapters in the manuscript and provided invaluable feedback. Similarly, we greatly appreciate the work of the anonymous external reviewer, for insightful and timely feedback on the manuscript. We also appreciate the support and expertise of our other colleagues at the University of Auckland, The University of Queensland, and Lancaster University, for peer talk and allowing us to draw on their expertise. Any remaining errors are our own.

We thank those who generously gave us permission to use their unpublished raw classroom data sets to draw from: Katherine Cao, Rhonda Oliver, and Rita Tognini. We also acknowledge the support of The University of Queensland Promoting Women Fellowship and the Department of Linguistics and English Language, Lancaster University, for financial assistance.

To our family and friends, without whom this book would not have been possible, thank you for keeping us going and cheering us on along the way.

1

DEFINITIONS, DESCRIPTIONS, AND UNDERSTANDINGS OF PEER INTERACTION

Why a Book on Peer Interaction?

In spite of the many hours of class time that learners spend in pair and group work with other learners, we still continue to think about and evaluate the usefulness of this time in comparison to whole class interaction with the teacher. Often our reference point is the principles developed from research on interaction between native speakers and nonnative speakers, between teachers and students (Block, 2003; Ellis, 2008; Mackey, 2012). Yet, as we'll see, teachers are teachers and peer are peers—as partners in interaction, they are likely to offer quite different kinds of learning opportunities. Now that there is a growing body of research on peer interaction, it is time to take a step back and consider peer interaction in its own right. What is it really like? What are its strengths? What are the limitations? Specific to instructed language learning, how can we make the most of peer interaction? This is the principal purpose of the book: to examine what the literature to date has to say about peer interaction as a context for language learning, within a range of classroom settings. We'll explore how peers contribute to language learning, acknowledging this context as highly dynamic and complex and unlikely to be readily understood from any one perspective.

The central focus of this book then is a particular context. Within the classroom environment as a whole, peer interaction is a context in which the participants are all language learners who are together for the purpose of learning. As we will see, the nature of this context is somewhat of a kaleidoscope: It changes with the shifting combinations of those involved, how they relate to one another, the activity in which they are engaged, their purposes and means, and so on. In this book, we explore the complex patterns of peer interaction and its potential contribution to second language (L2) learning by children, adolescents, and adults within the classroom setting.

In traditional language classrooms, peer interaction wasn't considered a context for learning. Teaching was solely the province of the teacher, and peers were no more than classmates. Perhaps this was largely due to a very different conception of teaching and learning. The view of *learning* as essentially transmission of "knowledge" from teacher to student has now changed dramatically. Current theories describe learning as being less about transfer of knowledge (what the teacher tells the student) and more about learners' appropriation of the new within existing understandings. This is realized not in the sole context of the teacher's instruction to a class of students, but through a diversity of contexts. This view emphasizes the role played by learners themselves in the teaching and learning process (Duchesne, McMaugh, Bochner, & Krause, 2013; Wray, 2010).

Child, adolescent, and adult language learners, in second or foreign language contexts worldwide now spend significant amounts of time interacting with other students in the class, rather than only with the teacher. One reason that peer interaction has been advocated in language classrooms is because it is different from teacher-learner interaction and, therefore, allows for different types of language use and practice. Long and Porter (1985), for example, suggested that peer interaction allowed for learners to practice communication patterns beyond the "teacher-led lockstep" mode, granting learners opportunities to engage in negotiation as well as to take on new conversational roles. Harmer (2001) points out that teacher-learner interaction in a full class setting guarantees each learner very little time to actually speak, but talking time for any one student is dramatically expanded in peer interactions.

This greater reliance on peer interaction as a context for language practice and use is matched by a steadily growing multidisciplinary body of research, from social, cognitive, and other perspectives. It includes research within the field of education on the role of peer interaction for learning and, more recently, in the field of L2 acquisition. This richness of perspective is vital, as O'Donnell (2006), speaking of the role of peers in learning, notes: "No single theoretical perspective on peer learning (. . .) can explain how knowledge and skill is acquired in the widely varied tasks and demands of the classroom" (p. 781). For this reason, this book endeavors to represent the contribution of peer interaction from a range of perspectives.

This first chapter provides a platform from which to explore the contribution of peer interaction to L2 learning and its limitations. We begin by considering what we mean when we talk about "peers" and peer interaction, including the varied types of peer learning, and common goals in the use of peer interaction in the classroom. We then briefly outline cognitive and social perspectives of peer interaction and learning as these underlie the research surveyed in this book. We conclude with an overview of the structure of the book, which is based on three key dimensions shaping the nature of peer interaction. This provides a framework for considering strengths and limitations of peer interaction within the classroom setting.

What Is Peer Interaction?

We describe as peer interaction any communicative activity carried out *between learners*, where there is minimal or no participation from the teacher. This can include cooperative and collaborative learning, peer tutoring, and other forms of help from peers. Blum-Kulka and Snow (2009) describe peer talk as having a "collaborative, multiparty, symmetrical participation structure." It is collaborative in the sense of participants working together toward a common goal. It is multiparty, in that it can involve at least two, but often more, participants. And it is symmetrical, in contrast to the teacher-student relationship, in which the latter is vested with a certain authority and is perceived to hold greater knowledge and experience.

"Peers" can be defined in a number of ways, for example, in terms of equivalence of age, skill, proficiency, or class group, yet they may differ for any of these categories. Specific to the context of this book, a fundamental characteristic of peers, as we describe them here, is that they are *L2 learners*, not native speaker peers and not teachers (although peers may adopt a teaching role at times).

The Role of the Teacher

Although we acknowledge the significant role of the teacher in successful management of peer interactions, it is beyond the scope of this book to discuss this in any detail. We focus particularly on those situations in which there is minimal assistance or intervention from the teacher. Suffice it to say that teachers play an essential, if sometimes unseen, role (e.g., Dörnyei & Malderez, 1997; O'Donnell, 2006). They are an obvious and ever-present participant in the classroom, setting the tone by how they set up the peer work, providing motivation, and equipping students with both linguistic and relational skills. They may provide a model prior to peer work, as well as guidance and correction during it. They can facilitate progress through encouragement when confidence or interest flags. They may intervene when peer talk becomes unproductive, in situations of off-task behavior, conflict, disengagement, exclusion, or dysfunctional interaction. After peer talk, teachers help learners to evaluate their progress and provide feedback on unresolved issues in language use. Research on peers in group learning in school settings emphasizes the necessity of training for effective interaction to take place (see, e.g., Mercer, 1996; O'Donnell, 2006), and the same may be true of adults (Dörnyei & Malderez, 1997).

Types of Peer Learning

There are many varieties of peer learning, but those most common to language classrooms are collaborative learning, cooperative learning, peer tutoring, and peer modeling. Collaborative learning involves a strong sense of mutuality and joint effort (Damon & Phelps, 1989a, 1989b; see also Topping & Ehly, 1998)—that is, it does not simply refer to learners seated together and who work on the same task (Galton & Williamson, 1992). Students must depend on one another to complete the task. An example of this often occurs through dictogloss tasks (Wajnryb, 1990), involving group reconstruction of a short text. In this task, the pace of the dictation precludes accurate or complete notation but allows students to glean the principle ideas of the short text and to record key vocabulary items and phrases. Working together in groups, students then share notes to reconstruct the text. This task promotes attention to language form and a need to connect form and meaning. Swain (2000) describes such collaborative dialogue as "dialogue in which speakers are engaged in problem solving and knowledge building" (p. 102). She argues that such dialogue mediates language learning; the students are socially constructing their understanding of the language in the text, as they talk and write together. Although not guaranteed, mutuality is more likely in such collaborative tasks where students have to share opinions and listen to one another to complete the task.

Cooperative learning is used as an umbrella term that includes collaborative learning. It is also often used as a synonym for collaborative learning (McCafferty, Jacobs, & DaSilva Iddings, 2006); however, cooperative learning does not always involve mutuality to the same degree. It essentially involves peers working together to a common goal, though not necessarily together. An example of cooperative peer interaction often occurs in a jigsaw task, in which a group of students individually contribute information to complete a task. Students are each assigned a particular topic to research or a piece of information to read or listen to. They each work on their individual assignment; then, as "expert," they report back to the group as a whole. By piecing together the information through discussion and feedback, the group problem-solves the task to produce a report on what they have discovered (sometimes with assigned roles such as scribe, leader, and reporter). The following example, from a class of undergraduate university students learning French as a foreign language, is from a listening jigsaw murder mystery task in which pairs of students first listened to select segments, before coming together as a group to piece together the information. In this extract, Sal and Al report on the movements of two of the suspects in the story to other group members who compare with their own notes.

Example 1.1

Sal: il a dit que il ah le premier avec les Blancs XX et ils rentraient à 18 et 30

   [He said that he ah the first with the Whites and they came back at 18:30]

MI: pardon?

   [sorry?]

Sal: 18 et 30

Al: ah um et aussi M Le Blanc um dit a dit um il était um avec sa femme et aussi doux autres um so donc *[ah um and also Mr. Le Blanc um says said um he was um with his wife and also two (mispronounced as soft) others um so then]*

S1:   Mme Martin

Al: yeah Mme Martin et M Brown et sa femme ah sa femme

[Yeah Mrs. Martin and Mr. Brown and his wife]

S1:   avec sa femme

[with his wife]

Al: ah M Brown

S1:   qui

[who]

S2:   M Brown

Al: M Brown et Mme Martin so

S2:   well mines the same

Al: right

S1:   Mme Martin

S2:   cos we're all together

Al: right OK at least we've got that

S1:   how about I do mine XX elle a dit qu'elle est qu'il rentrait à apres 6 heures (..) oh um XX ils ont Monsieur et Madame LeBlanc XX

[she said that she had that he was coming back at after 6:00 oh um XX they have Mr. and Mrs. LeBlanc]

(Philp, 1993, unpublished raw data)

Such tasks require learners to depend on one another for information. They may or may not be equals in this task, in terms of competence and/or proficiency, and mutuality may also vary. For example, group members may each actively participate, listen to one another, and take account of one another's suggestions. Alternatively, certain group members may take control of working out how everything fits together, to the exclusion of others. Peer interactions that are "characterized by high degrees of both equality and mutuality" (Damon & Phelps, 1989a, p. 18) have been found to foster active involvement in problem solving and exchange of ideas, by researchers in both education (e.g., Damon & Phelps, 1989a) and applied linguistics (e.g., Storch, 2002).

A common form of peer-assisted learning includes *peer tutoring*, in which one peer assumes a position of tutor and instructs or assists the other in some way. This includes peer review of a writing or performance task. Typically, this involves a more proficient learner (expert) with a less proficient learner (novice). This is associated with the Vygotskian notion of a more expert person providing scaffolding to support the performance of a novice learner (O'Donnell, 2006). Researchers of mainstream classroom contexts (Damon & Phelps, 1989a; Topping & Ehly, 1998) note key differences between the peer tutor and the teacher, and these are equally relevant to contexts of instructed language learning. The advantage of peer-assisted learning compared to teacher-learner instruction is that the peer tutor is less removed in status than the teacher, less distant a model in terms of competence, and closer in age and experience. For these reasons, peer tutors may be more approachable and more easily contested in their feedback, thus giving the novice a chance to try out options and experiment with their language.

Additionally, peers may offer particular insights into difficulties of classmates that the teacher does not have by virtue of his/her expertise. Further, the expert peer may benefit emotionally in being placed in a teaching role, and linguistically and cognitively through having to articulate explanations to the partners (van Lier, 1996; Watanabe & Swain, 2007). A potential threat to positive peer assistance is the risk of increasing social status differences in the classroom, where "expert" students are perceived as having more to contribute or being more valuable members of the class (O'Donnell, 2006).

Peer tutoring is illustrated in Watanabe and Swain's (2007) study, which compares writing between unmatched pairs. Interestingly, when working with a higher proficiency partner (Chie), Mei perceives her partner as being of equal proficiency, and their dialogue reflects high mutuality. After the session, Mei acknowledges ways in which working with Chie assisted her writing, both in language and strategy. Working with this peer, Mei appears comfortable to contribute equally with Chie and to accept her suggestions (this study is discussed in more detail in Chapter 5).

Example 1.2

Mei: I noticed that Chie corrected my mistake [of adding "*s*" to "*make*"]. I always forget to put "*s*" so I appreciated her help. Then I was absorbed in extending the thesis statement and was struggling with it. But Chie told me that we now need to write about specific examples. I thought like "yeah, you're right" (laughing).

(Watanabe & Swain, 2007, p. 123)

Peer modeling is often reflected when heritage learners, who have been exposed to the target language in the home environment, are matched with L2 learners who have only experienced target language use in classroom contexts (heritage learner interactions are further discussed in Chapter 5).

There are many potential problems in peer work in language classrooms: relational, linguistic, and cognitive. To some extent, such problems are resolved or exacerbated through choices of group size, assignment of roles, the goals of the task, the use of incentives or level of accountability, the relative ability within the group, and the physical arrangement (Johnson, Johnson, Holubec, & Roy, 1984; O'Donnell, 2006). Given the many practical books on classroom management of cooperative learning and group work (e.g. Dörnyei & Murphey, 2003; Johnson et al., 1984; McCafferty et al., 2006), this is not a focus of this book.

Having explained the scope of this book, and what we mean by peer interaction, we now explore the theoretical rationale for peer work as a context for L2 learning in classrooms. We will consider this from four perspectives: interactionist theories of L2 learning, sociocultural theories of L2 learning, language socialization, and age-related differences in learning.

Perspectives on Peer Interaction and L2 Learning

Within L2 acquisition theory, interaction per se is seen, from both cognitive and social theoretical perspectives, as a prime context for language acquisition and development. By interaction, we refer to either dyadic or multiparty talk that has a primary focus on communicating meaning, rather than on language form in isolation. Early interactionist research on peer interaction was often carried out under experimental conditions and focused on particular communication strategies employed by the participants to address difficulties in mutual comprehension. These strategies involve adjustments to both language form and the structure of the conversation itself. This is seen in Example 1.3 below (Duff, 1986) in which two learners, "J" and "CH," debate the topic of age and wisdom. In response to CH's questions, J repeats key words and reformulates his language to assist comprehension.

Example 1.3

	J: . . . Bad bad influence (3) . . . Experience sometimes uh worked for people for people as a MAL influence
CH: Influence?	J: Yeah. . .mal
CH: More?	J: Bad-bad influence . . . mal influence
CH: Oh (2) I don't know what do you meaning?	J: Mal means bad
CH: M-A-L? (looks in dictionary). Oh I see . . . mal oh MAL influence Your meaning is a	J: Even if the same experience
CH: Yeah	J: One person uh
CH: Can get some useful idea but other can get some bad idea from that	J: Yeah

(Duff, 1986, p. 178)

From a cognitive perspective, Long's (1983, 1996) interaction hypothesis proposes that such interaction facilitates learning. Specifically, as Pica (1992, 2013) notes, in *negotiated* interaction participants adjust how they express meaning in response to communication difficulties (e.g., through repetition, restructuring, or rephrasing of language). This promotes mutual comprehension and provides learners with opportunities to hear the target language, to pay attention to how meaning is expressed in the target language, and to try out that language themselves (Mackey, 2012; Philp, 2012; see Mackey & Goo, 2007, for a meta-analysis of research on interaction and learning). As illustrated in Example 1.3, J treats the prefix "mal" as if it were a single word, a complication of peer interaction is the potential introduction of non-targetlike input and feedback. This is one reason why teachers and students alike have questioned the benefits of peer interaction for language learning.

Complementary to cognitively oriented research is work based on sociocultural perspectives of L2 learning. This research emphasizes the social nature of interaction and the co-constructed nature of learning. Within an interactionist perspective, learning is primarily seen as something unique to, and situated within, the individual's own mind. It is an outcome or product of interaction with others. From a sociocultural perspective, learning is a jointly developed process and inherent in participating in interaction. Thus, Swain (2000) describes problem solving and knowledge building through collaborative dialogue as *learning*. In the following example, she illustrates this notion of co-construction. Two learners in the process of reconstructing a text together are puzzling over partitives (des or de) and adjective agreement (masculine or feminine) in the non-targetlike phrase "des nouveaux menaces" (new threats). They do not achieve this simply through individual reflection; it helps them to verbalize each possibility and try it out. Ultimately, they solve part of their problem by finding the gender of the noun in the dictionary. Swain argues that it is through verbalizing the form reciprocally, trying to produce the phrase correctly, that they come to reflect on language form, identify knowledge gaps, and find solutions.

Example 1.4

17 Rachel: Yeah, nouveux, des nouveaux, de nouveaux. Is it des nouveaux or de nouveaux?

[new, "des" news; "de" news (checking which partitive form to use) is it "des nouveaux" or "de nouveaux"?]

18 Sophie: Des nouveaux or des nouvelles? (masculine plural form of the adjective or feminine plural form)

19 Rachel: Nou[veaux], des nou[veaux], de nou[veaux]

20 Sophie: It's menace, un menace, une menace, un menace, menace ay ay ay! (exasperated) *[It's threat]* (then checking if threat is masculine or feminine)

(. . .)   (they look up "mece" in the dictionary)

22   Sophie: (triumphantly) C'est des nouvelles!

          [Its "des nouvelles"!] (i.e., the feminine form)

23   Rachel: C'est féminin; des nouvelles menaces.

          [Its feminine "des nouvelles menaces."]

(Swain, 2000, p. 299)

After finding the gender of the noun "menace," they successfully apply this knowledge to supply correct adjective agreement ("nouvelles"). As such, learning is the very substance of interaction, the co-construction that evolves through collaborative dialogue, as much as it is an outcome for each individual learner. As we will see in later chapters in this book, peer interaction is a primary context for such "languaging," as Swain (2010) calls it, because of the very nature of peers' social interaction—as nonexperts, they must puzzle through things together. Sfard (1998) emphasizes the dangers of seeing learning only in terms of acquisition by an individual or only in terms of participation. In this book, we see both cognitive and social perspectives as essential to understanding the contribution of peer interaction to L2 development.

Another view, important to understanding the contribution of peer interaction to L2 learning relates to work on language socialization and language identity, and the process of becoming a member of a community of users of the target language (Miller, 2003; Pavlenko, 2002; Swain & Deters, 2007). From this perspective, for example, peer interaction in first language (L1)–medium schools is an important context in which immigrant children and adolescents negotiate their identities and how they are seen by others. In this process, they appropriate or reject the discourses of their peers, and they become accepted or marginalized in the school community, with positive and negative consequences for L2 learning.

Another difference in perspectives on peer interaction relates to age and developmental factors. Research on peer interaction among children is quite distinct from the literature on peer interaction among adults. There is a large body of literature within educational psychology concerning peers and learning, and much of this is highly relevant to our understanding of peer interaction and L2 learning in the school years. As described in Chapter 7, the maturational trajectory of social and cognitive development from childhood to adolescence to adulthood manifests in qualitatively different ways of thinking and behaving (Duchesne, McMaugh, Bochner, & Krause, 2012; Muñoz, 2007) and thus has implications for the nature of peer interaction and its contribution to L2 learning among children of different ages. We draw on these four perspectives in order to understand the potential contributions of peer interaction to learning.

Organization of This Book

This book is arranged in three sections, reflecting the different dimensions that we suggest shape the nature and outcomes of peer interaction: language, participants, and task. In Section I, we describe three main ways in which learners engage with language in the context of peer interaction and the potential outcomes for language learning. In Section II, we explore factors associated with the participants in interaction. In Section III, we conclude and discuss factors associated with the purpose and mode of interaction. The final chapter of this book brings together what we consider to be the principal contributions of peer interaction, based on research to date. Although the majority of this book focuses uniquely on peer interaction, in this concluding chapter, we consider the relationship between peer interaction and the wider context of the classroom, including how it functions in relation to teacher-student interaction.

Peer Interaction as a Context for Learning

A primary premise of this book is that peer interaction is a context for language learning and use, and it is a context within the wider setting of the classroom. Although we focus here uniquely on peer interaction, it is crucial to retain the fact that peer interaction operates as it does because of its place in the classroom setting. That is to say, peer interaction is *one* of other contexts for learning, including teacher-student interaction. Peer interaction itself is thus nested within the framework of the classroom, and its contribution to learning is colored by this. As such, peer interaction is both influenced by and complements other types of interactions and experiences that occur, most notably teacher-student whole class interaction. We return to this idea in Chapter 12.

Peer interaction tasks can take various guises, encompass different aims, and accordingly, have diverse advantages (and disadvantages). The value of some types of peer interaction stems from an *unequal* relationship between peers during the task, where one peer is more competent than others. The potential of this is best understood from Vygotskian-based principles (Berk, 2013; Corden, 2000; Duchesne et al., 2013) and the notion of working within the learner's zone of proximal development (ZPD). The ZPD represents the range of performance between a learner's ability to complete a task unassisted and achievement with the assistance of a more expert partner. Other types of peer interaction have alternative benefits when they involve learners of *equivalent* levels of proficiency or competence for the task. Understood from a cognitive perspective, particularly from a Piagetian heritage, peers contribute to learning by providing a context in which they may challenge one another's preexisting conceptions. This conflict provides the impetus for interlanguage change, in a process of continual construction and reconstruction in response to their experience of language use. Throughout this book, we explore these differing aspects of peer learning. In addition, we illustrate the varied goals of formally organized peer interaction in the language or content-based classroom, including the practice or rehearsal of forms pretaught by the teacher (see Chapter 4); the provision of correction and feedback (Chapters 3 and 10); and the use of problem solving, creative language production, and exchange of information (Chapters 2, 9, and 10).

The nature of peer interaction as a context for learning is shaped not only by the wider framework of the classroom, but by other dimensions too, such as the central emphasis of language use in the interaction (e.g., experimental, corrective, or fluency based); the participants within the group (e.g., their social relations, age, experience, and proficiency); and the medium and mode of instruction (whether oral or written, face-to-face, or online), including the task (purpose, specifications, and content). The structure of the book is based on these three dimensions.

Section I: Language Use, Misuse, Modification, and Development

The first section of the book explores the role of peer interaction in promoting different aspects of the language-learning process. The three chapters in this section each explore one aspect of language use and the potential contribution of interaction as a result, from sociocultural, cognitive, and information-processing perspectives. Chapter 2 investigates peer interaction as a site for linguistic exploration, for learners to stretch their linguistic resources, notice gaps in their interlanguage knowledge, and try out or further explore new forms. Chapter 3 examines the occurrence of corrective feedback and other types of focus on form during peer interactions. It investigates the role of peer interaction in promoting mastery of linguistic form. Chapter 4 presents an evaluation of peer interaction as a site for language practice to promote automaticity, from the perspective of skill acquisition theory. These are three areas of language use identified in the literature as contributing to language learning. Each chapter pinpoints benefits of peers and limitations in these areas, based on research findings. This section as a whole highlights those areas in which peer interaction is most likely or least likely to be of benefit.

Section II: The Participants of Peer Interaction

The three chapters in the second section each focus on attributes of the participants in peer interaction and how they may make a difference to the nature and outcomes of the interaction. Chapter 5 explores the effects of L2 proficiency and L1 use. In some contexts and for some learners, L1 use can be a hindrance, but in other contexts, L1 use may provide a useful scaffold for target language production. What is interesting here is the *reciprocal* influence of each participant's respective nature because every participant influences the interaction in association with all others. When learners of matched proficiency interact, high or low proficiency is not necessarily predictive of particular outcomes. Rather, L2 proficiency and individual difference characteristics such as personality, affect, and motivation contribute to the shape and outcomes of the interaction in complex ways.

Even when homogenous groups are all working on the same task in a class, the quality of each group's interaction and the outcomes for learning can differ, simply because the members of the group and how they relate to one another differ. Hartup (2011), an educational psychologist, makes the point that peer interaction "always involves specific [individuals] with unique socialization histories, differing histories of interaction with one another, specific content (what the interaction is about), and a unique setting (a situation in time and place)" (p. 8). Although these differences are evident, it is not clear to what extent peers' relations with one another underlie the potential contribution of peer interaction to learning. Chapter 6 investigates how learners' perceptions of themselves and their peer interlocutors, and their relationships and past experiences with one another can affect the way in which they interact together. Chapter 7 concerns peer interaction among school-age learners and differences due to age. We examine differences and similarities in younger and older children's interaction in terms of their engagement with the task, with one another, and with language, including linguistic feedback to one another.

Section III: The Purpose and Mode of Peer Interaction

Peer interaction operates in different modes. Most common perhaps is oral interaction, but learners may also be involved in written interaction with one another, in either face-to-face environments or through computer-mediated communication. Another distinction in types of interaction concerns formality and the role of the teacher. Peer interaction can be formally created, for example, pair or group work set by the teacher for purposes of assessment or practice. Conversely, it may be informal and spontaneous, for example, a whispered conversation between two friends during whole class interaction (see Batstone & Philp, 2013). Often a combination occurs—for example, during an assigned classroom practice activity, partners may go "off task" to talk about their social life. Thus, the term *peer interaction* covers a wide spectrum of activity in which learners converse or engage with one another for a common purpose, either orally or by a written medium.

This final section considers relationships between the task, purpose, mode, and nature of peer interaction. Chapter 8 considers the dynamics of peer interaction according to task, including the type, structure, and complexity of tasks, and how these features impact outcomes of interaction. Chapter 9 provides an overview of research on computer-mediated peer interaction, including synchronous, asynchronous, and multimodal environments. This chapter gives insights into the particular benefits of virtual interaction in contrast to face-to-face contexts. Although interaction research has tended to focus on oral interaction, in classroom settings peer interaction often occurs as learners collaboratively engage in reading and writing tasks. Interestingly, this appears to be beneficial in ways that are different from those found in

Chapters 2–4. Chapter 10 focuses on how peer interaction shapes and is shaped by engagement in reading and writing. Finally, Chapter 11 provides an overview of the use of peer interaction for assessment purposes and issues concerning validity, reliability, and the appropriateness of peer interaction in assessment.

The concluding chapter of the book evaluates the implications and applications of the research on peer interaction for theory of instructed language learning and for language pedagogy. It reflects on the limitations of the research to date and important directions for new research. We discuss the potential of peer interaction for L2 learning in different contexts and the limitations: As noted in L1 research on peer interaction, peer interaction cannot be assumed always to be beneficial or to have blanket effects (De Lisi & Golbeck, 1999), and thus we consider how the dimensions of language, participants, and task may mediate the nature of peer interaction and its outcomes for L2 learning. In particular, we reflect on combinations of features of peer interaction that appear to either promote or inhibit learning. Finally, we discuss the relationship between peer interaction and teacher-student interaction, and how these two contexts complement one another, in ways not often researched or discussed with regard to L2 development.

SECTION I

Language Use, Misuse, Modification, and Development

2

PEER INTERACTION AS A CONTEXT FOR EXPERIMENTING WITH LANGUAGE

Introduction

One of the strengths of peer interaction is its role as a context for experimenting with language. As learners use the target language with one another, they experiment with possibilities for expressing meaning. Through this process, they develop their understanding and ability to use the language in various ways. Starting with the language they know, learners may collaboratively revise words and phrases in response to the one another's feedback. They may draw from explicit knowledge of rules of the language as they do this, try out new possibilities by trial and error, and depend on one another for help. In this way, learners work together to solve the linguistic difficulties they encounter in communicative language use. Peer interaction is typically more symmetrical in nature than teacher-learner interaction, and this gives rise to differences in the nature of the interaction (Allwright, 1998b). Without the teacher's presence, learners may explore language use with less anxiety of correction and with greater autonomy. This chapter considers the cumulative effects of this process for second language (L2) development and its benefits and limitations. We begin by exploring different ways in which learners may resolve the difficulties they encounter when experimenting with language. We then discuss the theoretical rationale for understanding the potential benefits of this aspect of peer interaction. This is followed by examples from research and reflections on the contribution of experimentation to learning.

Variety in Language Experimentation

The chapter begins with four examples of learners experimenting with language. Each example suggests a different way in which learners solve the problems they encounter. The first illustrates joint construction. In Example 2.1, two learners work together on the first sentence of a collaborative essay-writing task. They add to and reformulate one another's words to construct the sentence. Each learner's turn appears to trigger the partner's, as they try to express a shared idea: as if they verbally push out the words they hold mentally. This type of collaborative task with a peer provides an opportunity to explore the language they know to jointly form a sentence.

Example 2.1

69 M: [. . .] Music make me ah make people . . .

70 C: (writing) Makes

71 M: Makes

72 C: People

73 M: Happy . . . comma . . . relaxing, relaxed? Relaxing? Which one? . . . Relaxed?

74 C: Relaxed, relaxed . . . and exciting.

75 M: Excited?

76 C: Excited.

77 M: And in other hand? Ah no uhm . . . so, so, people . . . so, people use music, music at different times, no . . . this one.

78 C: So

79 M: And, and, and, another reason and

80 C: I think it's specific reason [that we have to write next]

81 M: Yeah.

(Watanabe & Swain, 2008, pp. 122–123)

The second example illustrates feedback and reformulation. In Example 2.2, during a communication task, NNS2 does not understand the information given. NNS1 modifies his/her initial utterance in response. This example shows how communication difficulties in experimenting with language through peer interaction can prompt learners to revise their production in more targetlike ways.

Example 2.2

NNS1: annd [sic] two small bottle

NNS2: two small what?

NNS1: bot (0.6) small bottles

NNS2: yeah

(Shehadeh, 2001, p. 456)

Example 2.3 illustrates the use of peers' collective knowledge to solve problems. As the two learners E and Y jointly construct a text, in line 4, Y suggests inserting the definite article *the* before *Soviet Union*. They test out their ideas by recalling another example *the United States*. The two learners use both their metalinguistic and intuitive knowledge to reflect on possibilities and as a basis for agreeing or disagreeing with their interlocutor's suggestion. This episode indicates that experimenting with language with a peer prompts learners to resort to the knowledge they possess collectively as a means of resolving problems encountered in L2 use.

Example 2.3

189 Y: like Soviet Union . . .

190 E: like Soviet Union

191 Y: wait a moment . . . do we have to put the article in the Soviet Union?

192 Y: The Soviet, Soviet Union . . . the Soviet Union, Soviet Union. Yeah

193 Y: the Soviet

194 E: are you sure?

195 Y: the United States

196 E: ah yeah . . .

197 Y: the United Nations

198 E: yeah, yeah

199 Y: the Soviet Union

200 E: you're right

(Storch, 2008, pp. 103–104)

The final example (Example 2.4) involves formulaic language use. It is different from the previous examples. The two learners practice reflexive verbs with the infinitive form of the verb given as a prompt for each question. Peer interaction provides an opportunity to practice formulaic language learned in class with their fellow learner and try it out in a communicative exchange.

Example 2.4

1 Std D: Tu te réveilles à quelle heurie?

          [At what time do you wake up?]

2 Std C: Je me réveille à sept heures.

          [I wake up at seven o'clock.]

3 Std D: A quelle heure tu te lèves?

          [At what time do you get up?]

4 Std C: Je me lève à sept heures.

> *[I get up at seven o'clock.]*

(Tognini, Philp, & Oliver, 2010, p. 12)

The previous examples show four aspects of how learners explore and experiment with language through peer interaction: (a) to try to express what they know; (b) to revise the language form they know in response to difficulties; (c) to revise by referring to their collective knowledge about the language; and (d) to practice and appropriate the formulaic language learned in class for communication. In the following section, we will consider the theoretical foundation of experimentation.

Theoretical Foundations

The theoretical foundation of the process of experimenting with language is largely drawn from Swain's (e.g., 1985, 1995, 1998, 2000, 2005) output hypothesis. This evolved out of criticism of Krashen's (1985) input hypothesis. Based on research on Canadian immersion programs in schools, Swain (1985) argues for the insufficiency of comprehensible input alone. She noted that students in such programs have ample opportunity to receive comprehensible input and develop high L2 proficiency. However, even after years in the program, students retain glaringly obvious grammatical errors, including inappropriate use of grammar forms in a given context. Swain claims that for grammatical development, learners need to be "pushed" into making their output more precise, coherent, and appropriate (the comprehensible output hypothesis). She argues that while comprehension of a message can take place with little syntactic analysis of the input, production forces learners to pay attention to morpho-syntax and to process the language more deeply. Swain (1995), in a later revision of the comprehensible output hypothesis, suggests three functions that output serves (in addition to fluency). Output promotes (a) a noticing function, (b) a hypothesis-testing function, and (c) a metalinguistic awareness function. In the following section, we explain these functions and explore how they might be facilitated in the context of peer interaction.

Noticing Function

It is widely acknowledged that attention and noticing play a crucial role in L2 learning (e.g., Schmidt, 1995, 2001). Carrying out communicative tasks, such as information gap tasks, can be a context for learners to notice connections between form and meaning. For example, when misunderstandings arise or difficulties in comprehending a partner occur, or when there are problems expressing meaning coherently, these brief hurdles in communication can draw learners' attention to language form. Noticing these problems is a catalyst for change

(Gass & Varonis, 1994; Schmidt, 2001; Schmidt & Frota, 1986). Learners come to realize the things they did not know and pay attention to things they knew were "not quite right." An interlocutor's signals for clarification requests, comprehension checks, and confirmation checks can highlight problems. In peer interaction, learners' signals may not be as straightforward because learners themselves seem uncertain of their signals as illustrated in Example 2.5.

In Example 2.5, P3's non-targetlike pronunciation causes confusion, taking six further turns to resolve. L's confirmation check in turn 2 to clarify P3's initial statement led to L's clarification in turn 3. In response to P3's clarification in turn 3, L repeats his/her confirmation check. L finally understood P3's initial statement after P3 repeated it in turn 7. As Pica, Lincoln-Porter, Paninos, and Linnell (1996) point out, in peer interaction, learners' signals tend to involve simple segmentations of each other's prior utterances. The learners' repeated exchanges of requests for clarification and confirmation through segmentation indicate that both learners became aware that something was "not quite right."

Example 2.5

1	P3:	When I met him, he said to me, "da da da" and then.	
2	L:	He dead?	← confirmation check
3	P3:	What?	← clarification requests
4	L:	He dead?	← confirmation check
5	P3:	No.	
6	L:	He died?	← clarification request
7	P3:	Dead? No, I said and then.	← resolution
8	L:	Oh then, I thought you said and dead. Sorry.	

(Williams, 1999, p. 599, commentary added)

Hypothesis Testing

In attempting to express themselves through the target language, learners consciously and unconsciously try out what they know about the language, using their existing knowledge and discovering how it works, as we saw earlier in Examples 2.1 and 2.3. Swain (1995, 1998, 2000) argues that this is a process of forming a hypothesis and testing it out. The hypothesis may be confirmed and/or disconfirmed through interaction, as shown in Example 2.6. In this example from Swain and Lapkin (1998), the two learners (Kim and Rick) jointly construct a story based on a series of pictures. Rick is not sure about the correct word for alarm clock. First, he haltingly tries out the word *rêve-matin* (turn 9). Subsequently, he experiments with his partner's word *réveille-matin* (turn 56), repeating it after her. Although she confirms its use, he has difficulty producing it again later (turn 70), and Kim again provides explicit feedback on its use in turn 71. Rick appropriates the word in the following turn; however, 10 turns later, he has reverted to a form more similar to his earlier word. Kim's use of the targetlike version (turn 94) appears to trigger further uncertainty about the word "rêve-matin," and Kim provides further disconfirmation of his use, stressing the word "reveille" in turn 95. This reflects the cumulative nature of learning.

Example 2.6

9   Rick: Elle est en train de dormir après que ... la rêve-matin est encore sonné. Et le rê- ... rêve-matin dit six heures un.

[She is sleeping after the alarm clock rang again. And the alarm clock says one minute after six o'clock.]

(46 turns)

55   Kim: ... il y a un réveille-matin.

[... there is an alarm clock.]

56   Rick: Revéille-matin?

[Alarm clock?]

57   Kim: Revéille-matin.

[Alarm clock.]

(8 turns)

66   Rick: Se réveille à cause ... du son ...

[Wakes up because ... of the sound ...]

67   Kim: Réveille-matin.

[Alarm clock.]

68   Rick: A cause du ...

[Because of ...]

69   Kim: Du réveille-matin qui sonne? Does that sound OK?

[Of the alarm-clock that rings? Does that sound OK?]

70   Rick: Or what about ... Jacqueline se lève a cause du ... du réveille- ... yeah, qui sonne.

[Or what about ... Jacqueline (the girl in their story) gets up because of the ... of the alarm— ... yeah, that rings.]

71   Kim: OK. Or you can say du réveille-matin or du sonnement du reveille matin.

[OK. Or you can say of the alarm clock or the ring of the alarm clock.]

72 Rick: No, réveille-matin qui sonne.

[No, alarm clock that rings.]

(19 turns)

92 Rick: Sur la rêv- . . . rêv-matin.

[On the alarm clock.]

93 Kim: Sur le réveille-matin our arrêter le sonnement.

[On the alarm clock to stop the ring.]

94 Rick: Rêve-matin?

[Alarm clock?]

95 Kim: REVEILLE-matin.

[Alarm clock.] (Stresses component meaning "wake.")

(Swain & Lapkin, 1998, p. 329)

Exploring and experimenting with language through peer interaction assists learners with this process of hypothesis testing because it allows them to try out what they know and confirm and disconfirm use through peer assistance. As the example shows, among peers this can be a very lengthy process with many successive short turns and repetition of the same language item as the learner incorporates a new form more consistently in his or her interlanguage use. Thus, peer interaction can provide opportunity for cumulative learning of new forms.

Metalinguistic Awareness

The third function, metalinguistic awareness, has been recently articulated through a sociocultural perspective of language learning (Lantolf, 2000a; Lantolf & Thorne, 2006). This perspective sees learning taking place through social interaction (Vygotsky, 1978). Language functions as a tool for thinking as well as communication. Knowledge is understood as being socially constructed, and dialogue serves as a transitional mechanism from the social to the internal plane of psychological functioning, as well as an occasion for language learning (Swain, 2000).

These ideas have led to claims that language production is not in and of itself the outcome. Rather, the process of putting thoughts into words ("verbalization") allows learners to become aware of the limits of their knowledge, to predict linguistic needs, and to set goals for further learning (e.g., Swain, 2005). Verbalization is mediated through social interaction and, for this reason, is referred to as a "collaborative dialogue." When involved in collaborative dialogue, learners engage in explaining, reflecting, and describing to solve linguistic problems. Swain and Suzuki (2008) refer to this process as "languaging," and to the process of co-constructing knowledge with peers as "knowledge building." In fact, learners *"use* language to *learn* language" (Swain & Suzuki, 2008, p. 565).

As we have seen in the examples provided, learners experiment with language through trial and error and by discussing how to express what they want to say, exploring and sometimes explaining their choice of forms. This collaborative effort mediates language learning, as it supports the process of internalizing information from the shared discourse, which Donato (1994) refers to as "collective scaffolding." It is with the assistance of others that learners stretch the boundaries of what they can do in an L2, even though they may be far from being able to do it independently. Many researchers associate this with Vygotsky's concept of a zone of proximal development (ZPD) (e.g., Swain, Brooks, & Tocalli-Beller, 2002). Originally, Vygotsky (1986) used the term ZPD to describe the cognitive learning potential reached through collaboration between novice (child) and expert (adult or older child). This term has since been extended to descriptions of L2 learning through collaboration between peers (whether asymmetrical in ability or symmetrical) (Lantolf & Thorne, 2006; see also Chapter 1).

For example, Donato (1994) has shown that learners are able to offer each other assistance regardless of their linguistic abilities, as shown in Example 2.7. Here, three second-year university students studying French are working together on a project during class. As they attempt to translate "you remembered" in French, they meet a number of grammatical issues to resolve. In turns A2–A4, they each seem to be trying out the form, saying it aloud. When Speaker 3 then queries it as a reflexive verb, this leads to a chain of possible forms, in search of the correct reflexive pronoun and the correct auxiliary to use. Speaker 2 changes the auxiliary verb *avoir* to the targetlike use of *être*—in the second person form *tu es*, at the same time dropping the reflexive marker (*te*) in turn A6. All three interlocutors try out this new form *tu es*, until turn A10 when Speaker 1 comes up with the full targetlike form *tu t'es*. In this way, the resolution of the problem is collaborative, each contributing steps toward targetlike expression of what they want to say. In the transcript, a star indicates non-targetlike use.

Example 2.7

A1   Speaker 1: . . . and then I'll say . . . tu as souvenu notre anniversaire de mariage . . . or should I say mon anniversaire?

[you remembered* our wedding anniversary . . . (. . .) my anniversary?]

A2   Speaker 2: *Tu as . . .*

[you + auxiliary]

A3   Speaker 3: Tu as . . .

A4   Speaker 1: Tu as souvenu . . . ← contributes lexis

[you remembered?*]

A5   Speaker 3: Yea, but isn't that reflexive? Tu t'as . . . ← identifies need for reflexive pronoun

A6   Speaker 1: Ah, tu t'as souvenu.

A7   Speaker 2: Oh, it's tu es   ← identifies need for auxiliary être

A8   Speaker 1: Tu es

A9   Speaker 3: Tu es, tu es, tu . . .

A10 Speaker 1: T'es, tu t'es   ← includes reflexive pronoun

A11 Speaker 3: tu t'es

A12 Speaker 1: Tu t'es souvenu.   ← complete target like utterance

[you remembered]

(Donato, 1994, p. 44, translation and commentary added)

As the example shows, the presence of the peer allows experimentation with language by repeating, resorting to knowledge about the form, correcting, and suggesting an alternative form. The learners use their collective resources of metalinguistic knowledge and intuition. They appear to solve it in stages, each contributing elements of the final solution. Their ability to do so suggests that these learners are comfortable trying out things, without anxiety about correction and with increasing autonomy (the social dynamics of interaction is explored in Chapter 6). As shown in Example 2.6, the process of coming to a solution can be lengthy in peer interaction, unlike teacher-learner interaction difficulties, which can be solved more directly and with authority by the teacher. However frustrating the process, collective experimentation among peers allows them to pool their resources and to try out different alternatives. In so doing, peers assist one another in gaining greater control of the language. In this regard, peer and teacher-learner interactions play complementary roles: the former for experimentation and the latter for authoritative instruction. This will be discussed further in Chapter 12.

Studies based on sociocultural perspectives investigate how learners assist each other through scaffolding and building knowledge together. This process helps learners to perform at a level beyond any one individual's ability, developing knowledge and use. In contrast, an interactionist view focuses on linguistic data that learners receive from their interlocutors during interaction. In particular, the emphasis is on individual acquisition, based on all the different types of language input received through interaction with others. Recently, some scholars have articulated functions of output in L2 acquisition processes from a psycholinguistic view, referring to Levelt's speech processing model (de Bot, 1996; Izumi, 2003; Muranoi, 2007). According to de Bot (1996), output plays an important role in the transfer of declarative knowledge (factual information about language, such as rules) to procedural knowledge (unconscious and automatic use) (Anderson, 1983; Ellis, 2008). The process of producing language assists in its automatic use. The research on this perspective concerns not only the quantity and quality of the information exchanged through interaction, but also various moderating factors such as tasks, interlocutor proficiency, context, and so forth, which may have an impact on the quality and quantity of interaction (e.g., Gass, Mackey, & Ross-Feldman, 2005; Iwashita, 1999, 2001; Philp, Oliver & Mackey, 2006). These aspects are discussed in later chapters. In this chapter, we mainly (though not exclusively) focus on studies based on sociocultural perspectives and will draw from psycholinguistic and cognitive-interactionist perspectives in Chapter 3.

Benefits of Peer Interaction Through Experimentation

The way that learners experiment with languages, and the process by which their experimentation leads to L2 development, has most often been studied in alignment with the three functions of output explained previously: noticing, hypothesis-testing function, and metalinguistic awareness (e.g., Swain, 1995, 1998, 2000), whether from an interactionist or a sociocultural perspective. The benefits of experimenting with language could be considered in regard to two (overlapping) aspects: first, how learners attend to form during interaction; and second, the outcomes of learners' struggles to get meaning across. Examining attention to form, researchers have tended to identify "episodes" or significant turns in which there is a brief move from attending to meaning to attending to form. Some researchers identify these in terms of "form-focused episodes," that is, "occasions where there was attention to linguistic form (i.e., grammar, vocabulary, spelling, discourse, or pronunciation)" (Ellis, Basturkmen, & Loewen, 2001, p. 294). This is more commonly used in research on teacher-learner classroom discourse. Other researchers identify "language-related episodes" (LREs) in which participants, most often pairs or groups of learners, specifically "talk about the language they are producing, and question their language" (Swain & Lapkin, 1995, p. 326). As shown in earlier examples, by identifying these episodes, researchers have been able to gain insight into the characteristics of peer interaction: what learners attend to and how learners resolve the linguistic problems that arise through interaction. Researchers have used descriptive, qualitative analysis to examine the struggles learners have to use language coherently. We will consider noticing of language form and resolution of problems in relation to L2 development. First, with regard to learners' attention to form, we explore various types of LREs identified in the research.

Characteristics of LREs

In the research, what it is in particular that learners attend to during interactions has been identified through categorization of LREs as, for example, form-based LREs (discussion of morphology or syntax), as seen in Example 2.7; lexical-based LREs (discussion of word meanings and word choices), Example 2.8; or mechanical LREs (discussion of spelling and punctuation) (e.g., Storch, 2008). In some studies, each type of LRE was further classified into subtypes (e.g., form-based LRE: verb morphology, choice of articles, and noun plurals). In Example 2.8, a group of four learners is discussing a possible outline of a section of the movie

Toy Story 3 after viewing the segment. C1 asks the word for 쓰레기 봉지 (trash bag) in English. This is classified as a lexical-based LRE.

Example 2.8

C1: and they are about to (.2); mmm. What is the 쓰레기 봉지 *[trash bag]* in English?=

H2: =Trash bag

C1: Trash bag?

H2: Yes

(Choi, 2011, p. 29)

Research of categorization of LREs in peer interaction suggests that learners do pay attention to a wide range of forms; however, lexical LREs tend to be far more prevalent (e.g., Choi, 2011; Philp, Walter, & Basturkmen, 2010; Williams, 2001).

Another feature of LREs that has been examined concerns how they are resolved. In Example 2.9, the word *honor* in C2's statement led L2 to revise it to *owner*. C2 then acknowledges L2's correction, repeating the word three times. The linguistic problem was resolved with the assistance of the other learner.

Example 2.9

C2: Daisy was the honor of the baby doll?

L2 (Linda): Owner: 아니에요?

[Isn't it Owner?]

C2: Yes Owner:: Owner . . . Owner . . .

(Choi, 2011, p. 31)

At times, learners may not be able to resolve their difficulties or may reach a non-targetlike solution. Example 2.10 illustrates this. When the first learner asked whether the phrase (*Il-bon-eh-suh*) [in Japan] was a correct expression, her interlocutor did not know the answer.

Example 2.10

1 S1: 연구하기로 해서, 일본에서, 맞아요?

(Yun-goo ha-gi-ro hae-suh, Il-bon-eh-suh, Ma-ja-yo?)

[Decided to research (about butterflies) in Japan, Is it correct?]

2 S2: 일본에서? 음, 마음대로 쓰세요.

(Il-bon-eh-suh? Umm, Ma-um-dai-ro ssu-sae-yo.)

[In Japan? Umm, write whatever you want.]

3 S1: 나도 몰라.

    (Na-do Mo-la.)

    [I do not know either.]

(Kim & McDonough, 2008, pp. 218–219)

These examples illustrate research findings showing that learners do attend to different aspects of language within LREs and use a variety of resources to resolve difficulties, including first language (L1), metalinguistic, and implicit knowledge. Trial and error often occurs, with input from all participants during collaborative activities. Finally, LREs between learners can end in varying degrees of success, and this is discussed in further detail in the next chapter. In the following section, we consider the contribution of LREs to learning and the relative importance of incidence and resolution of LREs in peer interaction as an indicator of learning.

Production of LREs

A substantial number of studies have investigated learners' experimentation with the language in peer interaction through provision of LREs. Whether and how often learners attend to form or lexis, and whether and how problems are resolved, differs considerably. A variety of factors—task, proficiency, group/pair dynamics, and time can have mediating effects and can all intersect to influence what learners pay attention to and how they do this. In one context, with certain peers, and on particular tasks with plenty of time, reasonably proficient learners may be encouraged to solve difficulties through talking about language per se (e.g., Leeser, 2004; Swain & Lapkin, 1998). Conversely, much less proficient learners in another context, with different peers, on another type of task, and with less time, may simply struggle with language use, grapple with language options by trial and error, and in doing so become more aware of language gaps, while not actually articulating or resolving them. Generally however, studies conducted in classrooms have found that in pair and group work, students do not always engage in discussion about language, and consequently, the frequency of LREs is not as high as found in laboratory studies (e.g., Philp et al., 2010; Tognini, 2008; Williams, 1999).

Philp et al. (2010), analyzing 12 hours of university French classes over 3 weeks, found relatively few LREs during peer interaction (between two and six per session), most of which were based on lexis. Interview data revealed that the low number of LREs could be partly attributed to learners' attitudes toward group work with fellow learners. Social considerations, such as feeling awkward about correcting others, have also been reported in a number of classroom studies on corrective feedback (e.g., Fujii & Mackey, 2009; García-Mayo & Pica, 2000) as noted in Chapter 3. The study shows how social factors influence the way learners engage in interaction, and this affects the degree of experimentation and the opportunities to learn. This will be discussed in further detail in Chapter 6.

Level of Engagement

A few studies found some variation regarding the quality of LREs in terms of the level of engagement with language form. For example, the prolonged interaction (Examples 2.11–2.13) found in Storch's (2008) study shows the learners' extensive involvement in discussion of the form. Storch investigated links between the level of engagement and subsequent language development. In her analysis of the metatalk of learners working in pairs on a text reconstruction task, she found that learners who discussed language at more elaborate levels were involved in more instances of learning/consolidation than those taking part in LREs with limited levels of engagement. In her study, learning/consolidation was examined in terms of whether the form discussed in the first task was correctly used in the subsequent task engagement. Elaborate engagement was operationalized as instances where learners deliberated and discussed language items containing lengthy explanations, and the interaction included communication strategies such as clarification requests and confirmation checks, as seen in the subsequent examples. In Example 2.11, the learners discussed, over several turns, whether the adverb "particularly" or the adjective "particular" should be used. Both interlocutors were involved in solving the problem by questioning (turn 72), explaining (turn 73), and agreeing (turn 77).

Example 2.11

69   M: the immigrants particular

70   C: south

71   M: is particularly

72   C: why is "ly"?

73   M: or in particular . . . because is, is adjective and in this context this not adjective here

75   C: mm (some agreement)

76   M: yeah . . . particularly . . . in south . . . maybe in . . . in

77   C: the immigrants particularly

(Storch, 2008, p. 101)

On the other hand, limited engagement was defined as instances where one learner made a suggestion and the other repeated it, acknowledged it, or did not respond to the suggestion as shown subsequently. In Example 2.12, S acknowledged J's suggestion with "ok," and then J continued on.

Example 2.12

48 J: of . . . emigration, emigration . . . yeah . . . reasons of . . .

49 S: ok

50 J: study . . . find that since 1947

(Storch, 2008, p. 102)

Depending on each learner's engagement, limited engagement was further classified into L+L (low and low) (with both participants showing limited engagement) or only with one participant showing limited engagement as shown in Example 2.13. In this example, the two learners K and A discussed punctuation of the sentence, and the discussion continued only for a few turns. For both learners, engagement in the task is equally short.

Example 2.13

37 K: in 1947 and then full stop

38 A: You want full stop and here capital

39 K: One, one in five Australian

(Storch, 2008, p. 102)

Storch's analysis revealed that the level of engagement varied according to particular linguistic features. While verb morphology, choice of articles, and word forms elicited elaborate levels of engagement, noun plurals and pronouns solicited few elaborate discussions. Storch explains that this was because of the relative difficulties of the rules of usage and the factors governing these rules. In the case of lexical-focused LREs (unlike form-focused LREs), prepositions gave rise to more than 50% of the LREs in total, yet few of these involved elaborated engagement. This was partly because, while there was not much discussion about the choice of prepositions, there was plenty of discussion about the complex rules of language. The analysis shows that learners who discussed language forms at more elaborate levels were more likely to demonstrate correct use of forms and lexis in subsequent interaction. On the other hand, limited engagement about linguistic choices by both learners (L+L) tended to lead to learning/consolidation for the learner *making* the suggestion, rather than the person *repeating* the suggestion. The study shows that quality of peer interaction could vary according to the level of engagement, which has some impact on L2 development.

Grappling With Language

Studies of LREs in learner interaction provide useful information on what learners attend to as they experiment with the language. As noted previously, not all studies reported frequent production of LREs. However, even in the absence of LREs, learner interaction itself can be valuable for learning: Simply talking and having to communicate meaning may help learners attend to language form and notice problems to a greater extent than just listening. Van Lier stresses this active nature of learning:

> I conclude that our interactions with others constantly provide pedagogical moments or learning opportunities. For teachers this means that interactions with learners in classrooms should allow learners to be perceiving, thinking, acting, and interacting persons, rather than passive receivers of knowledge.

> (van Lier, 1998, p. 142)

In this section, we discuss evidence from three studies undertaken in very different contexts that suggest that peer interaction with few LREs may nevertheless support L2 learning. First, Philp and Iwashita (2013) examined whether the process of interacting in an L2, versus observing others interact, may differentially affect learners' awareness of language. The study involved 26 university students of intermediate-level French. Two experimental groups, *interactors* and *observers*, engaged in three sessions of dyadic task-based interaction. The tasks elicited use of noun-adjective agreement and the *passé composé*. While interactors carried out tasks with other learners, observers watched the interaction among learners. Although the interactors provided little feedback to one another, subsequent interviews suggest differences between groups as to what they were thinking about during interaction, with the interactors paying more attention to language form because they needed to make active use of it, as shown in Examples 2.14 and 2.15.

Example 2.14

a. Interactor: Um oh yeah I remember at that point I was I was trying to ah um I was trying to think of a way that to say that um he he came up through he came up through the ground through a kind of like a underground passage.

b. Observer: So I'm, like, oh, yeah, that makes sense – that was a good way to describe it.

Example 2.15

a. Interactor: I can tell you what I was thinking there. I was very impressed that he knew the word "s'échapper" *[to escape]* which I didn't know.

b. Observer: I think I remember when she said "frisé" *[curly]* I was thinking oh that's the word cos I'd forgotten it.

(Philp & Iwashita, 2013, p. 12)

Interactors were significantly more likely to report that they were thinking about *how* to express their intended meaning in French or to report a focus on a particular vocabulary item. On the other hand, observers tended to focus on understanding the content of interaction. These findings are consistent with Swain's output hypothesis (e.g., Swain, 1995, 2000) and suggest that active language production itself (rather than passive observation) pushes learners to think about how to express meaning in the target language. That is, whether or not learners engage in solving linguistic problems, experimenting with language and thinking about what to say next can orient learners to pay attention to connections between form, meaning, and use.

Second, Tognini (2008) examined peer interaction data from 10 foreign language (FL) classes in both secondary and primary schools. She investigated L2 use and language choice among peers in these classes. The video recorded data of five lessons from each of the classes, and interviews with learners were analyzed in terms of context and purpose. The results show that a great deal of peer talk consisted of preformulated and scripted language. This was seen in both language practice activities and focused communicative tasks. Tognini (2008) also reports some brief instances of spontaneous language use. The following examples illustrate this.

Example 2.16 is taken from a role-play activity of booking accommodation. While the interaction is largely an exchange of formulaic language (*je voudrais*) with appropriate substitutions of vocabulary, there were some opportunities for feedback. For example, Student A's initial turn contains a number of instances of non-targetlike use (e.g., the wrong indefinite article with *lit* and *bain*, omission of *payer* after *voudrais*, and the incorrect fee for the room). Student B, however, focuses on the content and only corrected the fee in the subsequent turn.

Example 2.16

1 Std A: Je voudrais une chambre – à une lit et avec une bain – s'il vous plaît. Je voudrais quatre-vingts francs.

    [I'd like – at* a single with a* bath, please. I'd like 80 francs.]

2 Std B: No, soixante. (Discussion in English – indecipherable)

    [No sixty.]

3 Std A: Je voudrais une chambre – à une grande lit et – une bain – s'il vous plaît. Je voudrais payer – cinquante francs.

    [I'd like a room with at* a* double* bed and a* bath, please. I'd like to pay 50 francs.]

(Tognini, 2008, p. 223)

In Example 2.17, three learners of Italian are compiling questions to ask visiting exchange students from Italy. This activity requires the learners to experiment with language beyond preformulated language. Students L and M jointly construct the question *Ti piace l'Australia?* (Do you like Australia?) (turns 1–3), but Student O has some doubts about the sentence (turn 4) and offers an alternative sentence (turn 8). This prompts Student L to produce the grammatically acceptable sentence (turn 9). Although such interaction tends to be brief and contains fragments, students' attention is nevertheless drawn to issues of form in a meaningful way.

Example 2.17

1 Std L: Ti piace – ti piace -

[Do you like – do you like]

2 Std M: l'Australia

3 Std L: Ti piace l'Australia?

[Do you like Australia?]

4 Std O: Uuum.

5 Std L: (Repeats the sentence as she writes it down.) Ti piace l'Australia? Is it "dell" Australia?

[Do you like Australia? . . . of Australia?]

6 Std M: Uum, probably.

7 Std L: No, I don't know.

8 Std O: Could you write, "Che cosa ti piace fare l'Australia?"

[. . . What do you like to do Australia?]

9 Std L: First, "Cosa ti piace dell'Australia?" What else? – uum.

[. . . What do you like about Australia? . . .]

(Tognini, 2008, p. 244)

As shown in Example 2.18, learners engage in negotiation and attend to forms when they resort to their shared L1. In this information gap activity in a secondary school class, the students encountered difficulties and try to negotiate (see turns 4, 6, and 7) but, in doing so, revert to L1 to keep the exchange going. The switch to L1 is likely due to their low proficiency. In the foreign language context where there is less exposure and fewer opportunities to use the target language outside the classroom and where learners share the same L1, learners may inevitably switch to L1 to solve linguistic (and task management) problems more efficiently and keep the central conversation going. This issue is further discussed in Chapter 5.

Example 2.18

1 Std A: (Possibly reading from worksheet.) Est-ce que il y a une – cuisine?
   [Is there a kitchen?]

2 Std B: Umm – la cuisine – est –chez le – premier étage.
   [Umm – the kitchen – is – at* the first floor.]

3 Std A: Umm, umm – une peut – on peut -?
   [Umm, umm – a can (sounds like "a little") can one –?]

4 Std B: What did you say?

5 Std A: on peut?
   [Can one?]

6 Std B: I don't know what you're actually doing.

7 Std A: I don't know. Umm *(Laughs)* – Is this all right?

8 Std B: You have to say, what time is it open till?

9 Std A: Yeh, I say, au premier étage.
   [on the first floor.]

(Tognini, 2008, p. 232)

As shown in the previous examples, the learners in the study by Tognini (2008) did not discuss linguistic problems (such as suggesting a past-tense form or a particular word to describe the content of a picture, or correcting the ending of a verb), unlike that observed in other studies of adult learners with higher proficiency (e.g., Examples 2.11–2.13 from Storch, 2008). Rather, peer interaction is largely used as contextualized practice, using preformulated language for a communicative purpose. Tognini (2008) suggests that this type of practice is particularly helpful for beginner learners and may potentially assist learners to proceduralize explicit knowledge and develop fluency (e.g., de Bot, 1996; DeKeyser, 1998). This issue will be further discussed in Chapter 4.

Third and lastly, Example 2.19 illustrates how talking with peers can promote noticing. This data was originally collected by Cao (2009) in an English for Academic Purpose (EAP) pretertiary classroom in New Zealand for a study on willingness to communicate. Here the students are collaboratively working on writing a health questionnaire. Despite earlier assistance by the teacher, the group is struggling with how to express the question "how many times have you had . . ."; their struggle continues for a further 26 turns worth of negotiating how to say it.

Example 2.19

127 JO: How how many times did you (..) do (..) a plastic surgery, maybe one
      time

128   [4 turns later]

129 SW: Did you do did you have did you have maybe have

130 JO: I think have you gone I think have you gone, because it's already fin-
          ish, surgery

131 SW: How many times did you

132 JO: Have you gone a plastic surgery, I'm not sure but

(Cao, 2009, unpublished raw data)

Their deliberations in the comparatively equal context of peer interaction lead them in some false directions (JO introduces the non-targetlike collocations *do* and *go*), but they are clearly engaged with this form. In peer interaction, learners are trying out language, manipulating the forms in imperfect ways—but their attention is on how to say it. Their focus here sets them up to pay attention later when the teacher resolves their problem. In this way, peer group interaction works hand in hand with the teacher-group interaction. We will discuss this further in Chapter 12, in relation to the complimentary nature of peer and teacher-fronted interaction.

Experimentation with language among peers alone can appear limited because of a lack of focus on grammatical forms and, often, a sole focus on meaning. On the one hand, peer interaction can contain non-targetlike use and miscorrections. On the other hand, even where incorrect resolution of language problems occur, interactions between peers that do contain an element of difficulty and experimentation may promote eventual learning. These problems lay the ground for these learners to notice possible solutions that may arise in later interactions with the teacher or other peers.

The three studies discussed previously show how peer interaction may assist learners in attending to forms even in the absence of frequent and targetlike corrective feedback. Trying out language, albeit inexpertly, may yet promote L2 development.

Conclusion

This chapter explored characteristics of learners' experimentation with language during peer interaction and how their experimentation may promote L2 development. As learners experiment with language in various ways during peer interaction, learners negotiate or attend to different aspects of language within LREs (e.g., morpho-syntax, lexis, pronunciation, and punctuation) and used various resources to resolve difficulties, including shared L1, metalinguistic knowledge, and implicit knowledge. Through this process, learners are deeply engaged in the problem and its solution; it is trying out the language themselves that leads them to seek help. However, various contextual and learner factors, such as task type, classroom versus laboratory, learner proficiency, age, and pair dynamics, shape the characteristics and success of interaction for L2 development. In the absence of frequent corrective feedback or discussion of language problems, experimentation with language may involve rehearsing preformulated language to convey meaning and the lengthy procedure of patching together short utterances and fragments, collaborating with their peers to accomplish the task. These processes may ultimately assist learners to proceduralize their explicit language knowledge of the target language, a topic explored in Chapter 4. Perhaps a primary strength of peer interaction is that it allows learners the space to experiment with language, to try out language forms without being corrected, to struggle a little and discover the limitations of their knowledge, and to confirm or query the ways they express things. Most significantly, it can promote noticing of form and awareness of gaps to be resolved in due course.

3

PEER INTERACTION AS A CONTEXT FOR CORRECTING LANGUAGE

Introduction

In the previous chapter, we noted that one role of peer interaction is to provide an opportunity to experiment with language form and use, through communicating and collaborating with other learners (Philp & Tognini, 2010). This chapter focuses on fostering targetlike production through interaction, and on the strengths and limitations of peer interaction in this regard. Using the target language for communicative purposes can push learners to produce more complex or accurate language forms, reflect on the forms they use, and modify or correct their language output (Gass, 1997; Long, 1996; Mackey, 2012). To what extent is this potential realized in peer interaction? We will explore three ways that peer interaction could provide opportunities for learners to address non-targetlike use of language: in the form of feedback, in the form of modified output, and in the form of the learners' own reflections and revisions of language use. We will explore each of these in turn in the context of peer interaction and reflect on differences with teacher-learner interaction. In this chapter, we focus exclusively on oral interaction; peer written corrective feedback will be addressed in Chapter 10.

In order to explain what we mean by feedback, we begin this chapter with five examples. In this book, corrective feedback refers to an interlocutor's response to a non-targetlike utterance. It includes implicit and explicit correction. Corrective feedback constitutes a type of input that learners receive from their interlocutor during interaction. Input refers to any language, written or spoken, that learners are exposed to, but corrective feedback is different from other types of input as it is given in response to a perceived non-targetlike utterance. In that sense it is reactive. In contrast, output refers to any language that learners produce.

Example 3.1 shows the learner (L3) simply correcting his/her peer's utterance without advising the interlocutor that his/her utterance contained an incorrect word choice. The corrective feedback provided by L3 is referred to as a recast. It provides "positive evidence" of what is acceptable and, by juxtaposition, implicitly corrects the former term (Long, 2007; Mackey, 2012). Thus, L3 does not explicitly mention L1's incorrect choice of the verb "stopped"; the recast of the verb "stopped" to "turned off" implies correction. L1 incorporates the feedback in the subsequent turn, suggesting that L1 perceives it as corrective.

Example 3.1

L1: if they stopped!

L3: turned off

L1: if they turned off yeah

(McDonough, 2004, p. 216)

Although less common in peer interaction, correction can be explicit, as seen in Example 3.2. Here, B explicitly corrects A's choice of the verb "disturb" and suggests "blocked" instead. A incorporates the new word.

Example 3.2

A: quickly he /distu:rb/

B: No, not "disturb" you can say . . . ehm "blocked"

A: Ah, yes, blocked, blocked, the the . . .

(Bruton & Samuda, 1980, p. 53)

Implicit correction such as recasts (Example 3.1) and explicit correction (Example 3.2) are usually provided when the meaning of the utterance is clear, but the form used is non-targetlike (Oliver, 1995). In contrast, another type of feedback, negotiation moves, such as clarification requests or confirmation checks, is often given simply to clarify the meaning of the utterance (Long, 1983). This feedback can result in modified output. In Example 3.3, two learners are carrying out a picture drawing task. H8's clarification requests prompt H7 to segment and rephrase his initial utterance a number of times. Pica (1994) argues that this kind of feedback can serve to make language form and structure more salient for the learner.

Example 3.3

H7: Eeto, sono ki no aida ni onnanoko ga naiteiru.

[Well, between trees, there is a girl who is crying.]

H8: Nani ga arimasuka? (Clarification Request ← prompt)

[What is there?]

H7:   Naiteru onnanoko. (Modified output)

  [The girl who is crying]

H8:   Nani o shiteimasuka? (Clarification Request ← prompt)

  [What is she doing?]

H7:   Sorede naiteimasu. (Modified output)

  [She is crying.]

(Iwashita, 1993, p. 31, commentary added)

Although modified output in Example 3.3 is initiated by the interlocutor (listener), modified output can be initiated by the speaker. This type of modified output may be referred to as self-repair or self-initiated modified output. A confirmation check is a negotiation move following the previous speaker's utterance to confirm that the utterance was understood or heard correctly as shown in Example 3.4. In this example, two confirmation check moves are identified. In turn 4, the learner H7 simply repeats H8's previous utterance to confirm the meaning of the statement. However, in turn 8, H8's utterance was modified by H7. In each case, they serve to ensure mutual comprehension.

Example 3.4

1 H8:   "G"

  [G]

2 H7:   "G" wa doko?

  [Where is "G"?]

3 H8:   "B" no tsugi?

  [after "B"?]

4 H7:   "B" no tsugi?   ← confirmation check

  [after "B"?]

5 H8:   Hai.

  [Yes]

6 H7:   "G" wa nan no?

  [What is G?]

7 H8:   "G" wa sannin wa kuruma no mae ni tatteimasu.

  [In "G" three are standing in front of the car.]

8 H7:   *"Kuruma no naka?"*   ← confirmation check

  [In the car?]

9 H8:   Kuruma no mae.

  [In front of the car.]

(Iwashita, 1993, p. 30)

Some confirmation check moves, however, can serve a corrective function when given in response to communication difficulties associated with non-targetlike use, as shown in Example 3.5. Here, B corrects the verb form used in A's previous utterance to confirm the meaning of the statement. A then repeats B's statement himself ("Yondeimasu" [*She is reading*]), indicating recognition of the modification, or "uptake" (Lyster & Ranta, 1997).

Example 3.5

A: Etto, onnanoko wa hon ah o yo-yomimasu.

    [Well, a girl will read/reads a book.]

B: Yondeimasu?

    [Is (she) reading?]

A: Yondeimasu.

    [She is reading.]

(Iwashita, 1993, p. 37)

The previous examples show that learners do not just practice the language in interaction. Importantly, they receive information about the coherence, appropriateness, and accuracy of their language use in the context of communicating meaning, and this happens in ways that allow them to make and strengthen form/meaning connections. This has been well documented in native speaker–learner interactions (Mackey & Goo, 2007), but less so in peer interaction. The question is the extent to which feedback and opportunities to modify output happen in peer interactions. A further issue is the reliability of such feedback. Teachers and students alike express concern that learners may receive non-targetlike input from other learners and be unable to correct each other if they do (e.g., Kim & McDonough, 2011; McDonough, 2004; Pica, Lincoln-Porter, Paninos, & Linnell, 1996). At the heart of these questions is the crucial issue as to whether peer interaction meets the needs of learners for refining their linguistic knowledge. That is, whether input provided by learners through feedback is reliable in terms of quality and quantity.

In the following section, theoretical orientations toward understanding a potential role of peer interaction in second language (L2) development will be discussed, followed by a review of empirical studies in this field. Throughout the chapter, we focus on studies of corrective feedback, negotiation of meaning, and modified output, specific to the context of peer interaction. Our main focus in this chapter is to explore the extent to which peer interaction may be effective in terms of correcting and modifying language and to explore benefits and limitations of peer interaction for L2 development. In order to examine these issues, we review studies that compare peer interaction with native speaker–learner or teacher-learner interaction. To date, there is relatively little research comparing teacher-learner and peer interaction. For this reason, we will depend somewhat on the native speaker–learner research, which is laboratory based.

Theoretical Foundations

Interaction Hypothesis

The theoretical basis for drawing a connection between learner correction and L2 development largely draws upon Long's (1981, 1983, 1996) interaction hypothesis. Long proposed that conversational modifications, offered in response to communication difficulties, promote L2 learning. Reviewing negotiation studies, Pica (1994, 2013) suggested that learners attend to both message and form during negotiation, and is particularly helpful in promoting a focus on language form. She arguesd that negotiation can "help make input comprehensible to learners, help them modify their own output, and provide opportunities for them to access L2 form and meaning" (Pica, 1994, p. 520). In an update of the interaction hypothesis, Long (1996) stressed the facilitative role of implicit negative feedback in conversational interaction because such feedback draws the learners' attention to mismatches between input and output. Through peer interaction, learners provide feedback to one another and receive opportunities for modified output (Pica, 1994). Modified output provides learners with an opportunity to reflect on their language use as they are pushed to produce more accurate and appropriate forms in response to the feedback they receive (see Chapter 2 for further discussion on the role of output in L2 learning). These processes draw learners' attention to form and promote cognitive processing of target language grammar (Mackey, 2007, 2012; Pica, 2013).

This model of how interaction facilitates L2 learning was initially proposed based on interaction between native speakers and learners and was primarily conducted under experimental conditions, rather than by using naturalistic classroom data. A question arises as to the extent to which this model can appropriately be applied to peer interaction in classrooms.

Sociocultural Perspectives on Interaction and Feedback

Research on corrective feedback and modified output has been mainly undertaken within the interactionist framework as outlined previously. However, as mentioned in the previous chapter, an increasing number of studies have drawn on alternative theoretical foundations, namely, on sociocultural perspectives of L2 acquisition (e.g., Lantolf, 2000a; Lantolf & Appell, 1994; Lantolf & Thorne, 2006). As explained in Chapter 2, this alternative view suggests that learning first takes place through social interaction between the novice learner and the expert interlocutor (Vygotsky, 1978, 1986). Through joint construction, novice learners are enabled to do what they could not do on their own. This is described as a gradual move to greater self-autonomy, with the transfer of "other regulation" (e.g., when task performance is structured and completed through another's as-sistance) to "self-regulation" (when task performance is structured and completed by the individual alone).

Within sociocultural perspectives, corrective feedback and negotiation of meaning are contextualized within a collaborative process, where the dynamics of the interaction itself shape the nature of the feedback and inform its usefulness to the learner (Lantolf & Thorne, 2006). Example 3.6 illustrates this point. The two students (Becky and Hal) are engaged in a translation exercise in which each student takes a turn to initiate a Japanese sentence. In this example, Becky is try-ing to form a sentence (*My brother wants my father to take him to Japan*) in Japanese. Hal regulates Becky's production through co-construction in a number of ways: in turn 6, by adding the particle "e"; in turn 14, by adding a verb; and in turn 15, by reassuring Becky as she hesitantly attempts to put the words together. Thus, corrective feedback and negotiation of meaning are provided in the collaborative process as the two learners work through the problems encountered.

Example 3.6

1 B: Otoosan, (.) watashi wa=

   [Father ((honorific)), (.) I=]

2 H: =(What she want?)

3 B: uh, what she wants you// to do

4 H: Your father. Your father. // (Understand?)

5 B: Oh, watashi no oko ((laughs)) watashi no chichi wa, (.) nihon (.) ah (..) niho::n

   [Oh, my oko ((laughs)) my dad (.) Japan (.) ah (..) Japan.]

6 H: E   ← adds missing particle

   [to]

7 B: Ni? E.

   [to ((either ni or e is correct))]

8 H: Nihon e?

   [To Japan?]

9 B: Oh nihon ni?

   [Oh to Japan.]

10 H: Oh nihon ni?

   [Oh to Japan?]

11 B: [Niho:n ni:, (.)

   [To Japan: (.)]

12 H: Nihon ni.

　　　　[To Japan.]

13 B: Tsurete: hoshii to omotte imasu.

　　　　[Wants ((somebody)) to lead ((him)) to Japan.]

14 H: Tsurete itte hoshii to omo//tte imasu.   ← adds missing verb

　　　　[((adds the missing verb "itte" [go] to Becky's utterance))]

15 B: Tsurete itte?

　　　　[To take along?]

16 H: Hai.   ← confirms correct use

　　　　[Yes.]

17 B: Tsurete: itte hoshii to omote imasu.

　　　　[((Becky repeats Hal's line 14 utterance))]

18 H: Hai.   ← confirms correct use

　　　　[Yes.]

(Ohta, 2000a, p. 63, commentary added)

From a sociocultural perspective, the feedback that learners receive is considered "other regulation" because learners who receive feedback are guided toward more targetlike language use, just as Hal assisted Becky in revising the statement in turn 14 in the previous example. It is finely tuned to provide assistance within the zone of proximal development and encourages the learner to move to "self-regulation." Following Vygotsky (1986), this process is achieved through expert assistance to the learner. However, as noted in Chapter 2, in L2 acquisition research, this process may also occur between learners through collective scaffolding (Donato, 1994) (See Example 2.7 in Chapter 2).

Provision of Feedback and Modified Output

We have briefly outlined how correcting and modifying language may contribute to learning, from an interactionist and from a sociocultural perspective; we now explore this process in more depth. We will first look at early research on peer feedback and its impact on L2 development. Early studies compared negotiation moves observed in peer interaction with native speaker–learner interaction in laboratory settings. Both Varonis and Gass (1985) and Porter (1986) found that learners negotiate for meaning with other learners more frequently than with native-speaking interlocutors. They claimed that there were opportunities to investigate learners' responses and repair when communication broke down in the peer interactions. However, a question remained as to whether learners provide useful feedback, and whether their peers are able to actually make use of it. In fact, Porter (1986) found the amount of correction made by native speakers and learners alike to be very low (6% and 1.5%, respectively), and in some instances, learners miscorrected errors. Furthermore, as Mackey, Oliver, and Leeman (2003) point out, the frequent negotiation moves observed in the early negotiation studies were not always given as corrective feedback. As the primary purpose of negotiation is to achieve comprehension of the utterance, a negotiation move can be given in response to an utterance containing both targetlike and non-targetlike forms. Example 3.7 illustrates this point.

As learner J interviews learner S, we see a focus on meaning rather than form; the interlocutor attends to lexis rather than grammatical form. It is the word used or the content of what the learner says that the interlocutor queries (e.g., "retire," "institution," "ingress"), not non-targetlike use itself, although there are frequent errors (e.g., "But he work with uh uh institution," "The name I s ... some thin like eh control of the"). This is consistent with findings of classroom-based research (e.g., Tognini, 2008; Williams 2001); unlike teacher-learner interaction, peer interaction is not typically associated with corrective feedback, and negotiation sequences tend to revolve around lexis. This poses a limitation of the role of peer interaction in L2 development through corrective feedback and modified output.

Example 3.7

140 J:	And your what is your mm father's job?	
140 S:	My father now is retire.	T
140 J:	retire?	I
140 S:	yes.	R
140 J:	oh yeah	RR
140 S:	But he work with uh uh institution	T
140 J:	institution	I
140 S:	Do you know that? The name I s ...	
	some thin like eh control of the state	CC, R, T
140 J:	aaaaaaaaah	RR
140 S:	Do you understand more or less?	C
140 J:	State is uh ... what what kind of state?	I
140 S:	It is uhm	R
140 J:	Michigan State?	I
140 S:	No, the all nation	R/T
140 J:	No (back channel) government?	I
140 S:	all the nation, all the nation, Do you know	
	for example is a the the institution mmm	

	of the state mm of Venezuela	I
140 J:	ah ah	RR
140 S:	had to declare declare? Her ingress.	T
140 J:	English?	I
140 S:	No, English no (laugh) . . . ingress, her	
	ingress I	R

Note: R = Response, I = Indicator, T = Trigger, RR = Reaction to response, CC = Comprehension check

(Varonis & Gass, 1985, pp. 78–79, note added)

The focus of peer interaction research in the 1980s was on feedback in the form of negotiation arising from communication breakdown. There were few studies that investigated learners' ability to provide one another with feedback on grammatical accuracy or the types of strategies they typically employ to achieve this. One exception is Bruton and Samuda's (1980) small-scale descriptive study of video-recorded classroom interaction data over one week. Students worked together on problem-solving tasks without teacher support. They found that in addition to self-correction, learners were able to correct each other's errors and used a variety of strategies including implicit/explicit corrections, which often prompted the interlocutor to revise their initial statement. However, non-targetlike utterances were not always corrected, and learners were not consistently aware of communication breakdown or the need for repair. Frequency of correction was not reported in this study, and so it is not clear how often learners were able to attend to the errors or whether these particular errors were associated with communication breakdown.

Similarly, Gass and Varonis (1989) examined repairs observed in the data collected from 10 dyads of first language (L1) Japanese learners at intermediate level in an intensive English language program. They found that these intermediate-level learners were able to provide corrective feedback to one another on a variety of aspects in the target language and found that learner repairs were primarily in the direction of the target language. Although not able to produce targetlike forms, learners were able to recognize what was correct or incorrect during interaction with peers.

Such early studies indicate that learners are able to correct others and also recognize what is correct and what is not, even in the absence of a native speaker, and even when their own forms are not always targetlike. However, neither the frequency of the feedback nor the learning outcomes of peer feedback exchanges is clear. Recent peer interaction studies on feedback present some further insights into corrective feedback, negotiation of meaning, and modified output, and their link with L2 development. This will be discussed later in the chapter (e.g., Adams, 2007; Adams, Nuevo, & Egi, 2011; McDonough, 2004; Toth, 2008).

Comparison With Native Speaker–Learner Interactions

Researchers, teachers, and students alike question the reliability of the learner to consistently provide targetlike feedback or to self-correct with accuracy. A considerable number of studies have compared opportunities for corrective feedback and modified output observed in peer interaction within native speaker–learner interaction. Though these studies were undertaken under experimental conditions, and not in intact classes, their findings provide useful insights into differences between corrective feedback employed in peer interaction and in teacher-learner interaction.

For example, Pica et al. (1996) compared feedback and modified output produced by peer interaction with those in native speaker–learner interactions. Their analysis of data drawn from 10 peer and 10 native speaker–learner dyads raises a number of concerns. They found that learners tended to provide corrective feedback and to modify their own utterances by segmenting individual words and phrases of previous utterances and by repeating. However, unlike native speaker interlocutors, they rarely provided alternative words and paraphrases or made structural changes as seen in Example 3.8. Here, Shunta's question repeats part of Yakahito's statement. Similarly, Yakahito's response is a segment of his initial utterance. Although such exchanges seek to clarify the meaning, neither the intention of Shunta's initial question nor the meaning of Yakahito's response is clear.

Example 3.8

Yakahito	Shunta
First picture when she is standing	
in front of gass	when she is? [signal]
Standing yea standing in front	
of gas [response]	

(Pica et al., 1996, p. 72)

In contrast, the interaction between a native speaker and a learner, in Example 3.9, clearly shows the intent of the question and draws attention to the problematic form ("glass"). In Example 3.10, confirming the meaning of the learner's statement, the native interlocutor paraphrases the learner's statement instead of segmenting it.

Example 3.9

Learner	NS Interlocutor
around the house we have glass	you have what? [signal]

uh grass, plants and grass

[response]

(Pica, 1992, p. 2)

Example 3.10

NNS: and tree with stick

NS: you mean the trees have branches?

NNS: yes

(Pica, 1992, cited in Pica, 1994, p. 515)

More recent studies have shown that factors such as context and age influence the way that learners engage in interaction as well as the ways that interaction differs when a learner works with a native speaker or a peer. For example, Mackey et al. (2003) compared native speaker–learner and peer interactions in both adult and child dyads. The analysis of the data drawn from task-based conversation of 24 dyads in each group showed that even though native speaker interlocutors provided a significantly larger amount of feedback in the adult dyads, the difference in the child dyads was not significant. Although the interlocutor type (native speaker or learner) did not differentiate the amount of modified output in the adult dyads, it did lead to a significant difference in the child group. The lower incidence of corrective feedback and the higher incidence of signals requiring learners to modify their own initial utterance (i.e., clarification requests) may be attributable to sociolinguistic and affective factors (such as saving face for the interlocutor), as well as the learners' limited linguistics resources. The findings reveal differences between peer interaction and native speaker–learner interactions, and also some mediating effects of factors such as context and age on provision of corrective feedback and modified output in peer interactions.

Similarly, Sato and Lyster (2007) compared feedback types (reformulation vs. elicitation) and modified output in eight peer dyads and four native speaker–learner dyads, as well as learner perceptions of the interactions. Although native speaker interlocutors provided more reformulation feedback than learner interlocutors, it was the opposite in the case of elicitation feedback. Significantly more instances of modified output were produced in peer dyads than native speaker–learner dyads. Sato and Lyster explain these findings in terms of different comfort levels that learners experienced according to interlocutor type and their perceptions of the native speaker interlocutor. This issue is further discussed in the next section.

Characteristics of Peer Interaction

Unlike the negotiation studies in the 1980s, recent studies on corrective feedback, modified output, and negotiation in the context of peer interaction report a clear difference between peer and native speaker–learner interaction including fewer instances of corrective feedback and, in the former case, a preference for modified output over corrective feedback. This does not mean that learners are not actually able to correct other learners' non-targetlike use. Fujii and Mackey (2009), for example, found through interview data that learners may deliberately avoid correction. When replayed specific segments of peer interaction, learners reported that they deliberately avoided negotiation of meaning and did not indicate their difficulty in understanding others' utterances in order to save face. Instead, they relied on guesswork as to what others were trying to say, assisted by shared L1 and common context. Similarly, other classroom-based research (e.g., Foster & Ohta, 2005; Philp, Walter, & Basturkmen, 2010; Tognini, 2008) reports a reticence among learners to provide corrective feedback to peers, for a number of reasons, including perceived inappropriateness, low proficiency, face-saving, and the desire to focus on communication rather than grammatical accuracy. This is reflected in Examples 3.11 and 3.12 from interviews with undergraduate students of French in a foreign language context.

Example 3.11

Ben: . . . I don't want to be uhm I make mistakes myself so uhm I don't want to say oh no no no you can't say it like that you're meant to say blablablablabla because I'm a stu . . . student too and I'm not better than them than them so uhm I don't want to be better than them I'm just another student

(Philp et al., 2010, p. 272)

Example 3.12

Eva: Like if she says choix or choisi because I can understand what she's really want to mean so I just don't like interrupt

(Philp et al., 2010, p. 272)

Such research suggests that peer interaction can be an unlikely context for provision of corrective feedback. In contrast, it may be a better context for modified output than native speaker–learner interactions (Mackey et al., 2003; Sato & Lyster, 2007). As noted previously in the studies of native speaker–learner versus peer interactions, greater modified output among peers in comparison to native speaker–learner dyads may be related to the type of feedback given: The native speaker provides recasts and reformulations of non-targetlike utterances, whereas peers tend to repeat rather than modify one another's errors. Ellis (2012) makes this point when he differentiates between input-based feedback (which provides a reformulation, e.g., a recast) and output-based feedback (which solicits reformulation by the original speaker). Many of these comparison studies were conducted in L2 settings, where learners are not reliant solely on the classroom for target language input. However, the results of those studies are consistent with other work conducted in foreign language settings. In the Sato and Lyster study (2007), learners produced more output when they interacted with their fellow learners than with native speakers, as they felt that they had more time to plan their utterances in peer interaction. Conversely, with a native speaker, learners made less effort to self-correct, but rather depended on their interlocutors to be able to guess their intended meaning In Example 3.13, the learner relies on body language to communicate with the native speaker interlocutor but with the fellow learner feels more relaxed and has time to work out what to say.

Example 3.13

I really wanted to use body language to explain to him what I wanted to say when I was doing the task with my native speaker partner. When I was communicating with Risa, however, I thought like I had time to think so why don't I take time before I say anything.

(Sato & Lyster, 2007, p. 139)

Example 3.14 shows one learner's reliance on the native speaker interlocutor to guess what she has to say, reducing the need to try hard to make herself understood.

Example 3.14

I don't know why but I feel that native speakers are good at guessing what we want to say in English.

(Sato & Lyster, 2007, p. 138)

The examples show that learners seem to employ different strategies in communicating with a native speaker than with fellow learners, and this may be true of teacher-learner interaction. With other learners, they make a greater effort to be understood or are at least less reticent to try things out. These strategies are likely to benefit their learning. On the other hand, with a teacher or a native speaker, they may undermine their learning opportunities by reducing effort or attention. These differences highlight the point discussed throughout this book that peer interactions are not necessarily inferior or superior to teacher-learner interactions. Rather, they each have benefits and limitations that should be considered when creating communication opportunities in language classrooms.

Strategies Employed During Interaction

The peer interaction studies discussed previously show that learners are able to correct other learners' errors and modify their own utterances in response to other learners' signals, but on the whole, the incidence of corrective feedback is not high (although, see Chapters 8, 9, and 10 for effects of task and mode). However, the frequency of feedback varies according to combinations of factors including context, age, tasks, proficiency level, and participant. This may also be associated with sociolinguistic factors, such as a reticence to disturb conventional roles of students and teachers (Allwright, 1998a).

Many of the previous studies conducted in-depth analysis of the interaction and collected learner perceptions in order to explain the low instances of feedback. Innovations in research, such as the use of stimulated recall, have led to a greater awareness of the complexity of the relationship between feedback, modified output, and L2 development. For example, learner perception data provide some explanation for differences in provision and use of feedback in peer versus teacher-student interaction as well as in peer versus native speaker–learner interaction. In addition, a broader analysis, including a sociocultural rather than an interactionist perspective, reveals variation in the strategies employed by learners, including completion (co-construction), continuers, self-correction, and active listening.

The most common strategy used by learners is the completion strategy, in which learners complete each other's utterances together, as shown in Example 3.15. This strategy is often referred to as "co-construction" in sociocultural theory-based studies (Foster & Ohta, 2005). Here, G's incomplete utterance was completed by Sr, by adding the verb *shimasu* (do).

Example 3.15

1 G: Watashi no uchi:: no uh chikaku de (.) uhh booringu:

   [Near my house, bowling:]

   (G's sentence is correct so far, but is missing the accusative particle and verb.)

2 Sr: o shimasu?

   [do?]

   (the verb "to bowl" is "booringu o shimasu")

3 G: Hai.

   [Yes.]

(Ohta, 2001, pp. 94–95)

These completion/co-construction devices may not be intended as corrective, but simply as completion. The two learners assist each other in completing the task. Instead of correcting, when the interlocutor seems in trouble, his/her partner jumps in and takes over the turn to help build the utterance. The task is jointly constructed. In this way, communicative oral interaction may be better suited as a context for co-construction rather than correction. Symmetry between peers underlies such cocompletion as equals; the learners can accept or refute the effort.

Correction or completion by the teacher, however, carries the authority of the expert and thus carries a different weight.

Other- and self-correction are also frequently observed in peer interaction. Foster and Ohta (2005) found that although there are very few instances where learners need to negotiate for meaning to achieve comprehension, learners are able to correct their own utterances without being prompted. This is generally referred to as self-initiated repair and was also the most frequently observed repair type in studies by Buckwalter (2001), McDonough (2004), and Shehadeh (2001). Buckwalter (2001) identified repair strategies in the dyadic discourse of tertiary learners of Spanish, employing the broader definition of repair borrowed from conversation analysis (Schegloff, Jefferson, & Sacks, 1977)—that is, repair occurring in the absence of errors, as well as in presence of errors. Buckwalter (2001) details frequent observation of self-initiated repair as a self-regulatory process.

Other strategies employed by learners are "continuers" (Foster & Ohta, 2005) and "active listening" (Fujii & Mackey, 2009). An instance where an interlocutor takes an interest in the speaker's utterance and encourages him/her to continue is coded as a "continuer." Active listening is a listening strategy where trained learners become skillful partners in giving feedback by using verbal/nonverbal methods of active participation in conversation, such as back-channeling and the use of "wh" questions to help the speakers to continue (e.g., what?, where?, who?, when?, why?) (Fujii & Mackey, 2009).

In summary, strategies employed during peer interaction to promote mutual comprehension highlight the differences between peer and native speaker–learner interaction. Learners use different means of assisting one another when working through language difficulties. Reformulation, for example, a common strategy used by more proficient speakers, is beyond early L2 competence. Peer interlocutors at low and intermediate levels have limited target language knowledge and so provide less information about target language grammar through feedback. However, through co-construction or completion strategies, they assist one another to keep the conversation going and to complete the task. Taken in sum, these distinctions demonstrate the different strengths of native speaker–learner and peer interaction, rather than deficiencies. In the absence of native speaker models and corrective feedback, the focus of much of peer interaction is practice and pro- ceduralization of knowledge. These concepts are further discussed in Chapter 4.

Effects of Peer Correction on L2 Development

Although rare, a handful of studies investigate the effects of peer interaction on L2 development (e.g., Adams, 2007; Adams et al., 2011; McDonough, 2004; Toth, 2008). Despite substantial differences in study design, sample size, settings, target language features, and proficiency, all show that peer interaction can support L2 development, but to a limited extent. The authors interpret the findings in light of: learner perceptions of corrective feedback; learners' limited L2 knowledge which resulted in miscorrection; and individual variation in learner performance. Earlier research suggests that learners engage in a similar number of instances of interactional modifications and feedback to that of native speaker–learner interactions; however, the more recent studies call into question whether this in fact leads to similar learning. In other words, surface similarities in interactions may not actually be equivalent in terms of learning potential.

In a small-scale study of a foreign language class in Thailand, McDonough (2004) reports that most of the interactional modifications observed in peer interaction were self-initiated, which is quite different from modified output observed in native speaker–learner interaction which is largely other-initiated. Furthermore, the participants did not perceive the peer interactions to have assisted learning (according to questionnaire data). They also commented that peer interaction was useful for practicing oral communication skills, but less useful for learning English grammar. Instead, they believed that explicit instruction and practice activities were helpful for learning grammar. These concerns were also shared by the teacher. Other concerns reported by McDonough included environmental conditions (e.g., class size and position of student desks) that made it difficult for the teachers to monitor and provide feedback and the perceived mismatch between peer work and exam content.

In an experimental study of peer interaction in a laboratory setting, Adams (2007) found that although nearly 60% of the feedback episodes included in the tailor-made posttests evidenced learning (which was measured with acceptability of items and picture-labeling items), the rate of learning of the tested items varied from item to item, with past tense being the highest and locative the lowest. Close examination of the interaction data also revealed that even over the three treatment sessions, some target linguistic items had become salient, which may have assisted the learner in building form-meaning connections. Although facilitative, some feedback episodes offered incorrect solutions to linguistic problems, which resulted in the learning of non-targetlike items as shown in Example 3.16.

Example 3.16

Learner 1: John arrive, arrove, arrove or arrive?

Learner 2: arrove is in past.

Learner 1: arrove airport. Or arrived.

Learner 2: arrove is in past.

Learner 1: I mean arrove or arrived.

Learner 2: arroved the airplane.

Learner 1: arrived or arrove.

Learner 2: arrove.

Learner 1:   arrove the airport at 8:30 am.

(Adams, 2007, p. 49)

In this example, the learners who are collaboratively writing a picture story discuss the past-tense form of the verb "arrive." Initially, Learner 1 was unsure of whether "arrove" or "arrived" was the right form, but Learner 2 maintained "arrove" as correct and corrected Learner 1's use of "arrived" despite Learner 1's continual questioning of the form. In the posttest, Learner 1 ticked as "correct" the statement "John arrove at the airport last night."

In a classroom experimental study with a large sample size ($N = 71$) and longer treatment (nine task-based conversations over three sessions), Adams et al. (2011) found that the feedback that experimental group participants received from other learners was not focused exclusively on the target items, but rather, that it varied and included lexical items, articles, verb tenses, voice, and pronunciation. As the feedback focused on multiple and disparate items, target forms may have been less salient and less effective for learning. As found in Adams and McDonough's studies discussed previously, feedback observed in peer interactions was not always perceived as corrective. Adams et al. (2011) argue that feedback in peer interaction may have different functions from that provided in teacher-learner interactions. In the latter case, the learner can assume both that feedback is only given on non-targetlike utterances and that the feedback presents targetlike information. In peer interaction, neither of these conditions can be assumed. Because of this, even explicit correction may be interpreted as a signal to discuss linguistic form rather than as feedback.

Although the three studies discussed previously all sought a possible link between feedback and L2 development, Toth (2008) compared the effects of teacher-led and learner-led interactions on L2 development. Seventy-eight L1 English-learners of Spanish from six university classes were randomly assigned to a learner-led discussion group, a teacher-led discussion group, or a control group. Treatment group learners carried out two communication tasks preceded by grammar instruction over seven weeks. Learners in both treatment groups outperformed the control group in grammatical judgment and oral production tasks. Furthermore, participants in teacher-led discussions did significantly better in both tasks than those in the learner-led discussions.

Qualitative analysis of the discourse revealed that learners' attention to form in peer interaction was more broadly focused on a number of linguistic issues than in teacher-led class interactions as shown in Example 3.17. The target linguistic item in the study is the anticausative clitic *se*. As Toth (2008) explained, the learners' attention was mainly focused on the past-tense form as shown in line b, and an overgeneralized form appeared, but discussion on the correct use of *se* did not appear until later in line f. The example shows that peer interaction might not have allowed for the same procedural assistance in using the target form that was afforded to learners who were led by their teacher.

Example 3.17

a Student 2: ¿C´ omo se dice "wind"?

   [How do you say "wind"?]

b Student 1: Viento. Ok, you could say, maybe, "Se, se entra *[overgeneralized se]* viento en la casa," like—

   [Wind. Ok, you could say, maybe, "Wind [se], [se] enters the house," like—]

c Student 3: Se, uh, entró, ¿verdad?

   [It [se], uh, entered, right?]

d Student 1: Se entró viento en la casa.

   [Wind [se] entered the house.]

e Student 3: Se entró.

   [It [se] entered.]

f Student 2: Oh, se—¿Se entró?

   [Oh, [se]—It [se] entered?]

g Student 1: Se entró. Oh, but would you use se with that?

h Student 2: You wouldn't.

i Student 1: No, because that's a subject. Right. Viento entré, entró en la casa

   [Wind enter, entered the house.]

j Student 3: Sí.

   [Right.]

(Toth, 2008, p. 260)

These four studies have shown clear limitations of peer interaction despite some gain observed in the posttest results. Where such interaction allows learners to participate collaboratively, it may promote learner autonomy and encourage learners to rely on their own resources to correct one another and modify output. However, corrective feedback was not always frequent and corrective, nor focused on target linguistics items. In some cases, learners resisted peer feedback and did not perceive it as corrective. In contrast, the teachers' intervention was more timely and focused. A further benefit for teacher-learner interaction was that the teacher's frequent observations and assistance were given directly to the learners during the time of production, rather than well after the difficulty had occurred.

Conclusion

This chapter examines correction and modification observed in peer interactions. It explores what is different about peer interaction with regard to correction compared to teacher-learner interaction and to what extent peer interaction promotes or limits language development.

Recent studies suggest that although feedback may occur in peer interaction, this occurrence may not be very promising for learning. On the other hand, peer interaction tends to encourage more modified output than native speaker–learner interaction. Lower incidence of corrective feedback in peer interaction is partly due to learners' limited linguistic and attentional resources, as well as sociolinguistic factors such as face-saving measures and the desire to focus on communication rather than grammatical accuracy. Although corrective feedback is found in peer interaction, it may simply not promote learning in the same way as teacher-learner interactions. However, other aspects of peer interaction, such as the frequent self-correction that occurs as learners strive to communicate with their limited-proficiency peers, may add benefits not found in teacher-learner interactions. Chapter 2 argued that peer interaction is a particularly good context for learners to experiment with language, allowing new forms to emerge. Chapter 4 will further argue the advantages of peer interaction in terms of providing language practice opportunities that promote fluency. This chapter has highlighted both strengths and weaknesses of peer interaction in terms of pushing learners to refine their language use, in order to make it not only more coherent but also more accurate and appropriate. In this process, they pay greater attention to language form. This underscores the need for teachers to consider carefully how to employ peer interaction in the classroom and how to complement it with teacher-learner interaction to promote accurate language use. This is certainly an avenue for further research.

4

PEER INTERACTION AS A CONTEXT FOR POLISHING LANGUAGE

Introduction

Fluent language speakers are able to produce language without much effort, like accomplished musicians who can play the instrument without looking at music sheets or the instrument. The process of producing beautiful sound seems automatic. Words such as *fluent* and *automatic* are also frequently used to characterize advanced/native speaker performance in speech production. What does "automatic" mean, and what is involved in the process of becoming automatic or fluent? What does it mean to say that one's speech production is automatized?

In the previous two chapters, we explored the opportunities learners encounter as they practice using the target language with one another and found both benefits and limitations of peer interaction for second language (L2) learning. In Chapter 2, we were concerned with how learners experiment with language through discussing language problems encountered during collaborative activities and how they grapple with language as they work out what they want to say in the target language. We found that a major benefit of peer interaction is that learners are more likely to make connections between form and meaning through trying things out, reflecting, and modifying their L2 production with reference to their language knowledge resources. In contrast, in Chapter 3, we focused on peer responses to non-targetlike use through corrective feedback and other types of focus on form. Although some research suggests learners can recognize their own and others' non-targetlike use and correct each other's and their own non-targetlike use during peer interaction, we also found that the quality and quantity of corrective feedback is not the same as that observed in native speaker–learner interactions. Apart from the learners' limited linguistic resources, this is also due in part to sociolinguistic factors (e.g., inappropriateness of correcting fellow learners) as well as learner perception of task purpose (i.e., for communication). One of the greatest concerns among teachers and students alike of peer interaction is the provision of inadequate or misleading feedback. Although these can be limitations of peer interaction, the unique characteristics of peer interaction may promote L2 learning in other ways. Two important aspects of peer interaction, and ways that these interactions compliment the strengths of teacher-learner interactions, are (a) the opportunity to grapple with language (as discussed in Chapter 2) and (b) the opportunity to practice.

This chapter explores how peer interaction as language practice provides a context for polishing L2 use, that is, for increasing automaticity in production. A consistent finding of studies comparing teacher-learner and peer interactions is that learners produce more language in peer interaction. They have more turns, and produce longer turns, when interacting with a peer than a teacher (e.g., Pica & Doughty, 1985a). There is an old saying that "practice makes perfect." In this chapter, we explore the ways that extra opportunities to practice producing language in peer interaction may promote learning. We will turn our attention first to the role of practice in promoting automaticity and then to frequency effects.

Fluency and Automaticity

Many learners study a language wishing to gain fluency so that they can communicate with speakers of the language and also carry out various tasks in the target language. In Chapter 2, we explored how the three functions of Swain's output hypothesis contribute to L2 learning, but we did not examine how another function of output, that is, "practice," can promote the development of fluency.

For our purposes, and with a focus on functions of output, we limit the scope of fluency here to speech production. Fluency in speech production is described in terms of the speed, fluidity (smoothness and freedom from interruptions), and accuracy (Segalowitz, 2000). Fluent speech is often characterized as "smooth" and "effortless" with regard to listening and understanding the message in the speech. In contrast, disfluent speech contains many pauses, false starts, and repetitions as learners grope for words, and this may strain listener attention. Beginning learners' speech often shares many of the characteristics of disfluent speech as shown in Example 4.1.

Two beginning learners of Japanese at university, Vicky and Rose, exchange information from pictures to create a story during a jigsaw task. Their production is characterized by multiple repetitions, false starts, and self-correction. Both learners repeat the words a few times and then correct the ending. For example, in turn 2, Rose repeats the female name *Saki san* ("Saki") twice and the verb *kowareru* ("broken") twice after uttering a part of the verb once to produce a short sentence ("Saki's mother is looking at broken eggs"). Similarly, Vicky repeats the verb *aruite* ("walking") as she is not sure of the correct ending of the verb for the progressive form. Producing a simple sentence or two to describe a picture seems very effortful work for both learners.

Example 4.1

1 Vicky: Saki san wa tamago o ryoo- ryoote ni motte imasu. Saki san no inu wa soba de matte imasu. Saki san wa kutsu ga nukete imasu, nukeru.

[Saki holds eggs in her both, both hands. Saki's dog is waiting beside her. Saki is taking taking off her shoes]

2 Rose: Saki san- - Saki san no haha wa- - . . . kowa- kowareru- - kowareru tamago o mite imasu.

[Saki, Saki's mother is watching looking at bro— broken, broken eggs]

3 Vicky: Saki san to Saki san no inu wa tanoshikute arutte- aruite- aruite iru.

[Saki and Saki's dog is happily, walk, walking, walking]

(Iwashita, 2011, unpublished raw data)

This disfluency is partly symptomatic of working "online." Learners must attend to many different demands at the same time, both linguistic and cognitive (e.g., comprehension of the picture, looking for appropriate words, correct ending of the verbs, correct particles, word order, and pronunciation of the words). The process of identifying appropriate words and using appropriate forms and particles to form a sentence is not automatic, but effortful and slow. Fluency improves when processing is more automatic. This sort of processing is usually referred to as fast, effortless, and/or unconscious processing (Segalowitz, 2010). Clearly, the process of producing a sentence by the two learners in Example 4.1 is not automatic.

Researchers who view L2 acquisition primarily as skill acquisition similar to learning to drive or to playing a musical instrument are concerned with how automaticity can be promoted in the learning process (DeKeyser, 2001; Segalowitz, 2003). To become a skillful driver, a competent musician, or a fluent L2 user, a number of different cognitive skills are required. For example, to be a proficient speaker, learners need to tacitly understand structural aspects of the language (i.e., syntax and morphology), the sound system, word meaning, and appropriate use of the language according to the context in which the language is used. In order to produce a sentence appropriate to the context, the speakers' attention is drawn to all aspects of the language. For advanced learners, some operations are automatic (e.g., using the past-tense form to describe a past event), but other learners, especially those at beginning levels, may need to attend to everything—phonology, lexis, and morphology among other components.

de Bot (1996) explains this process of speech production based on Levelt's (1989) model. According to Levelt, speech is produced through a process of three interconnected systems: conceptualizer, formulator, and articulator. Once a message is formed at the preverbal level (conceptualizer), a speech plan is formed by retrieving appropriate words/lexis and then by applying grammatical rules (formulator) before the message will be produced in speech form (articulator). The automatic operation of the three processes generates fluent speech. For beginning learners, very little is automatic: Retrieving lexical units/words and applying them to appropriate grammatical rules will require learners' conscious operation searching for words, grammar, and sound.

Beginners like Rose and Vicky in Example 4.1 may know the word to refer to "break" in Japanese, but they will have difficulty in forming the verb in the passive ("broken"), as shown in turn 2 in the example. Rose seems to resort to her declarative knowledge of how to make a passive form, as the verb was repeated a few times. In contrast, more advanced learners are able to produce the passive form "broken" without conscious effort (Schmidt, 2001).

It is generally understood that to promote fluency and automaticity repeated practice is required (e.g., DeKeyser, 1998; McLaughlin & Heredia, 1996; Segalowitz, 2003). In skill acquisition theory, the goal of practice is automatization through transfer from declarative knowledge to procedural knowledge. Schmidt (1992) refers to "fluency" in speech production as automatic procedural skills. Fluent speakers are able to use their knowledge of how to do something (procedural knowledge) as well as their factual knowledge about something (declarative knowledge) (Anderson, 1983). According to Anderson's (1983, 1992, 1996) Adaptive Control of Thought model, learners go through three steps in the process of transforming declarative knowledge into procedural knowledge: a cognitive stage, where rules and items of factual knowledge are learned with effort in slow operation; an associative stage, where the learner works on putting this into practice; and then an autonomous stage, where execution of the skill becomes automatic and effortless.

Applying this model to L2 learning, instructed language learning can involve rule learning, but the initial application of these rules to production is effortful, sapping attentional resources from other aspects of production and resulting in disfluencies. However, continued practice eases the effort required, and eventually learners need to allocate far fewer resources to applying the rule, freeing up attention for other aspects of production and increasing fluency. Because peer interaction allows learners more opportunities to talk than teacher-learner interaction, it also allows them to make their processing more automatic.

Repeated practice will enhance this process of automatization, but this does not mean that mechanical drills or pattern practice typical of the audio-lingual method is advocated. Rather, as DeKeyser (1998, 2007) explains, the form to be learned has to be practiced in context, where the form is used to convey meaning. The problem of mechanical drills lies in the fact that "they do not engage the learner in the target behaviour of conveying meaning through language" (1998, p. 53). In other words, mechanical drills do not provide association between form and meaning (Gatbonton & Segalowitz, 1988; Segalowitz, 2000).

Role of Peer Interaction in Promoting Automaticity

As seen in Example 4.1, practicing language with other learners provides an opportunity to use the language in meaningful communication even if the learners' speech contains numerous repetitions, pauses, and fragments at times and requires a great deal of listener effort to understand the meaning of the speech. Repeated practice through peer interaction likely leads to two of the four effects of practice proposed by Ellis (2005)—(a) improved access and (b) schematization and script building. That is, as a result of practice, learners are able to retrieve knowledge with less effort. By repeating the same sequence, learners become a little more skillful and a little faster in producing target language forms and sentences. Cognitively, learners are able to form a schema or script about use of the form in the practice. Ellis (2005) explains this process by drawing an analogy from cooking: A novice cook will have become more skillful at making a béchamel sauce from a recipe by the second or third time, as the ingredients are found more readily and the progression through the steps is more routine. Explaining how to get to a train station in another language is easier and faster the second time than the first time, as the speaker is familiar with the words and forms to describe each step to reach the destination; in a sense, the script has already been constructed. The following example further illustrates this process.

The example is taken from Philp, Walter, and Basturkmen. (2010) in their analysis of interaction of 12 hours of University French classes over three weeks. Girard is talking about a hotel his mother had once stayed in and pays little attention to his grammar. Florence points out that he has used the wrong auxiliary "avoir" with the verb "rester" (*to stay*). He goes through a number of trials repeating the phrase and modifying his own output to include the targetlike auxiliary ("être") (turns 3 and 5). As Philp et al. (2010) noted, this lengthy exchange is partially to do with language difficulty but also to saving face for Girard who jokes around a little, aware of the problem but tripping up at times. His partner, Florence, makes placatory statements in turns 11 and 13. Nevertheless, the prolonged discussion demonstrates a learner walking through the process of becoming more consistent in the use of these forms. The discussion assisted the learner in deeply engaging in the problem and its solution.

Example 4.2

1   Girard: . . . Elle a resté à l'Hyatt Dubaï trop bien apparemment. Elle a resté à

                   [*She stayed (nonTL aux) at the Hyatt Dubai really good apparently. She stayed at (nonTL aux)*]

2   Florence: XXX

3   Girard: Elle est

                   [*She (TL aux)*]

4   Florence: XXX

5   Girard: Oui elle est restée mince c'est trop tôt du matin =

                   [*Yes she stayed (TL aux) god it's too early in the morning*]

6   Florence: = XX>

                    (Girard laughs)

                    (Teacher addresses whole class)

7   Girard: Elle est restée

                    [She stayed (TL aux)]

                    (Teacher addresses whole class)

8   Girard: D'accord

                    [Okay]

9   Florence: Bon allez

                    [Ok carry on]

10   Girard: (laughs) est restée

                    [. . . stayed (TL aux)]

11   Florence: C'est difficile

                    [It's hard]

12   Girard: Elle a =

                    [She has (non TL aux)]

13   Florence: = (tellement) = difficile

                    [(really) hard]

14   Girard: (puts on a silly voice) Elle est restée elle a resté elle est restée [normal voice] à l'hôtel du Piccadilly Circus so XX XX

                    [She stayed (TL) she stayed (non–TL) she stayed (TL) at the Piccadilly Circus Hotel]

                                                    (Philp et al., 2010, p. 269)

The above example illustrates an advanced learner becoming more automatic in the accurate use of grammatical forms that he was already highly familiar with. As we saw in Chapter 2, beginning learners often build up their procedural knowledge through using formulaic chunks with "slots" (Krashen & Scarcella, 1978). As illustrated in Chapter 2, Example 2.16 (Tognini, 2008), learners may repeatedly use a phrase, substituting different nouns or verbs: *je voudrais une chambre* ("I'd like a single room"); *je voudrais quatre-vingts francs* ("I'd like 80 francs"); *je voudrais payer . . .* ("I'd like to pay . . ."). This chunk *je voudrais* ("I'd like"), matches the subject with the appropriate morphological form of the verb "to want" in French, which is marked for person, number, and politeness, to politely or formally express personal wants. The connection between this noun and verb is continually repeated by the learners as they try it out in the imagined context of ordering a room. In this case, the learners work from a script, in a controlled practice activity that leads them to try out this phrase for different purposes.

Whether language practice with a peer strengthens form-meaning connections or enhances automaticity may depend on the task itself. Where the task recycles the same language over and over, this lends itself to increased automaticity (i.e., learners get better at processing language forms because much of the language remains constant). Other tasks may encourage creative language use and experimenting with form rather than practice of particular phrases (the relationship between tasks and language production is explored further in Chapter 8). Where most of the language is novel and changeable in structure, increased automaticity is unlikely because of the inconsistency of the language. Example 4.3 illustrates the language of a task that elicits predictable forms. Here a pair of child L2 learners (9–11 years) repeats the same question syntax many times, albeit with varying degrees of accuracy, while carrying out a very simple grid task.

Example 4.3

K: Jun a jungle>

B: Does horse live in a jungle? Say that.

K: Does horse live a jungle?

B: No> (. . .) does the horse live in the desert?

   (10 turns later)

K: Yes> the cow live a jungle?

B: No> the (. .) [laughing] desert desert [guessing the pronunciation]

K: Desert desert

B: The cow live in the desert?

K: No> the cow live a farm?

B: Yes>

(Oliver, Philp, & Mackey, 2008, unpublished raw data)

The task gives the learners an opportunity to practice the same syntactic structure with different lexical items in a context of authentic communication, allowing them to build fluency with structures they are beginning to master. Other tasks could be designed to allow learners to build automaticity in retrieving specific vocabulary or in using specific morphemes (Ellis, 2003; Nation & Newton, 2009). This highlights the importance of the teacher in peer interaction. Peer interaction in the classroom does not supplant teacher influence on learning. Rather, it challenges teachers to carefully consider the learning objectives and select or design tasks appropriately to meet them. The dictogloss tasks discussed in Chapters 2 and 10 would be appropriate if the objective is to have learners question and experiment with language use. Tasks that elicit repeated use of the same structure or particular vocabulary items, such as a spot-the-difference task or the grid task used in the previous example, are a better fit if the purpose of the interaction is to allow fluency building.

Formulaic Sequences in Peer Interactions

As shown in Chapter 2, Tognini's (2008) study of peer interaction in primary and secondary foreign language classrooms suggests that some learners predominantly use preformulated language in interaction with others (see Example 2.5). Using preformulated language in communication activities is not the same as mechanical drills. Gatbonton and Segalowitz (1988) suggest that benefits of the former include assisting speakers to initiate interaction and inviting a response from listeners. In addition, formulaic speech is a starting point for L2 development (Ellis, 1984; Myles, Mitchell, & Hooper, 1999; Wray, 2002).

The use of formulaic speech and its contribution to language development have been well documented in early descriptive studies of child L2 development. When they first begin to use an L2, learners appropriate "chunks" of language gleaned from the "noise" about them. Gradually, as the noise becomes more familiar and starts to acquire meaning, so too the learner's chunks become more analyzed. Thus Ellis (2003) describes the acquisition of grammar, at least, as the "piecemeal learning of many thousands of constructions and the frequency-biased abstraction of regularities within them" (p. 8). Wray (2000) provides the following general definition of a formulaic sequence:

> A sequence, continuous or discontinuous, of words or other elements, which is, or appears to be, prefabricated: that is, stored and retrieved, whole from memory at the time of use, rather than being subject to generation or analysis by the language grammar. (p. 465)

Qualitative research and theoretical work on formulaic sequences point to a number of important roles that formulaic sequences play in L2 development. First, formulaic sequences, ubiquitous for first language and L2 speakers alike (Nattinger & DeCarrico, 1992; Sinclair, 1991), serve to save the burden of processing novel utterances both for the speaker and the listener (Ellis, 2003; Pawley & Syder, 1983; Wray, 2000, 2002). For the L2 learner, using prefabricated strings saves on processing effort (Ellis, 2003; Wray, 2000, 2002; Wray & Perkins, 2000) and frees up attentional resources for attending to other aspects of input and output. More contentiously, formulaic sequences may also provide a database to learners for subsequent "chunk breakdown" and creative construction (Bardovi-Harlig, 2002; Ellis, 1996; Myles, Mitchell, & Hooper, 1999; Perera, 2001; Wray & Perkins, 2000). Myles, Hooper, and Mitchell (1998) and Myles et al. (1999) found evidence of this among older children, in a corpus-based study of 16 junior high school students learning French. Over two years, they observed that the students developed a substantial repertoire of formulaic expressions and used them for communicative purposes. Understanding the contribution of peer interaction to processing formulaic sequences, and developing greater creative use of language, will require longitudinal and regular data sets (Bohn, 1986). Myles et al.'s corpus-based research suggests this is a useful avenue for exploring such potential benefits of peer interaction.

Frequency Effects

When practicing language use through peer interaction, learners receive L2 input from one another. We consider here the effects of processing this input on language learning. Whether learners receive corrective feedback or not in peer interaction practice, grappling with language and practicing during collaborative activities expose learners to target language input. As discussed in the previous chapters, through interaction, forms in the input are often repeated, rephrased, and segmented (Pica, 1994, 2013), which assists enhancing saliency of input forms.

Opportunities to process L2 input promote learning through frequency effects; allowing for frequency-based learning has been hypothesized to be one of the ways that interaction with a native speaker may facilitate language learning (Ellis, 2002; Gass & Mackey, 2002). One way that input processing promotes automaticity is through "chunking." According to Ellis (2003), native speakers intuitively know how letters, sounds, and other language elements tend to co-occur in words and phrases (e.g., in English, there are many words in which the letters "t" and "h" co-occur in words like "this", "they", and "though"), and the word "the" is more likely to appear at the beginning of a sentence than the word "think". We implicitly learn how to chunk letters, sounds, morphemes, words, phrases, and clauses—bits of co-occurring language at all levels. With increasing exposure, these bits and pieces in chunks are gradually incremented, and eventually a larger proportion of target language form and words are correctly recalled. Ellis (2005) argues that this should also apply to the L2-learning process. That is, as learners are exposed to L2 input, sensitivity to the regularity of co-occurrences of words and forms is gradually acquired. According to Gass and Mackey (2002), this account of frequency effects can be applied to the interactionist view of L2 acquisition, as interactional modifications facilitate pattern identification, recognition (of matches and mismatches), and storage.

Frequency effects can further be explained in terms of dual mechanisms of learning (i.e., item vs. system learning) and the idea of restructuring from a connectionist account of L2 acquisition (e.g., Ellis 2003). As explained in Chapter 3, Adams (2007) found that learners who received corrective feedback demonstrated greater learning of three target language forms than those who did not receive feedback. Despite the benefit of corrective feedback for learning of the target language items, Adams (2007) explains that this type of learning in her study was likely limited to learning a specific form based on the concept of dual mechanisms of language learning (Ellis, 2003; Hulstijn, 2002). That is, although learning of specific items is a process that deals with learning each item separately, system learning deals with learning the abstract rules that underlie the use of linguistic items. For example, one learner in Adams's study learned the past-tense form of the verb "watch" during peer interaction. The past-tense verb "watched" registered as an item in memory and could be retrieved in test performance, but the peer interaction practice may not have assisted the learner's acquisition of the rule for past-tense forms (rule-based learning). Based on the connectionist view of L2 acquisition (Ellis, 2005), processing takes place in a network of nodes (or units) in the mind that are connected. Repeated exposure to the past-tense verb forms of various kinds strengthens these connections and facilitates learners' acquisition of the system as well as the item through frequency of exposure and connections.

Adams (2007) postulates that through constant exposure to the target item during peer interaction, learners who engage in peer interaction practice and receive corrective feedback may be able to strengthen form-meaning connections, and through this develop and refine their target language knowledge. That is, in her study, with reference to past-tense marking, feedback given during interaction assisted learners in acquiring a specific item, but repeated exposure to various items could help them make form-meaning connections and also facilitate building and strengthening associations among exemplars to assist system learning. As we saw above when discussing automatic processing, learners need opportunities to use the language to build frequency-based connections.

A critical difference between peer interaction language practice as a means of building automaticity and as a means of acquiring frequency knowledge is the distinction between learning from producing output and learning from processing input. As learners produce language, they are able to practice processing at each level of speech production—conceptualization, formulation, and articulation (Levelt, 1989)—enhancing their ability to produce language automatically. As they increasingly automatize their language production, they free up attentional resources to focus on the accuracy of their language use. Even if production attempts in peer interaction result in non-targetlike production that is not corrected by a peer, the opportunity to produce language has allowed for practice at mapping L2 words onto meanings, retrieving them from memory, and articulating them. Therefore, non-targetlike L2 use may still be beneficial in developing automatic processing.

However, the role of frequency knowledge in building fluency is based on subconscious processing of vast amounts of data from the input. In this case, there may be disadvantages for learning from peer interaction, in which some (and in some settings, much) of the input learners receive from their interlocutor is non-targetlike (Ortega, 2007). The benefits of practice for language learning therefore depend at least in part on the type of language learning. For building more efficient output processing, peer interaction seems to be a particularly good context because learners have so many more opportunities to produce language in peer interactions than in teacher-learner interactions. On the other hand, for building frequency-based knowledge, peer interaction may be less helpful. Peer reading and listening tasks, however, in which peers jointly work on understanding targetlike texts, may still be beneficial as practice to develop frequency-based patterns. (We discuss peer reading in Chapter 10.)

Practice Makes Perfect

So far we have explored the ways in which peer interaction practice might be facilitative of L2 development. It is worth noting that, although repeated practice in a meaningful context can be beneficial for L2 development, this process is not straightforward, and we should not expect a simple relationship between practice time and language learning (cf. Lightbown, 1985). Advancement and regression in fluent production is described as U-shaped behavior (McLaughlin, 1990). Based on an information processing approach, McLaughlin and Heredia (1996) explain that although complex behavior such as language learning builds on a number of simple processes and through practice automaticity is facilitated, the process is not linear. Learners go through cycles of analyzing rules and consolidation during this process. According to McLaughlin and Heredia (1996), there are two different effects that practice might have. First, through practice, various skills become more automatic. Second, however, increased practice can also lead to restructuring, which causes a decline in performance as learners reorganize their internal representations (McLaughlin, 1990). In this view, practice does not automatically lead to skilled performance; rather, this is a cumulative process in which learners develop more efficient procedures. Practice may make perfect, but building fluency in language use is not straightforward. This has implications for looking at the benefits of peer interaction: Outcomes may not be evident in the short term, as benefits are likely to be cumulative and incremental.

Conclusion

In this chapter, we explored how different characteristics observed in peer interaction may promote L2 acquisition. In the absence of frequent corrective feedback, and discussions of linguistic problems during collaborative activities, we have suggested other ways in which using language through communication practice with peers can contribute to learning. One benefit of peer interaction is the opportunity for extended and repeated production practice, allowing learners to move from effortful slow production with frequent pauses, false starts, and repetition to achieve effortless and smooth production (e.g., Ellis, 2005; Segalowitz, 2003), when communicating in the context of exchanging meaning (DeKeyser, 1998, 2007). In this sense, peer interaction practice during collaborative task activities is a means of promoting automaticity whether or not learners negotiate for meaning or form. Although the process of automatization is not linear and may reflect "U-shaped" behavior (McLaughlin, 1990), consistent practice through peer interaction provides a way forward. However, as discussed here, every aspect of peer interaction is not necessarily beneficial for fluency building. Teachers need to carefully balance classroom practice to provide learners with frequent exposure to meaningful target language input to allow learners to build and strengthen target-like connections among forms. This points to the important role that the teacher plays in designing and implementing peer and other interaction opportunities in the classroom.

This is an area that has received relatively little attention in the literature, despite the well-established findings that peer interaction allows learners greater opportunities for language practice. Peer interaction is a significant segment of many language classrooms and is considered a way to promote greater automaticity in L2 production. However, it is rare to find classroom-based studies, such as Myles et al. (1998, 1999), that focus on this aspect of learning through interaction. New research tools such as corpus linguistics, and new theories, including emergentism and connectionism, provide more promising means of describing language use and development over time, and of evaluating the potential benefits of practice more effectively.

SECTION II

The Participants of Peer Interaction

5

LEARNER PROFICIENCY AND L1 USE

Introduction

The previous chapters have focused on how peer interaction can impact on language learning. In this chapter and the following two, we turn the focus to the variation within peer interaction that occurs because of differences among peers. In this chapter, we discuss the role of second language (L2) proficiency on the way that learners engage in interaction. The use of the first language (L1) in peer interaction will also be discussed. The purpose of this and other chapters in this section (Chapter 6 on identities and relationships, and Chapter 7 on peer interaction among children) is to advocate for research that examines peer interaction in its own right, as a context for communication. If we are to understand how peer interaction may impact on learning, we need to study the variation among these interactions, rather than simply compare them to teacher-learner interactions.

This chapter considers how learner proficiency influences interaction and learning opportunities. A common concern expressed about peer interaction in the classroom is that conversational interaction is only appropriate for learners at certain proficiency levels (e.g., Swan, 2005). This chapter will consider empirical research that examines the interactions of learners at different levels of L2 proficiency, as well as research that examines how proficiency shapes interactions in mixed-proficiency dyads. As noted in the introductory chapter, peer interaction differs qualitatively from teacher-learner interaction because in peer interaction no interlocutor can be considered an expert on L2 use. However, even for learners in the same classroom, there are inevitable differences in proficiency, and this can shape the way learners construct and engage in interaction. Studies that examine peer interaction among mixed-proficiency groups can shed light on these processes, and we will review important findings here. We will also consider two constructs related to proficiency: learner heritage and L1 use. Learners of a heritage language often have higher proficiency or different proficiencies than their peers in L2 classrooms, so we will review here research on their interactions with nonheritage peers. The use of the L1 has been frequently linked to language proficiency as a compensatory strategy that allows learners to continue interactions despite the limits of their proficiency. We'll finish the chapter with a discussion of how the L1 is used in L2 peer interactions.

Language Proficiency and Peer Interaction

Relatively little research has looked into the impact of proficiency on learning, but the impact of proficiency on a range of interactional features has been investigated, including negotiation of meaning and focus on form, scaffolding, and patterns of communication. One of the earliest studies of the role of proficiency on learning was Gass and Varonis's (1985) study of negotiation of meaning in peer interaction. Their study included dyads that were mixed and matched for proficiency. Their findings suggested that it was not the level of proficiency that impacted negotiation of meaning, as both high-proficiency and low-proficiency dyads produced similar amounts of negotiation of meaning. However, having high- and low-proficiency learners in the same dyad led to more miscommunication and more work to resolve miscommunication through negotiation. Pairing influences not only negotiation but also the way that participant roles are assigned in a task. In Yule and Macdonald's (1990) study of peer interactions among mixed-proficiency dyads, for example, communication was strongly shaped by whether the high- or low-proficiency learner was cast in the dominant role for the task. Their task required one learner to give map directions to their interlocutor, who had a slightly different map. When high-proficiency learners were the direction givers, there was very little negotiation of meaning, and the low-proficiency learner participated very little in the conversation. On the other hand, when the low-proficiency learner gave the directions, both interlocutors participated more, as they collaboratively engaged in resolving miscommunication to solve the conflicts built into the task. This study illustrates the inherent complexity of studying a social phenomenon like conversational interaction, where different factors interact to shape how communication unfolds.

Mixed-proficiency dyads may also produce more modified output in interactions. In Iwashita's (2001) study, Japanese foreign language students in her study were paired in high-high, low-low, and high-low proficiency groups; Iwashita hypothesized that negotiation and modified output strategies would differ among groups, with the high-low proficiency group producing the most modified output. The findings did not follow predictions, however, with statistical tests failing to uncover differences among the groups in the types of negotiation moves given, and the high-high group producing the most modified output. Iwashita noted the high level of confirmation checks in her data, as illustrated in Example 5.1.

Example 5.1

HL8:   Kuruma?

      [Car?]

HL7:   Kuruma kara

      [Off the car]

HL8:   Kara?

      [Off?]

HL7:   Deru

      [Get off]

HL8:   Ah deru?

      [Get off?]

HL8:   Hai

      [Yes]

(Iwashita, 2001, p. 279)

Although this example came from a high-high dyad, similar data were found throughout the study. Iwashita noted that for low-proficiency learners in particular, it was difficult simply to form sentences in Japanese, so it was easiest for them to negotiate with confirmation checks, which are repetitions of an interlocutor's utterance, than to negotiate with clarification requests, which require learners to create a phrase. The prevalence of confirmation checks in the data limited opportunities for modified output, as confirmation checks often lead to simple affirmations. Although the findings were limited, there was a trend (but nonstatistical) for the high-low dyads to produce more opportunities for negotiation, and for low-proficiency learners in the high-low pairs to produce more modified output than similar learners in the low-low pairs. It is important to note though that higher rates of negotiation and modified output in high-low pairs may be moderated by learner preferences. The learners in Iwashita's study indicated that they preferred working in mixed-proficiency pairs.

The benefits of mixed-proficiency pairs have been called into question both by research on proficiency and scaffolding and by research on proficiency and focus on form. For scaffolding, although some studies have shown advantages to mixed-proficiency groupings, others have noted that these may stifle the less proficient learner. In a study of two Japanese learners engaged in a collaborative interaction, Ohta (2000b) found that the more proficient learner assisted the less proficient learner in coping with the linguistic demands of the task. However, this may not always be the case. Other evidence indicates that as the proficiency gap between high- and low-level students widens, the stronger student often excludes the weaker student from the interaction (Kowal & Swain, 1994). Taking a dominant role like this precludes scaffolding, limiting collaborative learning opportunities for both the high- and low-proficiency learner. However, the mode of communication may help promote scaffolding, even among mixed-proficiency dyads. Lee's (2008) study of scaffolding in online peer interactions among higher and lower proficiency Spanish learners uncovered frequent use of scaffolding behaviors that helped learners produce structures they could not produce on their own. Lee speculated that the visual nature of the interaction in text-based online chat may have made these moves more salient. She pointed out that learners used the written record of their interaction as an anchor for their discussion of form, as in Example 5.2.

Example 5.2

1 A: ¿Qué opina de los inmigrantes en este país?

   [What do you think about the immigrants in this country?]

2 G: Muchos son Mexicanos. En mi puebla ellos trabajan a Dunkin Donuts. No son contentos.

   [Many are Mexicans. In my town they work at Dunkin Donuts. They are not happy.]

3 A: De acuerdo. Algo no está bien en los verbos.

   [I agree. Something is not right in the verbs.]

4 G: No se. Mi gramatica es mal.

   [I don't know. My grammar is bad.]

5 A: Fijese en los verbos "ser"

   [Look at the verbs "ser"]

6 G: Hay dos. Cual?

   [There are two. Which one?]

7 A: El segundo verbo

   [The second one]

8 G: Estan? Ellos no estan contentos.

   [They are? They are not happy.]

9 A: Ahora si está bien.

   [Now, yes now it is right.]

(Lee, 2008, p. 60)

After the higher proficiency learner, A, comments on a need to correct a grammatical issue, the lower proficiency learner, G, expresses frustration with his grammar. The learner A then makes specific reference to the chat transcript, which G uses to find the indicated verb and guess at the answer. In this case, even though one learner's proficiency is clearly higher, the shared focus on the chat transcript allowed them to work together to produce grammatical language.

Focus on form may be more beneficial when learners are paired in matched, rather than mixed, proficiency dyads. Early research in this area established that higher proficiency was related to more focus on form. For example, Williams (1999) compared the number and type of language-related episodes (LREs) produced by eight ESL learners in naturalistic data from four classrooms, including one dyad from each of four proficiency levels ranging from low-intermediate to advanced. The results showed a steady increase in attention to form as proficiency increased, with learners at lower levels consistently producing fewer LREs than learners at higher levels. Although small scale, the study provided evidence that "the degree and type of learner-generated attention to form is related to proficiency level and the nature of the activity in which the learners are engaged" (p. 583). LREs were predominantly focused on lexical items, irrespective of proficiency level. The few LREs on morpho-syntactic forms tended to occur in structured activities and among learners of higher proficiency.

Increasing proficiency seems to increase focus on form and, in particular, focus on grammar. Leeser (2004) found that, as the combined dyad proficiency increased, so did focus on form. This suggests that Williams's findings show benefits for higher proficiency learners in peer interaction, rather than any advantage of matching proficiency. Leeser focused on the mix of proficiencies found within a single streamed class level. His participants were students from intact Spanish courses, whose teachers ranked them for proficiency. They were then paired up either in mixed- or matched-proficiency dyads and completed dictogloss tasks. Like Williams, Leeser found that attention to form increased with proficiency, with high-high proficiency pairs engaging in more LREs than low-low pairs, and high-low pairs falling in between. The learners' ability to correctly resolve LREs also increased with proficiency, suggesting that focus on form is not only more frequent but also more beneficial for learners as their proficiency increases. Similar to Williams' findings, lower proficiency pairs were more likely to attend to lexical forms, whereas higher proficiency pairs increasingly focused on grammar.

Learners may also change their communication style when paired with a mixed- or matched-proficiency interlocutor. In a small-scale study, Kim and Mc-Donough (2008) paired eight intermediate-level Korean learners with another intermediate learner for one interaction and with an advanced interlocutor for another interaction. Similar to the findings of Leeser (2004) and Williams (1999), when the learners interacted with a matched-proficiency learner (similar to the low-low dyads in Leeser's study), there was less overt focus on form than when they interacted with a higher level interlocutor (similar to the high-low dyads in Leeser's study). These findings give credence to Leeser's claims that the proficiency of each interlocutor in the interaction impacts on the way that the learners focus on form, and that increasing the proficiency in the dyad (e.g., by replacing a low-proficiency learner with a higher proficiency learner) leads to an increased focus on linguistic form.

Beyond the focus on form, however, the learners adopted different patterns of communication when interlocutors changed. Based on Storch's (2002) analysis documenting different patterns among learner dyads, Kim and McDonough compared the learners' patterns of interaction with each interlocutor to see if learners shifted their interaction style when their interlocutor's proficiency was higher. Storch noted four different patterns of interaction among learner dyads: collaborative, expert/novice, dominant/passive, and dominant/dominant. She noted that collaborative and expert/novice dyads engaged in more exchanges that promoted language learning, whereas dominant/passive and dominant/dominant dyads tended to squash each other's learner opportunities (we also discuss these ideas in Chapter 6).

Kim and McDonough (2008) found that learners whose interactional style was collaborative in their interaction with a similar proficiency interlocutor tended to become passive learners in a dominant/passive dyad when interacting with a more proficient learner. Indeed, several learners noted after the tasks that they felt stymied by their more advanced interlocutor and that the other learner simply took over the task, which limited their opportunities to participate and learn. Even though there were more LREs and LREs were resolved correctly more often when they worked with a higher proficiency learner, they did not perceive this as the best learning setting.

These learners' intuitions about their learning are corroborated by Watanabe and Swain's (2007) study, which also examined the interactional patterns of learners who engaged in interactions with learners of mixed- and matched-proficiency levels. Like Kim and McDonough, Watanabe and Swain avoided between-group comparisons. Instead, they focused on how individual learners' interactions were influenced when they conversed with more and less proficient interlocutors. The learners participated with both partners in a multistage task that involved peer writing, reformulation by a competent speaker, opportunities to notice the differences between their original writing and the reformulation, and finally individual text reconstruction. Similar to prior research on LREs, they found that learners discussed form more often when interacting with a higher, rather than a lower, level interlocutor in the task. However, in the noticing stage of the task, which is pivotal to the learning opportunities in the task, learners produced equal LREs with both partners. Watanabe and Swain point out that this is likely due to the difference in the number of reformulations. The texts produced by the learners with their lower proficiency interlocutors had more errors, and therefore more corrections were made in the reformulation. Each correction is an opportunity for students to engage in noticing and discussion of form, so this may have prompted more discussion of form in the lower proficiency interactions. Conversely, the learners also had higher scores on the text reconstruction when they worked with lower rather than higher proficiency learners. Like Kim and McDonough, Watanabe and Swain attribute this to the interactional patterns; they noted that regardless of the proficiency pairing, learners who had a collaborative style of interaction discussed form more, spent longer discussing form meaningfully, and had higher scores from the text reconstruction. Watanabe's (2008) follow-up study also found that learners who engaged collaboratively in interactions, regardless of the specific proficiency mix, perceived the interaction as being more beneficial than those with other interactional patterns.

Although proficiency certainly plays a role in shaping interaction, these findings suggest that interactional patterns may be more important. Dyads that engage in interactions collaboratively are more likely to learn through interaction than those that don't, regardless of proficiency. However, proficiency may play a mediating role in determining which type of interactional pattern learners engage in. Like Kim and McDonough, Watanabe and Swain noted that learners shifted their interactional styles with new partners. For example, one of the focal learners, Jun, was dominant in interaction with a less proficient learner, Shu, as illustrated in the subsequent example.

Example 5.3

170 Jun: "Music is important to many people to get energy and for healings," for healings, to get energy for healings ... because it's, because it's noun here.

171 Shu: for healings

172 Jun: Yeah, but yeah, I have some, what can I say, I wonder this sentence. Why we don't write down like here, like this? We can [write] "people can get some healing." Anyway some, some sounds, some [is] a little bit strange. But, people can get healing ... I don't know. For our essay, "people can get healing by listening to music." Ahh ... no no no, I don't know ... No, I don't think so.

173 Shu: can get healing ... mm.

174 Jun: Anyway, we can ... yeah, maybe it's better.

175 Shu: ... maybe it's better.

(Watanabe & Swain, 2007, p. 134)

In this example, Jun dominates the discussion, whereas Shu's contributions are mainly limited to echoic responses. There is little negotiation between them, and through the interaction, Jun seemed to conduct the task as though he were doing it individually, making few attempts to engage Shu and producing a large number of self-directed utterances. This pattern shifts though when he works with a more proficient interlocutor, Gou.

Example 5.4

265 Gou: [...] diminish, deplete like decreased? But not decreased.

266 Jun: Reduced?

267 Gou: Reduced, yes. "Although the carrying capacity of airplanes is smaller than that of ships" ... airplanes have reduced ... reduced ...

268 Jun: Time of?

269 Gou: Time?

270 Jun: I hope

271 Gou: I don't know ... time. What kind of time?

272 Jun: Time um time ... ah

273 Gou: Time of transportation? Not transportation

274 Jun: No no no ... time of the ... maybe quick

275 Gou: Quick?

276 Jun: Just time of trade?

277 Gou: Um-hmm. Right. Business letter is important for ... ah but we can use fax.

278 Jun: Hmmm. How about, I don't know, airplanes brought new products uhh which ... uh ...

279 Gou: What do you wanna say? Airplanes?

(Watanabe & Swain, 2007, p. 133)

When interacting with a more proficient interlocutor, Jun's style shifts. Rather than dominating the interaction, he collaborates. His long turns and self-directed utterances have disappeared, and he solicits his interlocutors' opinions on the forms they are discussing until they are able to solve the questions of form in ways that they both find acceptable. These findings call into question earlier research that indicated that mixed-proficiency pairs were superior in terms of engaging in negotiation of meaning (e.g., Gass & Varonis, 1985). Both pairs illustrated here are mixed-proficiency pairs, but negotiation of meaning and attention to form are related not to the mix of proficiencies but to how individual learners allow these differences to shape their interactional styles. As we have noted before, there is always variation in how task and individual factors influence peer interaction. Rather, the individuals in each interaction significantly shape how the interaction is carried out (we will discuss this theme in greater depth in Chapter 6). Having a high- and low-proficiency learner engaged in an interaction does not automatically lead to a dominant/passive interaction. Both Watanabe and Swain (2007) and Kim and McDonough (2008) noted mixed-proficiency pairs adopting collaborative patterns of interaction, as demonstrated in Example 5.3, or adopting expert/novice styles, illustrated in Example 5.5.

Example 5.5

333 Nana: What do you want to say next?

334 Emi: I want, I wanna say um . . . that um . . . actually I wanna say, how he, not how, I wanna say he's really um . . . good, good teacher of my life.

335 Nana: Yeah, yeah, yeah.

336 Emi: He taught me a lot.

337 Nana: Ah, I know that how important he is for you.

338 Emi: Yeah.

339 Nana: But ah . . .

340 Emi: Yeah but generally

341 Nana: Yes, I know, but ah in this paragraph, we have to write about how important thinking

342 Emi: about him

343 Nana: Yes.

(Watanabe & Swain, 2007, p. 133)

In this example, Nana (a more proficient interlocutor) works with Emi. Even though Nana clearly takes charge and leads the task, she actively encourages Emi's participation, overtly in the first turn of the example and implicitly by agreeing to other turns as the discourse unfolds. Nana uses her control of the interaction to foster, rather that squash, her interlocutor's efforts to communicate. These data highlight the complex relationship between proficiency, interaction patterns, and attention to form. Although proficiency differences may push learners to specific types of patterns, they do not determine them.

Indeed, it may not necessarily be a learner's actual proficiency, but rather each learner's perception of their partner's proficiency that shapes the choice of inter-actional patterns. Watanabe and Swain (2008) explore this with an analysis of one core learner, Mai, from their earlier study. Mai was paired with two learners, and the interactions were both expert/novice, but never in the expected direction. When Mai worked with a more proficient learner (Chie), she immediately took control of the task and played an expert role for most of the task. However, when she worked with a less proficient learner (Rina), she ceded control of the task to her interlocutor from the beginning, sliding into a novice role. Although the roles in both of these interactions were fluid, with the learners acting collaboratively at times, the overall pattern was for the less proficient learner to take the expert role in each. Follow-up interviews made it clear that Mai's perceptions of her inter-locutors' proficiency did not line up with test scores. For example, she considered Rina to be a stronger writer and so allowed her to control the collaborative writ-ing stage of the task. On the other hand, Mai found Chie to be very quiet, which she interpreted as a lack of confidence and low proficiency. Although this is a very small-scale study, the powerful effects of perceptions are reported by Philp, Walter, and Basturkmen (2010) in a classroom study and Lazareton and Davis (2008) in a study of proficiency effects in peer assessment.

These findings illustrate the difficulty of investigating the effects of proficiency on peer interactions. Although small, this body of research has shown that proficiency (and perceptions of proficiency) may affect interaction in ways that are difficult to predict. For example, negotiation of meaning increases when learners have different proficiency levels, whereas focus on form increases as proficiency increases overall. The effectiveness of conversational modifications in promoting learning also may be affected by proficiency. Working with a more competent speaker may increase a lower proficiency learner's opportunities to focus on form; however, these opportunities may not result in learning benefits. Learners at a lower level may not be developmentally ready to learn the forms they focus on with higher level learners (Leeser, 2004). Although we generally think of the higher proficiency learner as teaching the lower proficiency learner, it may actually be the higher level learners that benefit most. Higher proficiency learners are more likely to take on expert roles in interaction, and learners who act as experts may learn the most (Watanabe & Swain, 2007). This supports van Lier's (1996) assertion that students learn from teaching other peers. This suggests that proficiency may indirectly influence learning opportunities in the interaction; different proficiency mixes may prompt learners to assume particular roles in the interaction, and assuming these roles may increase their learning opportunities. This illustrates how factors like proficiency may moderate, rather than directly influence, interactional roles and learning in peer interaction.

Heritage Learners in Peer Interaction

Although proficiency differences exist in all classrooms, these differences can be exaggerated in contexts where heritage and foreign language learners both study. Heritage learners often have language experiences different from those of instructed learners and so in certain language domains may have much greater expertise than their interlocutors. We know very little about how heritage learners interact with one another and with other peers in language classrooms. One reason for this is the difficulty in classifying heritage learners. Valdés (2001) defines a heritage learner as "a student who is raised in a home where a non-English language is spoken, who speaks or merely understands the heritage language, and who is to some degree bilingual in English and the heritage language" (p. 1). This definition allows for a wide variety of experience with the home language, and indeed, heritage learners are a very heterogeneous group, with differences including their age of exposure to the L2, the context of their heritage language acquisition, and the amount of exposure to heritage language input they have experienced (Montrul, 2008). Any of these factors can affect their proficiency in the heritage language. Heritage learners' proficiency can range from learners who can understand a colloquial variety of a language (but not necessarily speak it) to learners who have speaking and listening competence in both colloquial and standard varieties and may even have had some education in the heritage language (Oh, Jun, Knightly, & Au, 2003).

Although heritage learners have early exposure to their home language, their learning opportunities are often limited, particularly with regard to education in the home language. They tend to have a restricted lexicon, lower sociolinguistic competence, and incomplete grammatical acquisition compared to monolingual speakers or balanced bilinguals (Montrul, 2008). Although researchers have frequently called for separate courses for heritage and other language learners in foreign language programs, this is rarely heeded for logistical reasons (Lynch, 2008). So although heritage and other learners may have different experiences, knowledge, and motivations for language study, they are often grouped in the same classrooms.

Heritage learners may be more likely than other language learners to act as experts in peer interactions. Blake and Zyzik (2003) paired heritage and nonheritage learners of Spanish in a jigsaw task to examine their discourse in text-based chats. They noted a trend in the data for heritage learners to assist their interlocutors more than their interlocutors were able to help them. Although Blake and Zyzik question whether the tasks were as beneficial for the heritage learners as the nonheritage learners, the heritage learners themselves reported that they found the task beneficial to their learning. These interactions may have improved the heritage learners' confidence because they were able to take on expert roles, whereas in their interactions with monolingual family members, they may perceive their proficiency as deficient. However, in light of Watanabe and Swain's (2008) findings (discussed previously), it's also possible that the more proficient heritage learners did benefit from the opportunity to teach their "novice" peers.

Although heritage and L2 learners both initiate focus on form during the interactions, the focus on form initiated by the heritage language learners may be less likely to be resolved (Bowles, 2011a, 2011b). This may be an indication of an imbalance in the benefits of the interaction, with L2 learners gaining more from their partners than their partners gain from them. However, benefits have also been uncovered in both directions, depending on the linguistic target (Bowles, 2011b). Heritage learners are more likely to receive help on orthographic issues such as spelling and placement of accents, whereas the L2 learners may receive help from their heritage learner partners on vocabulary and grammar. The learners in Bowles's studies had tested into the same level of Spanish courses, so their global proficiency was similar. For these learners, peer interaction was a time when they could use the differences in their learning backgrounds to help one another.

Work on peer interaction among heritage learners is an emerging area of research. In some ways, heritage/L2 learner dyads reflect the dynamics of higher/lower proficiency learners, even when their global proficiency is quite similar.

This highlights the complexity involved in determining proficiency and its effect on peer interaction. Although learners may have similar or different levels of proficiency overall, proficiency is simply a cover term for discrete knowledge about different aspects of a language. In any interactional exchange, global knowledge may be less important than specific knowledge about the linguistic items being discussed. As the heritage learners exemplify, different learning experiences and different exposure to the language leads to different levels of knowledge about specific linguistic items. Proficiency measured globally then cannot predict how learners will fare in terms of learning in an interaction.

L1 Use in the Interaction

Because neither speaker in a peer interaction has nativelike L2 proficiency, the L1 may be used as a fall back to allow communication to continue in interactions where learners share an L1. In the early days of communicative language teaching, the possible use of the L1 in the classroom was a frequent concern for teachers attempting to integrate interactional opportunities in foreign language classrooms and other contexts where many learners share a common language. Indeed, even recent studies on the implementation of task-based curricula in English as a Foreign Language contexts very frequently cite fears that students will rely mostly on the L1 in tasks as a barrier to classroom implementation (e.g., Eguchi & Eguchi, 2006).

As our understanding of peer interaction develops, however, these fears can be put into perspective. For one thing, there is evidence that as learners become accustomed and comfortable with engaging in peer interaction, they increasingly limit their L1 use. Most studies that have questioned the use of peer interaction in the classroom have been conducted among learners who were unaccustomed to peer interaction prior to the study (e.g., Eguchi & Eguchi, 2006; Li, 1998). Learners who have frequently been exposed to communicative teaching and to peer interaction approach tasks differently. Zhang (2007), for example, found that teachers who embraced interaction in their classrooms had students who were positive about interaction, preferred communicative teaching, felt that the L2 should be predominately used in the classroom, and avoided L1 use as much as possible in peer interactions and in communication with the teacher. Similar findings have been reported by Tinker-Sachs (2007) and Weaver (2007). So one answer to the concern that foreign language learners will overuse their L1 in peer interaction is not to give up. Although these interactions may not be very productive at first, each success in trying out the L2 can lead to greater confidence in communicating in the L2 with the peer.

Beyond practice, a teacher's classroom style may influence the ways that learners use language in peer interactions. For example, Chavez (2006) found that differences in teaching style impacted on student use of the L1 during interactions. The three teachers selected had quite different communication styles, including different uses of the L1 during teacher-fronted interaction. These differences clearly carried through to the students' use of the L1 and the L2. This effect was quantitative, in that students of the teacher who used the L2 the most also used the L2 proportionally more than other students. But more interestingly, these students also used a wider variety of language functions in the L2 than students in the other classes. Their teacher used peer interaction most often and indicated in interviews that she valued communicative practice over accuracy and formality in language teaching. Her students' language use followed this; they used the L2 frequently and used it to accomplish a wide variety of conversational goals. Their use of the L1 allowed them to communicate information they would not have otherwise and was primarily indicative of their genuine engagement in communicating meaning. The second teacher focused more on grammatical correctness. During their peer interactions, her students used the L2 less frequently and most often used the L1 to clarify confusion. The final teacher in the study tightly controlled language use, mostly through devoting the majority of class time to teacher-fronted discussions. When his students had opportunities for peer interactions, they mainly relied on language in their texts, mining it for terms to use and rarely using L1 or other communicative strategies to develop the conversation, relying instead on rote exchanges. We often think that peer interaction moves the classroom beyond the teacher's control. This study reminds us that the teacher sets the tone for the classroom, and student engagement in peer interaction will reflect that as well. This also reminds us that it is not possible to divorce peer interaction from the overall classroom context in which it occurs. Teacher-learner interactions in the classroom can influence later peer interactions.

Researchers who work under a sociocultural framework also note that the L1 can be used in a variety of ways in the classroom, and many uses of the L1 actually promote, rather than detract from, language learning (we give more detail on sociocultural theory in Chapter 2). Detailed analysis of how learners use their L1 while engaged in L2 peer interaction has questioned the assumption that L1 use limits learning opportunities. Several researchers, including Antón and DiCamilla (1998) have suggested that L1 use during peer tasks often plays a mediating role, allowing learners to establish understanding and to support each other as they co-construct the task talk. Using the L1 to facilitate L2 communication allows learners to discuss their own language production, a type of metatalk that may facilitate cognitive processing (Swain & Lapkin, 1998). L1 use during feedback and negotiation processes can enable learners to work together and talk about their communicative problems, helping them collaboratively construct solutions. It also helps circumvent communication problems that could end the conversation (Swain & Lapkin, 1998). Metatalk in task-based peer interaction also allows learners to engage in collaboration on the tasks (García Mayo & Alegria de la Colina, 2007). L1 use in peer interactions may support learner cognition, allowing for more in-depth discussion of task content and, therefore, a higher level of task completion (Storch & Wigglesworth, 2003). Beyond collaboration, Kibler (2010) noted that in her classroom-based peer writing study, use of the L1 allowed the learners to fluidly take on and switch expert and novice roles, supporting peer scaffolding and allowing peers to demonstrate expertise in language and content during the tasks.

Conclusion

Proficiency differences within and between groups of learners may moderate the amount and type of negotiation for meaning, but beyond surface features of interaction, the effect of proficiency in promoting learning is quite complex. Mixed-proficiency interactions can provide less proficient peers with opportunities to engage in scaffolding that allows them to stretch their communication ability. But their language use may also be cut off by higher proficiency peers who use their language abilities to control the interaction. The disparate findings presented in this chapter demonstrate the complex role that L2 proficiency plays in peer interactions. Its effects are mediated by the nature of the task as well as by social relationships among the participants themselves.

Proficiency and language heritage both seem to fall into the category that Laursen (2010) refers to as "moderators," which he defines as "settings that accelerate or impede outcomes, rather than as predictors that have direct effects on outcomes" (p. 898). Rather than determining how learners engage in interactions, proficiency and language heritage are factors that relate to learners' prior experience with the L2 and may alter the ways that learners view the interaction and their role in it. Similarly, L1 use during peer interaction (also related to learner experience with communication in the L2) can either promote or detract from learning, depending on whether learners use it to extend their abilities to meet the cognitive challenges posed by the task or to avoid attempting the challenge. Each of the factors discussed in this chapter can impact on the value of the interaction for learning, but in ways that are individually shaped by the communicative context constructed by each pair of learners.

6

THE SOCIAL DIMENSION OF PEER INTERACTION

Introduction

So far we have explored a number of ways in which peer interaction may promote second language (L2) development. We've seen that it provides a context in which to experiment and to try out new forms. Working collaboratively can draw learners' attention to form and scaffold language use. Peer interaction also allows for much needed time on task, simply practicing. On the flip side, peer interaction is not necessarily beneficial. For example, peer feedback can be inadequate, inconsistent, or misleading. Peer interaction can be a context in which learning is hindered—off-task behavior, negative attitudes, lack of collaboration, domination by individuals, and mismatched group members are all potential problems. Many reasons behind the benefits and limitations of peer interaction are only apparent when we consider the social dimensions of working together. In this chapter, we explore the relationships between peers and the ways in which those relationships may moderate peers' interactions and the contributions these interactions may make to L2 learning.

We will examine this theme from three different angles. First, we explore how relationships in peer interaction differ from teacher-learner interaction. In particular, we evaluate the extent to which peers' associations and past experiences with one another can affect the way in which learners interact together and the consequences of this for learning opportunities. Second, we explore the contribution of peer interaction to learners' perceptions of self and others, and to self-identity. With regard to this, we reflect on positive and negative aspects of L2 peer support for L2 learning. Finally, we discuss the dynamics of peer interaction, whether in whole class settings or in pair or group work. All three of these social dimensions to interaction shape learning differently according to age and context. We will discuss each separately in relation to child, adolescent, and adult learners, and to foreign language and L2 contexts.

Peer Interaction Versus Teacher-Learner Interaction

How do relationships in peer interaction differ from teacher-learner interaction? What difference does this make to possibilities for L2 learning? We will discuss these questions first in relation to children in primary school settings and then with reference to adolescents and adults.

Social and Linguistic Benefits of Child Peer Interaction

For child L2 learners in classrooms, there are clear differences between peer and adult-child interactions. This is best described in the field of educational psychology. Many educationalists, speaking of children in mainstream contexts, exhort researchers and practitioners to recognize and value the distinctively different nature of peer relations (e.g., Blatchford, Kutnik, Baines, & Galton, 2003; Pellegrini & Blatchford, 2000). Hartup (1989) and Laursen and Hartup (2002) emphasize that for children, peer relationships are fundamentally different from adult-child relationships, and that this is significant to the kinds of learning opportunities within children's interactions with one another. He argues that adult-child interaction tends to be "vertically" organized, in terms of status and knowledge, and for this reason is often associated with expert/peer frameworks. However, peer relationships among children are described as horizontal. Because of their relative equality—developmentally, physically, and socially—they share relatively common perspectives and interests. Hartup (1989, 2011) suggests that it is this *equivalence* between peers that provides a unique environment in which children can explore and practice the social and linguistic skills they partially acquire from adult-child contexts. Similarly, Damon (1984) and Damon and Phelps (1989a, 1989b) highlight the uniqueness of peer interaction for triggering *cognitive* change because of this parity in ideas and conversation. In particular, Damon (1984) points out four characteristics that assist learning, each one relevant to L2 development:

> [First,] children speak to one another on a level that they can easily understand. Second, they speak directly to one another, without hedging words. Third, they take the feedback of another child seriously and are strongly motivated to reconcile contradictions between themselves and other children. Fourth, informational communications between children often are less emotionally threatening than corrective advice from an adult. (p. 332)

In interaction among L2 learners, talk is often related to something concrete that the children are doing together, or experiencing together, whether in play or in structured tasks, and this facilitates L2 use and comprehension. This is reflected in Example 6.1, in a conversation between two kindergarten children during writing practice. Inga, whose first language (L1) is Russian, and Jerry, whose L1 is Cantonese, remark playfully on one another's work, pointing to their books as they do so. Fassler (1998) notes that Jerry, the Cantonese-speaking child "was try-ing hard to match the phrasing and rhythm of Inga's more fluent and colloquial English" (p. 380).

Example 6.1

Inga-Jerry: (Pointing repeatedly at Jerry's writing) I don' like *that*. I don' like *that*. *I* don' like *that*.

Jerry-Inga: (Grinning, points back at hers) I don' like *this*. I don' like *this*. I don' like *this*.

Inga-Jerry: I like *mine*. I don' like *yours*.

Jerry-Inga: So I don' like/I like *mine,* not/not *you!* (Inga laughs.)

(Fassler, 1998, pp. 379–380)

For L2 learners in mainstream contexts, many researchers have noted that native speaker peers provide models of target language use and a context for learn-ers to use that language productively to try out linguistic form and register as they gradually build up language gleaned through adult-child interactions (Philp & Duchesne, 2008; Wong Fillmore, 1976; Wray, 2002). However, in multilingual classrooms, L2 peers can perform the same functions, particularly where they are of mixed proficiency levels, in spite of L2 limitations. Unlike teacher-child in-teraction, where the teacher has a didactic agenda, in peer interaction the child's agenda is often primarily social—L2 use is part and parcel of gaining access to the classroom community. This is particularly important because the affective and social aspects of peer interaction contribute in unique ways to L2 learning (Bro-ner & Tarone, 2001; Cekaite & Aronsson, 2005; Philp & Duchesne, 2008; Wong Fillmore, 1976; Wray, 2002), and this is explored subsequently.

Benefits of Language Play for Children

An example of how the affective nature of many interactions between children may contribute to learning is seen in language play. Child peers share a common sense of what is funny and what is of interest. As we saw in Example 6.1, shared humor provides a "way in" to *participation* in the target language. At the same time, it provides a "way in" to *language*, as learners manipulate target language forms through language play.

   Cekaite and Aronsson (2005) provide the following example of shared humor from a Swedish reception class, a class for new arrivals. Example 6.2 involves a group of four children, aged 7–10, from different L1 backgrounds: three girls, Fusi (aged 7), Layla (10), and Rana (8); and one boy, Hiwa (8). They are playing a memory card game together—a game often used in this class to practice plurals. Their interaction includes singing, laughter, and distortion of language, as well as the practice and trial of the target forms. They instruct one another; Hiwa (line 5) commands Layla to play by the rules and name the card and then supplies the correct label for her, which Layla repeats. Then, Layla laughingly responds to Hiwa's funny-sounding non-targetlike production with the target phrase ("a pair of shoes"). Hiwa this time responds with the correct word for "pair," but repeats his funny-sounding word for "shoe" (*skol* instead of *skor*), and others join in, playing around with non-targetlike and nonsense forms together (lines 11–18).

Example 6.2

1 Fusi: Ah: NE:J! (picks a card that does not match)

          [O:H NO:!]

2 Hiwa: En få°gel (labels Fusi's card)

          [A bird]

3 Fusi: En få -_

          [A bi-]

4 Layla: En [eh eh (.) eh eh] ett pa:r

          [A [eh eh (.) eh eh] a pai:r] (picks a card of mittens; singing)

5 Hiwa: [E:i x såg! (.) sa¨g namnet!]

          [E:i x say!(.) say its name!]

6 Hiwa: Ett e:h vantar

          [A e:h mittens]

7 Layla: Vanta:r. (.) x qamiis

          [Mitte:ns. (.) x blouse]

8 Hiwa: E:n två sko:l (picks a card of shoes, smiley voice)

          [A: two shoe:l]

9 Layla: En he he par skor

          [A he he pair of shoes]

10 Hiwa: En par skol (smiley voice; picks a matching card)

          [A pair of shoel]

11 Fusi: Det [å r två skol he he he he he he

          [It [is two shoel he he he he he he]

12 Hiwa: [he he

13 Layla: (smiles)

14 Hiwa: En fågelskol [en fågelskol (picks cards, smiley voice)

          [A birdshoel [a birdshoel]]

15 Fusi: [Ne:j (looks at Hiwa)

          [No:]

16 Layla: xxx?

17 Hiwa: Khani mani (.) shanja kani he[he (playfully labelling the cards)

　　　　　 [hocus pocus (.) shanja kani he[he] (nonsense formula)

18 Layla: (to Hiwa) [he he

19 Fusi: Jag! (claims her turn)

　　　　　 [Me!]

(Cekaite & Aronsson, 2005, p. 176)

What this example demonstrates is that between L2 learners, language play can productively engage learners' attention to form, as they manipulate language for fun. At the same time, in this relaxed setting, without the teacher to calm them down, their collaborative play carries with it the pleasure of participating in the joke together. As Broner and Tarone (2001) argue, the affective quality of such language play contributes to its salience and memorability.

This example illustrates how peer interaction affords opportunities to play with language and practice new forms. It also demonstrates that interaction serves social goals—each child's desire to make friends, to be part of the group, and hold a position within it. The hilarity seen in the previous example contributes to affiliation between participants. Dunn (1999) emphasizes this, noting, "What is common across so many child-child interactions—and especially those between friends—is that they *matter* to the children; their emotional salience is unquestionable" (p. 270, original emphasis).

Benefits of Formulaic Sequences for Children

Research about L2 learners in mainstream and reception classrooms suggests that formulaic sequences, such as "my turn" and "I don't know", are a common feature of the learner's early attempts to participate as a successful classroom member (Wray, 2002). The linguistic importance of formulaic sequences was discussed in Chapter 4, but the use of these prefabricated chunks, when gleaned from monolingual classmates, brings both social and linguistic benefits because the use of their phrases aligns the child with his or her classmates. Most research emphasizes the role of native speaker peers in this process, but Willett's (1995) year-long study of four English as a second language (ESL) children in a mainstream first-grade classroom also suggests a role for L2 peers in the children's social integration in the class.

Willett found that the children's increasing participation was largely enabled through the use of formulaic chunks. In the classroom she observed, three ESL girls sat together and collectively made use of familiar classroom routines and formulaic language to participate in the same way as the native speaker children in the class. This allowed the children to "construct identities as competent students"

(p. 490). As Fassler (1998) also notes of L2 peers, such support for one another's use of English is "embedded in the children's peer relationships" (p. 381)—that is, in the social dimension of peer interaction. Willett contrasts the success of the three girls with the plight of another child who sat away from his L2 peers in the class and was unable to depend on them for help. He was perceived to be a struggling student by the teacher.

Similarly, Toohey (2000), describing elementary (K–3) classrooms, and Barnard (2009), an upper primary classroom (year 5), remark on the differential success of L2 learners in mainstream schools and the ways in which classroom practices, and teacher perception, may limit some children's opportunities to make use of the resources of more capable peers, whether L2 or monolingual peers. This research suggests that children who are in some ways excluded from peer activities, including associations with L2 peers, become further removed from the goal of being able to participate as members of the classroom community.

In these studies, all carried out in mainstream schools where the target language is the language of use inside and outside the classroom, we see that L2 peer talk is important not only because it provides (approximations of) target language input but also because it provides the context in which social goals of affiliation and social positioning are fulfilled, and thereby the motivation and context for L2 use (Philp & Duchesne, 2008). However, this is not the case in other settings.

Children and Teenagers in Foreign Language Settings

In foreign language contexts, these social goals are more likely to be negotiated in the L1. For example, based on naturalistic data from 10 primary and secondary foreign language (French and Italian) classrooms in Australia (Tognini, 2008), Tognini, Philp, and Oliver (2010) found that in interaction between peers, learners tended to switch to English for personal topics, as illustrated here by two secondary school students. In the following example (Tognini et al., 2010), two students stay on task using fairly restricted language from their text but switch to L1 for joking "off script."

Example 6.3

1 Std B: Qu'est-ce que tu aimes faire pendant les vacances?

[What do you like to do during the holidays?]

2 Std A: Pendant les vacances j'aime faire des promenades à vélo avec mon ami – *(snigger from questionner)* mon ami.

[During the holidays I like to go bike riding with my friend – my friend].

3 Std B: Your friend!

4 Std A: Why do you say that! *(Laughter and protestations)* Shut up.

(Tognini et al., 2010, p. 17)

For this reason, the potential benefit of peer interaction is substantially different in foreign language classrooms and in mainstream classrooms. In the latter, social goals interact with linguistic goals to shape peer interaction. In the former, the potential of peer interaction is primarily linguistic, as seen in the Chapters 2–4. Nevertheless, it is clear that in both contexts, the potential of L2 peer interaction depends greatly on the relationships between learners. In both contexts, peers may promote or hinder L2 learning. This will be discussed in detail later in the chapter with reference to identity and participation.

Social and Linguistic Benefits of Adult Peer Interaction

So far, we have discussed the social nature of peer interaction and its relevance to language learning only in reference to children. We now consider the nature of peer relationships among adult learners. Relationally, differences between peer interaction and teacher-learner interaction also arise, primarily because of the status of the teacher (Allwright, 1998b; Nunan, 1999), and the expert-novice dimension of teacher-learner interaction. The teacher constitutes an expert, whereas a peer is generally more of an equal, although of course students range in proficiency level, as discussed in the previous chapter, and expert-novice patterns are often evident during collaborative pair and group work (Storch, 2002). In Chapters 2 and 3, we noted that learners differ as to how they feel about practicing the L2 with peers and in their preferences for and against peer work and peer correction (e.g., Ewald, 2008; Garrett & Shortall, 2002; Fujii & Mackey, 2009; Philp, Walter, & Basturkmen, 2010; Tognini et al., 2010). In this section, we explore ways in which the potential benefits of interaction between adult learners are tied to the relationships between the interactors, including their perceptions of one another and their shared experiences and histories as students together.

As was found to be true of child peer interaction, adult L2 learners can be a significant resource for one another, precisely because of their relative equality as learners within a class. For example, they may seek assistance from peers rather than the teacher if reticent to ask questions during whole class interaction, as Cao (2009) found in a longitudinal study of willingness to communicate in adult English for Adult Purposes classes. Based on classroom observation and stimulated recall interviews, she notes that peer interaction provided a means of involvement when students were uncomfortable speaking up in the whole class setting. Cao reported,

> They normally wouldn't ask the teacher for help to clarify the meaning of unknown words especially in the whole-class situation, rather, they would turn to another student (usually the neighbor) for help (. . .) they reported (. . .) it might be a waste of the teacher's time and other classmates' time to ask about a word that might not be new to the majority of class.

> (Cao, personal communication, 2011)

Batstone and Philp (2013) in a descriptive analysis of Cao's data set, note that peer interaction in the classes takes on various guises, not limited to pair and group work, and functions in different ways to support L2 learning. Peer interaction often occurred concurrently with whole class interaction; struggling students whispered in asides to a neighbor (interacting within what the authors refer to as "private space"), as they tried to make sense of what was being said in the more public forum of teacher-led interaction. This is seen in Examples 6.4 and 6.5, in which all private talk is *underlined*. During a lesson involving a discussion about migration, one student, SH, asks the teacher to explain the word *refugee*. However, student S appears to lag behind the explanation and privately asks another student, ST, "What is it? refugee?" and ST briefly explains. The whole class discussion moves on, and the teacher elicits reasons for the plight of refugees. Once again, S takes the opportunity to privately ask a peer for further clarification, this time from J (line 56). We see that J and S's conversation parallels the class discussion, and ultimately, S herself ventures to take part in the whole class discourse. When her point is not taken up by the teacher, S and J respond to the teacher's question between themselves. We see in line 74 that S relates what is happening in whole class discourse to her conversation with J.

Example 6.4

53 T1: (writing on whiteboard) yes yes maybe ... But apart from war? ... War XX here here maybe ... crimes against humanity maybe ...

54 A: [Not enough food

55 S: *[Refugee? ((asks J))*

56 J: *[Refugee is a person who escape from war or*

57 T1: What else can be a reason?

58 J: So

59 T1: for them to become refugees?

60 A: Their country and

61 T1: for them to become a refugee?

62 SL: Political reasons

63 J: *(continuing his response to S) If if there a war in your country [you cannot live in your country*

64 T1: [political reasons yes, apart from political reasons, what else?

65 J: *So you want to go to another country ((to S))*

66 SL: Religion

67 T1: Yes and also economic reasons so if there's famine somewhere or drought no water

Example 6.5

68 S: *[If you come back to your country, you will be catched you cannot go to another country*

69 A: [no food]

70 J: *(To S?) Have to go other country because your country is very dangerous*

71 T1: Yep and also economic reasons X

72 SH: And the second word is it different from the first one?

73 S: [for that for the people if they go back they will die (to J)

    (a few turns later)

74 S: *I think we were talking about that? (quietly, to J)*

75 J: *Yes boat people [in Vietnam is Refugees (responding to S)*

(Batstone & Philp, 2013, p. 115)

This student, S, is able to use the new term *refugee* when later discussing her ideas during group work with another set of students. What is important to see here is that peer interaction socially mediates teacher-learner interaction (Lantolf, 2000a, 2000b): It is through talking to a peer (rather than asking the teacher), that S is able to make sense of confusing input. In the context of peers, she can explore ideas in a more immediate and personal environment and is ultimately able to make connections with the teacher-fronted discourse. Ohta (2001), in a study of teacher-directed and peer interaction in a Japanese classroom over two years, similarly demonstrates how "learners individualize the learning space by acting on affordances particular to their own needs" (p. 270).

Batstone and Philp (2013) suggest that peer talk in private space complements the teacher-fronted discourse in a number of ways. When classroom discourse triggers noticing of an unfamiliar or confusing form, whether lexical, phonological, or morpho-syntactic, the learner may seek help from a peer rather than the teacher. Public discourse necessarily involves being heard by everyone present and thus can be face-threatening (Peng, 2007), as noted previously, or culturally inappropriate for some students (Cao, 2009). In this class, learners made use of different contexts (e.g., small group, pair work, and private conversations) to elicit help from peers, once a particular learning issue had been identified. The process, which may begin in private space during teacher-led discourse, continued during group work at a later stage in the lesson. Thus, peers offer less intrusive space, individualized help, and for this reason, possibly, greater clarity. As with the studies on child classroom interaction reviewed previously, this study found that peer interaction among adults was shaped by social and pedagogical contexts, in terms of who they sought help from and in what way.

Adult Peers as L1 Resources

As noted in the previous chapter, research in foreign language settings has identified the use of L1 between learners as a useful tool for resolving difficulties (e.g., Anton & DiCamilla, 1998). In this L2 setting, Batstone and Philp (2013) also found that group peer work would sometimes include private asides between learners who shared a common L1. Once again, this allowed the co-construction of private space to resolve problems before then returning to the whole group discussion. In the following example, two of the four students in the group begin the task. Meanwhile, Y and C talk aside in Chinese (lines 6–13) before finally taking part in the task with the other students (line 14). It seems that Y needed first to resolve his difficulty with the difference between immigrate and emigrate (explained earlier in whole class interaction but not understood) before he could participate within the larger group. What is interesting here is the contingency of peer assistance (Foster & Ohta, 2005). Although the teacher had previously explained the difference, and although Y has a dictionary, he needs C to decipher the meaning more clearly, to provide individualized assistance, in the shared L1, and by using examples matched to his experience.

Example 6.6

18 Y: Which one, E-M-M, dan ci

[word]?

19 C: Cha Zi Dian

[Look it up in your dictionary]

20 Y: Zhe shi shen me yi si?

[What does this mean?]

21 C: Di er ge shi, bi ru ni yi ming dao xin xi lan ma, yi ming guo lai, ran hou ni dui xin xi lan lai shuo, dui xin xi lan de guo jia lai shuo ni jiu shi immigrate immigrate, ran hou ni dui zhong guo yi min chu lai de hua, dui zhong guo na ge guo jia lai shou ni jiu shi emi er emigrate.

[The second one is, for extract, you migrated to NZ, you migrated, then from NZ's point of view, you immigrate immigrate, then from China's point of view, you emigrate]

22 Y: Yi chu de

[emigrate]

23 C: Dui dui dui

[Yes yes yes]

24 SH: And you what do you think? ← SH directly involves Y

25 Y: What are you talking about?

26 SH: Immigration

27 J: Immigration
28 Y: I think immigration is er a big thing for the for the country, for extract, for NZ, lots of immigration immigrate take lots of money to this country and make the NZ much more stronger

(Data from Cao, 2009, p. 166 and unpublished raw data)

In summary, peer interaction can take different forms in classrooms, and as Batstone and Philp note, it may often serve a compensatory function where teacher-led discourse is unequal to the task of engaging all students and meeting their immediate individual needs. These private asides allow students the space to puzzle through problems that arise in whole class discourse, with the help of a peer in a way that is more aligned to their personal level of understanding (see Ohta, 2001, for a discussion of the use of private speech for similar purposes). Citing sociocultural work on classroom interaction (see Lantolf & Thorne, 2006), Batstone and Philp note that a benefit of assistance sought from a peer is the way it matches the learner's own agenda, rather than that set by the teacher. It proceeds in step with the learner's stated need—that is, at the time, the learner is focusing on the problem, in response to the learner's own focus, and without the stress of a wider audience. Equally, the peer who acts as a resource may also benefit from the process, in having to articulate the meaning of a new form or rephrase an argument provided during whole class interaction (Ohta, 2001; Topping & Ehly, 1998). Connected to this is the notion of choice and agency, the capacity to act on one's choices (Giddens, 1984). We discuss this in the following section: Who do learners choose to ask for help, and about what?

Peer Contributions to Identity and Participation

This second aspect of the social dimension to peer interaction stems from the relationships between participants and their experiences of working together. In this section, we explore notions of agency, identity, and participation and how peers may contribute both positively and negatively to the L2 learning context.

Descriptive longitudinal work of L2 learners adjusting to a new social context is characterized by heartwarming and heartbreaking stories of acceptance and rejection in this process (Norton, 2000; Norton & Toohey, 2001; Toohey, 1998), among both child and adult learners. What stands out in these stories is the mix of factors that shape what learners say and do through interaction. Such factors include investment—the degree to which learners are strongly motivated to learn or are willing to communicate. It is also mediated by personality traits such as openness, assertiveness, or gregariousness (Miller, 2003; Paradis, 2007; Strong, 1983; Wong Fillmore, 1976) and dynamics between peers. These factors all contribute to the emerging relationships that develop across the many interactions, sometimes promoting opportunities for learning and at other times preventing them.

Children

As noted earlier in the chapter, ethnographic and descriptive research among children aged 7–12 (e.g., Cekaite, 2007; Peregoy & Boyle, 1999; Willett, 1995; Wong Fillmore, 1976) documents processes of socialization and negotiation of identities within the school community that evolves through whole class and peer interaction (e.g., Cekaite, 2007). Across these studies, peers act as gateways to interactional opportunities (Pavlenko, 2002) because they contribute to perceptions of a child as "competent" or "struggling," "like us" or "different," and to opportunities for participation.

Cekaite (2007), in a longitudinal study of a 7-year-old Kurdish child in an L2 Swedish reception class for immigrants, notes how the child was seen differently by others over time, as she gained greater understanding and control over classroom practices, and as her interactional competence improved. The child's own agency is paramount in this study; the youngest in the class, she obstinately refused the teacher's affectionate label of *lille Fare* ("little Fare"), saying firmly *NEJ lille* ("no little"), positioning herself along with the older children in the class (p. 51). This child aligns herself with the community of peers to which she wants to belong. In mainstream classrooms, this could be the community of native speaking peers or a marginalized group of L2 learners. Studies on identity and participation more commonly focus on learners and native speaker peers; very few studies reflect on the role of L2 peers. This is certainly an area for further research both for children and adolescents, as we discuss in the next section.

Adolescents

In a longitudinal study of new immigrant students to Australia, Miller (2000, 2003) follows the progress of 10 adolescents, aged 13–16, over 18 months. Over this time, they move from an intensive language reception center to a bridging program to placement in mainstream local high schools. Miller reflects on their renegotiation of social identities within these new settings. She perceived that some of the students spent more time with native speaker peers and managed to become "legitimated as a speaker of English"; they made friends and became members of mainstream social groups. However, others, notably speakers of Asian languages, were marginalized and spent most time with L1 peers. Miller emphasizes that students had limited control in this process and were prejudged on whether "they sounded right." Yet this ability depended both on personal characteristics such as self-identity, investment, willingness to communicate, and personality, and on the willingness of native speaker peers to "open the gate" (Norton & Toohey, 2001). As Miller (2003) reports,

> For those students who were marginalised, high schools were not places where you met new friends as Nora had so fervently hoped, but places

where you were physically and socially isolated within the ESL unit; realised you didn't speak properly; had to catch up with the others; felt lost; didn't understand the tests, the texts, or the assemblies; and had to rely on L1 friends for all social interaction. (p. 181)

In this context, the role of L2 peers who share an L1 and/or similar experiences is a complex one. They can provide support and friendship, a means of surviving the challenges of negotiating a place in the community of target language speakers. At the same time, however, particularly for adolescents, relying on L1 peers may diminish opportunities for interaction with the native speaker peers. It is beyond the scope of this chapter to explore the literature on identity and acculturation (for review, see Harklau, 2007), but it is helpful to recognize the overlay for the adolescent as L2 learners of ethnic identity over self-identity. That is, along with the "achievement of a stable coherent, positive sense of identity as the major task of adolescence" (Harklau, 2007, p. 641), these youth must also make choices in acculturation between home and adopted culture. Age appears to make a difference in the identities learners choose, as we will discuss in the following chapter.

Adult Learners

Agency is equally important to remember when considering outcomes of adult peer assistance. Learners choose who they will and won't rely on for help, as well as who they prefer to work with given the choice, and these choices can be productive or limiting (Ohta, 2001). To date, there has been very little attention in the L2 literature about the impact of relationships between learners in the classroom, particularly its effects on the outcomes of peer interaction. Philp and Mackey (2010), examined 12 hours of classroom data of an adult foreign language French class of 30 undergraduate university students in New Zealand. This class was characterized by a wide range of ability, including heritage learners, students with 3–12 months L2 study abroad experience, and students with one year of instruction. The data provide a picture of the complexity of the social fabric of the classroom, in which students' past experience and histories with one another were contributing factors in their (un)willingness to work together and to provide or receive feedback. Philp and Mackey focused on the extent to which social factors may impact both positively and negatively on interaction in that class. Interview data, for which recordings of class interaction were used as prompts, provided insights into learners' perceptions of their interactions with peers.

On the positive front, some pairing of students was beneficial. Familiar peers often sat together and relied on one another, and some students developed expert-peer relationships where proficiency levels were unmatched. For example Eve, an L1 Chinese speaker, often worked with two male students, both heritage learners, whom Eve had known from the previous semester class. She eagerly depended on them for correction and explanation when she could and described them as "like lecturers." Yet, relationally she regarded them as different from the teacher. As Eve notes in describing the value of pair work, "Your neighbour is not—she, like, she's not a teacher or something and I feel like more relaxed" (Philp & Mackey, 2010, p. 218). However, this depended on the person; when paired with an unfamiliar person, she felt nervous, as seen the following comment:

Example 6.7

And so sometimes I feel quite nervous talking to her . . . she just doesn't seem to understand and so I'll be thinking well is this my pronunciation problem or like am I saying this correctly or yeah (laughter).

(Philp & Mackey, 2010, p. 217)

Similarly, Claude deliberately provides backup to his friend Matt, who was of lower proficiency in French. In a role play, Claude continually scaffolded his performance by saying Matt's "lines" for him before each turn. As Claude explains:

Example 6.8

He had told that it had been a while since he had done French [and] um (.) um I was just trying to make it a bit clear for him.

(Philp & Mackey, 2010, p. 218)

Other students felt that working with friends allowed them to make mistakes. Ben noted:

Example 6.9

When I talk to close friends ah it doesn't bother me if I've made mistakes or or it doesn't bother me as much.

(Philp & Mackey, 2010, p. 217)

These examples reflect the positive benefits of working with well-known peers: reduced anxiety, assistance, and reliance on a nonjudgmental attitude to mistakes.

However, negative elements also appear. Philp et al. (2010), in a study based on the same data set, found that some students reported they were less likely to correct one another in peer interaction. As noted in Chapter 3, for example, Ben, a high-proficiency student who noticed the errors his friends made in task-based pair work, deliberately avoided correction for reasons related to social positioning and the underlying equality of peers, noting:

Example 6.10

> I don't want to be better than them I'm just another student.
>
> (Philp et al., 2010, p. 272)

Research reviewed in Chapter 3 shows that productive corrective feedback may or may not be a feature of peer interaction. It seems that this depends on several factors, one of which is the students' relationships with their interlocutors and their past experiences together in language learning.

Philp and Mackey (2010)'s findings also show that there is a flip side to peer interaction: Groups can be relationally mismatched, with negative consequences. They reported one such group of three high-proficiency learners: Gerard and Florence, who were close friends and always worked together; and Robert, a heritage learner, well liked by other class members. They were placed together for peer role play on one rare occasion by the teacher. They were somewhat competitive, and, from unfortunate experiences in previous classes together, Robert and the pair had developed a dislike for one another. In the role play, Robert, as a waiter, said very little, whereas Gerard and Florence hammed up their roles and took their time deciding on what to order. Under the surface, there was great resentment as seen in Gerard's recollection of the scene in Example 6.11.

Example 6.11

> Uhm, I ordered the drinks . . . (. . .) and so she wanted to know which cheese. And like Robert was like oh yeah really f. . . . I don't care. Sorry if I'm being uhm he wasn't really into the whole exercise and um Florence didn't want to, was just playing it more and more, saying oh well . . . I want something strong and well you can always get the [Roquefort] and Florence was sort of like taken back and going like oh yeah really getting into this and I'm like oh yeah so inspiring [sarcastically] really getting into this aren't you?
>
> (Philp & Mackey, 2010, p. 224)

Similarly, Mackey et al. (2007) report that negative relationships between partners in pair work prevented positive outcomes. In Example 6.12, one learner explains that she was so irritated by one partner that she deliberately didn't listen to him:

Example 6.12

> I wasn't even trying to understand cause whenever Graham says anything I just kind of try to pretend he doesn't exist.
>
> (Mackey et al., 2007, p. 148)

These studies suggest that relationships between learners, built up over experiences of learning together in classes, sometimes over several semesters, strongly affect the outcomes of peer interaction, whether for better or worse. Students may be oriented to helping one another through modeling and correction, or they may habitually overlook errors, rather than engender perceptions of inequality. Damon and Phelps (1989a) note, of any kind of peer interaction,

> Dominance, jealousy, prejudice, defensiveness, and a host of other interpersonal dynamics can disrupt productive joint activity between people of any age, children included. (p. 14)

Similarly, Salomon and Globerson (1989) reflect on the cumulative perceptions of self and others, built up through interacting together in class:

> Students know each other, they have likes and dislikes of each other, they share (or do not share) a view of the task, they come to have expectations of each other and of themselves, and they compare their own performance with the performance of the others in the team. (p. 93)

Peer Dynamics

The third aspect of peer interaction that we explore here concerns peer dynamics. With regard to children in school, reports of large UK-based projects on pupil grouping in primary school classrooms (Barnes & Todd, 1977; Blatchford et al., 2003; Mercer, 2000) stress the importance of interpersonal relations for effective group work and particularly the need to foster social skills essential to effective group work, including trust, organization, and planning skills, as well as reciprocity and management of conflict and competition. This suggests that both cognitive *and* social skills need to be developed; neither can be taken for granted. Although this study focused on primary school children in mainstream classrooms, the findings are equally relevant for children and adults in language classrooms.

In the previous chapter, we saw that proficiency pairings can affect the dynamics of interaction. However, proficiency is just one part of the equation. To date, there has been very little L2 research of pair and group dynamics. A notable exception is Storch's (2002) study of patterns of interaction among pairs of adult learners in an L2 context. Storch identified four patterns of interaction between learners, based on Damon (1984), distinguished by degree of mutuality and equality. She found that the students engaged with one another in a particular manner, either as collaborators who listened to one another and were relatively equal in participation, as novice and expert, or in relationships of dominance or dominance and passivity. It was the first two patterns that Storch found to be most conducive, where there was greatest mutuality: in expert/novice pairs and in collaborative pairs. She suggests that in classroom peer interaction, pairs are best reassigned where there are unproductive patterns (i.e., dominant/dominant or dominant/passive).

Storch's (2002) study of interactional patterns among adults suggests that both linguistic and interactional skills contribute to the ultimate effectiveness of pair and group work. Part of the effectiveness of peer interaction relates to affiliation, as we've argued previously, but part of it relates to how well learners listen to and engage with one another. As noted in Chapter 8, in task-based language teaching research, a primary agenda has been the creation of effective tasks that promote maximum opportunities for L2 learning (for review see Ellis, 2003), but an important area for research, largely ignored, is the training of interpersonal skills essential to making these tasks work as intended (Dörnyei & Murphey, 2003). This is certainly an important area for further exploration.

Conclusion

In this chapter, we have reflected on the intrinsically social nature of peer interaction and three different ways in which relations between peers contribute to the potential benefits of peer interaction for L2 development. Each aspect of peer relations has implications for L2 research, and for pedagogy, in terms of fostering the positive contribution of peer interaction in the classroom.

First, we noted that the relatively equal status of participants in peer interaction makes it very distinct from teacher-learner interaction. For children, peer interaction provides unique contexts for L2 use because of a relative equivalence in cognition, interests, and perspective. With other children, they may engage in activities that are conducive to language learning, including pretend play, games, and language play. When adolescent and adult peers perceive themselves as equals, they may feel less anxious in making mistakes, more relaxed in experimenting with language, and more likely to hazard a guess or to ask for help from a peer in contrast to teacher-learner interaction. The flip side of this is that peers may resist correction by classmates because it disrupts the intrinsic roles of teacher and student within the culture of the classroom. Breen (1985) writes:

> The culture of the classroom insists upon asymmetrical relationships. The duties and rights of teacher and taught are different. More significantly, both teacher and taught may be *equally reluctant* to upset the asymmetry of roles and identities to which these duties and rights are assigned. (p. 146)

Peers by nature provide an alternative resource in the classroom to teachers, but in some classrooms, the rich potential of peer interaction is not fostered. Although the culture of any classroom is highly complex in terms of its construction, the teacher plays a key role. One way in which teachers nurture this potential is through promoting positive peer relations. Teachers also foster a culture of peer assistance by encouraging peer correction and by acknowledging the ideas and expertise of students where possible. Through recognizing peers as playing an important role in one another's learning, teachers are carefully intentional in their planning and management of opportunities for peer talk.

Second, we argued that peer interaction is a context in which learners negotiate their identity, role, and relationships within the classroom environment. Social and linguistic goals are inseparable, yet not often researched as such. This is a difficult but much needed area of research. L2 peer friendships can be empowering, but they can also prove a hindrance to L2 learning: When peers who share the same L1 take refuge in the support of L2 peers, they can also reduce opportunities to interact with native speaker peers. Although there is a growing body of research that documents interaction in the early and middle years of schooling, there appears to be little work on the effect of peers on L2 learning among adolescent learners. As Miller's (2003) research suggests, immigrants arriving in early to late adolescence may be most vulnerable to opt out of seeking participation in the community of majority language learners and rely more on their L1 and on L1 peers for support. A vital area for research, little explored to date, is the role played by peers in adolescent immigrants' experiences in mainstream high schools and how this intersects with empowering or limiting the agency and successes of L2 learners.

Finally, we noted that the potential of peer interaction is mediated by its participants: Past experiences and histories together, personality traits, willingness to participate, and interactional skills may all impact on the potential for pair and group talk to "work." This supports current practices of taking the time to foster group cohesion and to create positive classroom environments at each level of classroom dynamics—individual, group, and whole class (e.g., Dörnyei & Maldarez, 1997; Dörnyei & Murphey, 2003). It also suggests that it is worth reforming groups that persistently operate in patterns of low mutuality, where members are dominated by others. We cannot afford to ignore, either in research or in pedagogy, the fact that the potential outcomes of peer interaction in classroom settings—whether beneficial, negligible, or undermining of L2 learning—are mediated to a great extent by social relations and goals.

7

AGE-RELATED CHARACTERISTICS AND PEER INTERACTION

Introduction

This chapter represents a slight departure in the book from the treatment of aspects of peer interaction in general, including both child and adult second language (L2) learners. In the previous chapter, we made distinctions in aspects of peer interaction according to age. We now turn our attention to the uniqueness of the child language learner and consider age-related differences in peer interaction and implications for L2 development. Much of recent research on age-related characteristics of peer interaction emanates from the field of educational psychology and predominantly focuses on mainstream classes among monolingual children. However, we have incorporated some of these findings in this chapter where it is relevant to L2 learners in a range of contexts.

At different stages of childhood, from infant to preschool and from late primary school to early and final years of secondary school, peers make a difference. Who the peers are, the nature of their interactions with friends and classmates, and the importance of those relationships all differ according to age. Drawing from research in educational psychology as well as applied linguistics, this chapter looks at age-related characteristics of children over three periods of childhood in the school-age years. We consider how these characteristics might shape the nature and outcomes of interaction between L2 learners in the context of school. We will also explore the contribution of peers at different ages to the kind of input and feedback that they provide one another, and the use they make of it. The chapter concludes with a consideration of implications for theory, research, and language pedagogy.

Periods of Childhood

When thinking about the nature of peer interaction across the school years, it is helpful to reflect carefully on the marked developmental changes all children undergo—socially, intellectually, physically, and linguistically. Along with developmental differences, the context of learning changes, as do the challenges that schooling presents, cognitively, socially, and linguistically. Children move from an environment in which the family is central to one in which other adults and peers are increasingly important (Berk, 2013). For our purposes, we will compare children of school age over three main periods of childhood (see Philp, Mackey, & Oliver, 2008):

1. Early childhood (including children of 5–7 years of age, in the beginning grades of school);
2. Middle childhood (8–11 years, in elementary or middle school);
3. Adolescence (including early adolescents, 12–14 years, in junior high school, and later adolescents, 15 years+ in the final years of high school).

Although we use age as a marker here, this is intended as indicative not fixed: Children vary in the age they progress through certain stages of cognitive development. We note too variability within and between children in attainment of competencies. Although adequate for our purposes, recent research has questioned Piaget's notion of "stages" as an appropriate metaphor for describing child development (see for discussion, Berk, 2013; Duchesne, McMaugh, Bochner, & Krause, 2013). We will discuss each period in turn and consider the implications for peer interaction and L2 development. Characterizations of these periods of childhood are drawn from current developmental psychology texts (Berk, 2013; Duchesne et al., 2013), based primarily on Piagetian and Vygotskian perspectives on learning (De Lisi & Golbeck, 1999; Hogan & Tudge, 1999; O'Donnell, 2006). Both view interaction as a key context for learning and thus provide a platform for considering the contribution of child peers to L2 learning.

Perspectives on Opportunities for Learning Through Peers

In Piaget's view, the relatively symmetrical nature of interaction between peers is particularly conducive to cognitive development because it can lead each child to notice conceptual differences between their own and their partner's idea of things. Through interaction with an equal, each child may puzzle over anomalies autonomously, attempting to resolve cognitive conflict as it arises. In contrast, adult-child interaction may limit such opportunities, where an asymmetrical relationship is more likely to induce immediate acceptance of the more expert opinion, without question and therefore without conflict. We might infer that, with regard to L2 development, peer interaction may encourage change where anomalies in language arise between equals. In the following example (Oliver, Philp, & Duchesne, 2012), two young learners of English as a second language (ESL), aged 6–7, debate the senses of a snake as they fill out a grid on attributes of different animals. Their engagement in the topic leads them to reflect carefully and to articulate their thoughts as they work through the problem together. This also provides a context for meaningful L2 use.

Example 7.1

M: Does the snake have ear?

C: No

M: Yeah they are little . . . I think no be . . . I think I think I thinks they no they smell something OK let+

C: Yeah them smell with them tongue

(Philp, Oliver, & Mackey, 2006, unpublished raw data)

In contrast, the peer interaction shown in Example 7.2, between children of the same age as those in Example 7.1, is interrupted by guidance from the teacher (T). Initially, W appeals to his friend, M, for confirmation of what he is drawing. However, the sudden appearance of the expert reduces the need for any further reflection. The conversation is now dominated by the teacher's focus (completing the task with the right language) and, in this case, undermines the children's efforts to work through the challenge on their own. As we saw in the previous chapter, it is the children's essential equality that promotes exploratory talk (Barnes & Todd, 1977; Mercer, 1996).

Example 7.2

W: Square> like this like this?

M: No not circle square here yes square 1 2

W: This?

T: Yes, he's right. He's drawing 15 circles. But now you have to ask M, ask him, where are they.

W: Where are they?

T: Big voice come on.

W: Where are they?

T: Now where are they. What is this?

W: Car

T: Car, draw a picture of a car.

(Oliver, Philp, & Mackey, 2008, unpublished raw data)

It should be remembered, though, that a Vygotskian perspective places greater value on asymmetrical relationships as contexts for change (Vygotsky, 1978; see also Lourenço, 2012), as discussed earlier in Chapter 2.

Specific to peer interaction and L2 learning, interaction between a novice and more skilled peer may be beneficial when the novice's performance of a task is linguistically scaffolded and enhanced through joint construction. Yet, even in matched pairs we find this "collective scaffolding," as we saw in Chapter 2 (Donato, 1994). In the following example, two young ESL learners jointly assist one another to form a question. In this way, they pool their knowledge as they construct the question: C produces the main lexical items, and M provides the grammar.

Example 7.3

M: Do=

C: Giraffe

M: Does the

C: Giraffe has legs

M: Does the giraffe have leg?

(Oliver et al., 2008, unpublished raw data)

This collective scaffolding between peers occurs at all ages, as we saw in Chapter 2. Thus far, we have highlighted characteristics of peer interaction shared across age spans. We argue that where children are matched in maturity and ability, their interaction as peers has different potential benefits for L2 learning compared to adult-child interaction. Their equivalence promotes use of both exploratory talk, as learners try to sort out their thoughts (Barnes, 2008), and experimentation with language. The relative symmetry of peers allows for the possibility of collective scaffolding, in which all participants pool knowledge to express themselves in the target language. Speaking of the significance of symmetry of peers for learning in general, Duchesne et al. (2013) claim:

> First, peers are more willing to challenge one another's ideas than they are the views of an adult. Second, children are particularly motivated to resolve the difficulties as they form part of their relationships—whether it is a matter of being right, of maintaining a friendship, or of keeping the interaction going. (p. 75)

This might apply as much to linguistic as it does to factual or conceptual difficulties. Thus, for children, peer interaction provides a unique context for L2 use. Although this is true across ages, we also find age-specific differences in the potential ways in which peers contribute to learning. We now explore these differences as we discuss characteristics of children at each age span.

Characteristics of Age Spans

Early Childhood

The period of early childhood typically covers the ages of 2 to 7, corresponding roughly to Piaget's preoperational stage, during which children become able to mentally represent their world through symbolic activity, most notably through language. Their ability to represent their world is seen, for example, in make-believe play and in drawing. In this section, we confine our discussion to ages 5–7, when, with familiar objects and contexts, children can exhibit some of the features associated with Piaget's concrete operational stage, including logical understanding, the ability to categorize objects, and the ability to take another person's perspective (Berk, 2013; Duchesne et al., 2013).

As discussed in the previous chapter, children's interactions at this age often reflect their social goals of developing friendships, equality, and reciprocity. Philp and Duchesne (2008) describe a 6-year-old girl, Yessara, acquiring ESL in a mainstream kindergarten class. They emphasize peer interaction as a key context for the expression and negotiation of friendship and solidarity. This is seen in Example 7.4. Yessara shares both the eraser (*rubber* in Australian English) and her accent (rolled *r*) with her friends, Roberta and Sally.

Example 7.4

1   R: I've got a sticker

2   S: I've got a sticker

3   Y: hey Roberta

4   S: hey Roberta I'll tell you something

5   Y: rubber rubber

6   S: rubber rubber rubber (imitating rolled /r/ of Yessara)

7   R: rub rub rubber

8   S: rubber rubber rubber (attempting rolled /r/ without success)

(Philp & Duchesne, 2008, p. 95)

Such affiliative mimicry can occur whether the context of the interaction is classroom deskwork, as in the previous example, or in informal unstructured play. Example 7.4 illustrates affiliation in the peer interaction between monolingual children and their L2 classmate, but equally we see this among L2 peers. In the following example from a reception class of 6- and 7-year-old children, two children are identifying shapes in a picture. They take pleasure in pronouncing the unusual word "octagon". Although not represented in this transcription of just one pair, clearly audible on the recording is that this pair's delight was caught up by the other children in the room who were also working in pairs on the same task. Many of the pairs, on hearing their friends use the word, mimicked their repetition, using the same intonation and vowel distortion, their mouths forming a wide circle to pronounce the novel word.

Example 7.5

P: Ok … how many: … oc … oc (laughs)

I: (laughs) how many oc? (laughs) That's a circle

P: oo Octagon

I: Octagon

P: Octagon

I: Zero

P: Octagon

(Oliver et al., 2008, unpublished raw data)

Pretend Play as a Context for Language Use

It is particularly at this age that *make-believe* or *pretend play*, in which the child pretends to be something or someone, provides a context in which the L2 learner can start to use the language of peers and participate in interaction with others. This offers both linguistic and social benefits for the child (Philp & Duchesne, 2008). Ervin-Tripp (1991), speaking of first language (L1) and L2 acquisition alike, argues that linguistically, pretend play offers "a rich source of important language practice in different styles and vocabulary (. . .) it provides a chance to practice a range of speech acts, styles and registers" (p. 88). Engagement in pretend play is rarely as imaginative, as sustained, or as frequent as it is among children— playing with peers and siblings offers this singular opportunity. In the context of pretend play, children are able to practice specialized vocabulary and social registers that they would not use otherwise, for example, by taking on the role of teacher or other adult personae. In classroom settings, these scenarios include both real-world contexts and fictional characters, including shared stories.

It is because of the social importance of peer interaction at this age that pretend play affords such opportunities to extend language use. Fassler (1998), in a six-month participant observation study of an ESL kindergarten noted that "many early uses of English were embedded in children's sociability—their eagerness to communicate and their efforts to cultivate friendships" (p. 390). They acted out a variety of scenarios, taking on roles as a teacher or a doctor or personae from class stories, for example, sometimes using explicit metacommunication ("I'm doctor ok?"; "Say 'hi'") to initiate or maintain these roles. In the following example, as one child, Jerry, moves from comparing drink boxes (large, medium, and small in size) with his friends to pretend play, the drink boxes transform into members of a family. The children's participation in this play, as they each adopt a role, promotes the social goal of affiliation, as much as it promotes L2 use. Typical of much of children's pretend play, their linguistic efforts are here supported by props. As Ervin-Tripp (1991) points out, such play is often also supported by the predictable structure of this particular scenario. The speaker and specific interlocutor are indicated on the left of each turn.

Example 7.6

Jerry-Tracy/Inga:	I mommy father baby (Pointing to the drink boxes)
Tracy-Inga:	//I'm baby crying, whaaah. What // say [to] daughter?
Inga-Tracy:	Daughter, why ya crying?
Tracy-Jerry:	Jerry the fader [father] come back.
Inga-Jerry:	Father, come. Daughter want you. Wake up. [His juice box is lying down on its side on the table]
Jerry-Inga/Tracy:	I not up. Up. Help me out. Come on!

(Fassler, 1998, pp. 394–395)

Like pretend play, Ervin-Tripp notes that other forms of peer play also offer learners the chance to learn new vocabulary and to practice new forms as they collaborate on projects. Thus play offers the context to "negotiate what they want, (. . .) argue for their positions, and (. . .) explain plans and games" (p. 96). We see this more during middle childhood, where play often includes games with rules. Again, we see that it is the equivalence of peers that affords these opportunities.

Reciprocity

One of the many changes seen during the span of early childhood is an increasing capacity for reciprocal interaction, an essential element of successful peer talk. In an L1 acquisition study of collaboration between 36 pairs of children, aged 4–7, Ogden (2000) found clear differences according to age with regard to capacity for reciprocal interaction. Her work is as relevant to L2 contexts as it is to L1 contexts. Year 2 children (aged 7 years) demonstrated "greater capacity for sharing perspective and engaging in collaborative activity" (p. 222). Ogden attributes this to the developmental ability to beginning to think recursively. That is, the ability to think about what someone else is thinking and to understand others' thoughts and needs. Although this burgeoning ability is not fully attained until midadolescence (Miller, Kessel, & Flavell, 1970), it is evident in middle childhood. This is not to say, however, that younger children are entirely incapable of engaging in reciprocal interaction. Ogden also acknowledged the influence of contextual factors in enabling children to collaborate with one another at school (something they may already do with siblings at home in their L1). These factors include familiarity with the peer, and with the task, as well as their [school-based] experience of working with another child (Dunn, 2002). This has obvious implications for L2 peer interaction activities in the early years of schooling—peer tasks likely require scaffolding by the teacher and support through organization of the task (Gibbons, 2002). When frustrated by a difficult (or boring) task, children of this age often lack the resources to stay focused. Similarly, they may find personal conflicts hard to resolve, as seen in the following example between two 6- to 7-year-old L2 learners. These girls are [no longer] engaged in a matching task (Oliver et al., 2008).

Example 7.7

B: Red

A: Xx xx there's no red allowed to be on that

B: Gonna tell the teacher

A: Will you stop it . . . Will you stop it . . . Will you stop it right no::w (saying it in funny voice to tape recorder) (repeatedly names her partner)

B: I'm telling the teacher

(Oliver et al., 2008, p. 561)

In spite of these potential difficulties, peer interaction is an important means of allowing children practice in talking, unassisted by an expert. Makin, Campbell, and Jones Diaz (1995) suggest that at this age, peer interaction "enables conversational skills to flourish, with an increasing ability to share topics, take conversational turns and provide explanations" (p. 28). These skills continue to develop through the first few years of schooling.

Middle Childhood

By middle childhood, a child's L1 is highly developed, with increasing vocabulary and grammatical complexity. The span of years 7–11 represents a period in which children's thinking changes dramatically and becomes more adultlike, with a greater capacity for problem solving and greater attentional resources. Although not yet able to think abstractly, in this period, children have the capacity to think logically in a more ordered and organized manner about concrete and tangible information (Berk, 2013). This has implications for the kinds of tasks in which L2 learners may be expected to engage. For instance, children at this age also have a more advanced understanding of spatial concepts. Thus, they are able to manage language tasks involving maps and directions, as they develop the ability to mentally represent how someone else might walk from one place to another along a certain route. Socially, in middle childhood, peers are better able to take perspective—making use of a range of signals, they can more astutely interpret the feelings of others and take them into account. Much younger children can imagine themselves in the other person's place and express empathy, but in middle childhood, this ability is further refined and more complex (Berk, 2013). Prosocial acts such as helping and sharing increase. In addition, children of this age develop a wider range of strategies to regulate their own emotions and to adjust to the demands of different situations. This suggests a greater potential to work in groups and collaborate on tasks with others without teacher assistance.

Metalinguistic Awareness and Language Play

In terms of language, metalinguistic awareness develops to a much greater extent over this age span. Although not yet fully developed, L2 learners can use their metalinguistic ability in instructed settings to resolve difficulties with certain linguistic forms, if they are supported by contextualized use of these forms in meaningful contexts (White, 2008). Metalinguistic awareness in middle childhood is also reflected in their interactions with others, particularly in language play such as riddles, puns, and pedantic play (contrasting literal with illocutionary meaning). In peer interaction, language play serves both social and linguistic goals: Language play can provide the way to deflect conflict and to engage the attention and approval of peers (Cekaite & Aronsson, 2005). Engaging in language play together can also facilitate affiliation between peers. Philp et al. (2008), discussing the linguistic benefits of language play, connect these social benefits to linguistic spin offs:

> Language play promotes manipulation of form and meaning, imitation, and repetition, and may increase saliency of form (. . .) Moreover, because it is enjoyable, the affective strength of such play may potentially lead to deeper processing of the language. (p. 8)

These qualities of language play were illustrated in the previous chapter (see also Cekaite & Aronsson, 2005; Cook, 2000; Sullivan, 2000).

Growing Oral and Written Literacy

Through schooling, middle childhood is characterized by an increasing oral and written literacy. For L2 learners, literacy impacts on the kinds of tasks children engage with at this age and the linguistic demands of the task. Children's engagement in collaborative written reports and reconstruction tasks provides opportunities to extend their language use within different kinds of discourse, manipulate language form, and experiment with how to express their ideas in the target language. At this age, children make greater use of written texts as input for discussion and as models for their writing. This is seen in Example 7.8. Two L2 learners, aged 9–10, are together designing a habitat for a platypus in the zoo. They discuss the platypus enclosure and the writing of an appropriate sign. This example reflects their developing ability to include more formal language (moving from "don't touch it" to "please do not touch the platypus") and a growing lexical repertoire (e.g., "spur").

Example 7.8

P: this is going to be like the back and this is going to be . . . the front . . . no he won't . . . he wouldn't wander around the water and go out there so we don't need a gate there because he won't wander that far out

(2 turns later)

J: so if we have a sign that says . . . if you find a platypus take it . . . take him to . . . no . . . a staff member

P: no no . . . don't touch it . . . please don't touch it . . . yes yes that's what we'll do . . . we'll put . . . please don't . . . no . . . please don't touch platypus spine . . .

J: no . . . what is it/ . . . what is it? . . . its got something that's poisonous

P: so that'll make the people walk away . . . because they aren't going to take it home if its got something poisonous on it

J: please . . . please don't touch the platypus because it has . . . a poisonous *spur*

P: yes . . . please do not touch the platypus because of its spur . . . its spur is dangerous and you will have to be taken to hospital . . . right?

(Gibbons, 1991, pp. 27–28)

It is important to note the collaboration between the pair. Gibbons notes that through "their successful negotiation they produce a final wording for their notice that incorporates the earlier suggestions of both children. It is quite likely that neither child would have come to this final version alone" (pp. 27–28).

We see here an association between age-specific abilities and affordances created by peer interaction. This kind of task might occur in the classrooms of younger children, but usually in the context of teacher-fronted rather than peer interaction because of the challenges it presents cognitively and linguistically. Although younger children need scaffolding to attempt such a task, these older children can accomplish it between themselves. After repeated experiences at such tasks, or at an older age again, they might complete it individually.

Potential Quality of Peer Talk

Middle childhood differs from early childhood in terms of time spent in institutionalized settings and ratio of peers to adults (Berk, 2013; Philp et al., 2008). This means that children of this age are typically spending more time in the company of peers, and much of this time in unstructured settings. In her discussion of the previous example, Gibbons notes the complexity of the peers' use of language when left to themselves:

It is also striking how full of conditional language and explanations this short dialogue is, and correspondingly how much richer it seems than the language typically produced by children in a teacher-dominated classroom. (p. 28)

However, if language use between peers is to be as productive for learning as that seen in the previous example, it requires careful planning by the teacher with regard to task selection and management. Explicit training in cooperative communication skills is also vital (Mercer, 1996; O'Donnell, 2006). Years of observational and quasi-experimental studies in mainstream primary and secondary classrooms warn of the tendency for group work among peers to be little more than individual seat work (Galton, Hargreaves, & Pell, 2009; Kutnick et al., 2006). Mercer (1996) emphasizes that children are capable of collaboration but need to be explicitly given "the ground rules." That is, cooperation is a skill that can be nurtured and developed through instruction and modeling. He gives the following example from a teacher, speaking to a class of 10-year-olds:

So then you would have to accept someone else's opinion if it was different from yours, so you would say something like "Do you agree?" (. . .) or "I think that's wrong" (. . .) And the person who was going to disagree with you wouldn't just say "no," you have to have a **reason** for disagreeing. (p. 373)

In the same way, with regard to improving the potential of group work for L2 learning, children at this age benefit from modeling and explicit training that promotes mutuality, receptive listening, and cooperation.

Adolescence

Late childhood and early adolescence is a time of tremendous change: biologically, with the onset of puberty; cognitively; socially, in their relationships with adults and peers; and psychologically, in terms of identity and developing autonomy. In adolescence, from about age 11 and up, the capacity for abstract reasoning and thinking develops (Berk, 2006), as attentional resources improve and working memory capacity increases. Learners develop in their ability to store information temporarily while at the same time processing other information as they work on another task or aspect of a problem (Duchesne et al., 2013). Piaget described this as the formal operation stage. This ability includes a well-established metalinguistic awareness in all language domains, including the capacity to analyze language as object, and a growing ability to make logical inferences (Berman, 2007; Muñoz, 2003). They recognize subtle distinctions in language use and start to use and understand figurative speech and sarcasm. Adolescents have generally developed social and intellectual skills that better equip them for cooperative and collaborative peer work. Compared to younger children, they are better able to pick up emotional signals, to work cooperatively, and to stay on task. They are better equipped to exchange ideas by giving and asking for opinions as well as acknowledging the contributions of others (Berk, 2013; Duchesne et al., 2013; Hartup, 1983). These all suggest advantages for L2 learning through peer work. Reflecting on differences in interactional skills according to age, Muñoz (2007) suggests that although younger learners may require some kind of interactional scaffold from the teacher when working in groups, older learners do not. Adolescents generally have the social skills to cooperate efficiently and are able to organize their own roles in collaborative work. In addition, because of greater metalinguistic awareness, there is greater potential to focus on form-related difficulties, to articulate them and reflect upon them. In the following example, two L2 learners are involved in a paired grid task during a high school economics class. Their conversation reflects their ability to listen and respond to one another's ideas. When B misunderstands J's point (line 2), they negotiate over several turns before reaching a consensus (line 8). This task also reflects the high level of difficulty of content-based classes at this age.

Example 7.9

1 J: It's like sacrificing dead money (.) first and then they get when they get profit> you know revenue> and then get profit out of it> and then they keep on you know repaying the debt=

2 B: So debt keep= so the economy keep on paying paying their money bad debt not pay the debt

3 J: No I was talking about the firm

4 B: The firm?

5 J: Yeah

6 B: But the deficit cannot account for the whole economy not the firm?

7 J: Yeah I was referring to the firm, if the firm cannot operate like that the whole economy cannot operate like that then in the same way kind of idea

8 B: Oh you're right

(Ministry of Education, New Zealand, unpublished data, 2008)

Writing of L1 acquisition in adolescence, Berman (2007) notes that in school settings, "linguistic literacy is inculcated, expanded, and exploited. In all these respects—a growing repertoire of linguistic devices, social and cognitive developments, and increased schooling—adolescence constitutes a watershed in later developing knowledge and use of language" (p. 260). This is of course just as true of the L2 learner. Cummins (2000), writing of immigrant children in English schools, suggests that it takes a minimum of five years for a child to develop the age-appropriate level of academic skills of their L1 peers. Adolescents with onset of L2 learning in high school may well be disadvantaged compared to new start-ers in mainstream primary schools, in spite of superior metalinguistic knowl-edge, as they have less time to make up for lost input (Collier, 1987). However, Cummins also notes that the cognitive maturity of the adolescent learner has advantages in literacy-related skills. With their increasing awareness of linguistic registers, oral and written, they gain greater control over their linguistic repertoire and advance in their ability to understand and reproduce different discourse styles. These challenges face L1 and L2 learners alike, but L2 learners' limited linguistic repertoire may pose problems.

During adolescence, with greater autonomy and independence, even more time is spent with peers than adults or family members, within a wider social network and reflecting a greater reliance on peers. This shift in social spheres is reflected in a change in language use, extending beyond home and school set-tings to other social settings (Chambers, 1995). For children who immigrate to another country, peer choices (both by learners and by their peers) may to a large degree determine the richness of their L1 and L2 language environment and have consequences for language development. As we saw in Chapter 6, social relation-ship preferences may promote or reduce opportunities for L2 use and learning. In a longitudinal study of differences in language acquisition according to age of arrival, Jia and Aaronson (2003) explored the contribution of both maturational factors and social contextual factors. In their study, they monitored the richness of the English L2 environment and L2 acquisition of 10 Chinese L1 children (aged 5–9 years) and adolescents (12–16 years) over their first three years in the United States. Of relevance to understanding the contribution of peer interaction at different ages, the researchers suggested that experiences related to psychosocial variables/L1 and L2 exposure were important to the differential success in L2 acquisition between the child and adolescent learners (rather than maturational factors alone). For example, younger learners, who arrived in the United States before the age of 9 tended to switch to a preference for using English within the first two years of arrival. By this time, they had English-speaking friends and so enjoyed a richer L2 environment. By their third year, they were reading more texts in English and watching more L2 media than the older learners. However, adolescents who arrived after the age of 9 tended to maintain their preference for Chinese; they had higher L1 proficiency, more Chinese-speaking friends, and a richer L1 environment.

Szuber's (2007) study of 59 L1 Polish adolescent immigrants in the United States similarly found that those learners who arrived after the age of 9 were typi-cally exposed to less English at school and in the community. Those exposed to more English were also those who tended to use English more in their day-to-day interactions at school and with friends and in the neighborhood. These two stud-ies highlight the complex relationship between age-related characteristics, includ-ing psychosocial variables such as identity, and the potential of peer interaction for L2 learning. Consistent with other research reviewed in Chapter 6, these two studies suggest that L2 peers may actually reduce opportunities for target language input and use, particularly where this leads to avoidance of or exclusion by L1 peers.

In another setting, that of language immersion classes in Canada, Tarone and Swain (1995) also found differences by age in willingness to use the target language. Although in early childhood students happily used the target language with one another in class, by early adolescence learners showed great reluctance and stuck to their L1. Taking a sociolinguistic perspective, Tarone and Swain interpreted language choice to be related to issues of identity with a particular speech community: Their target speech community (teenager speak) was not represented in the classroom, except in English, their L1. Tarone and Swain give the following example from a former student in the program, who pointed out:

Example 7.10

S: . . . I speak differently to my friends than I do to my parents. It's almost a whole different language, and . . . they don't teach us how to speak [French] that way.

[later]

S: So I'd like to be able to sit in a classroom and have someone teach me how to say "Well, come on guys, let's go get some burgers" and stuff like that.

(Swain, 1993, pp. 6, 12, cited in Tarone & Swain, 1995, p. 172)

Although little research exists on this, it nevertheless underscores the social importance of language choice on the one hand and the significance of peers on the other.

Personality Changes

Adolescence is also a period of transitory change with regard to personality, as seen in a study of age differences in personality traits by Soto, John, Gosling, and Potter (2011). In this study, the Big Five Inventory (BFI) (John & Srivastava, 1999) was used to survey personality across a cross-sectional sample of 1,267,218 children, adolescents, and adults (ages 10–65) from English-speaking countries, gathered through the World Wide Web.

They found adolescence as a period of tremendous change; in some cases, personality traits were opposite to trends seen in childhood and adulthood. For example, four traits showed a negative trend from late childhood (ages 10–12) into adolescence (ages 13–17), with more positive trends in adulthood: *conscientiousness* (a trait associated with being hardworking, meticulous, efficient, organized, reliable, and self-disciplined; cf. Dörnyei, 2005); *agreeableness* and *extraversion*; and *openness to experience* (a trait characterized by imagination, flexibility, creativity, curiosity, novelty seeking, and originality; cf. Dörnyei, 2005). It is interesting to note that these four traits, found to show negative trends in adolescence, are also those associated with greater L2 use and success in learning in the literature (for review, see Dörnyei, 2005; Ellis, 2008; Strong, 1983).

Based on the developmental characteristics and competence gained by the end of adolescence, this appears to be a period of great potential in terms of positive outcomes of peer interaction for L2 learning. In comparison to younger learners, adolescents have a greater facility for metacognitive thinking, greater capacity for sustained attention, and greater flexibility in adapting their attentional resources to the demands of the task (Duchesne et al., 2013). Linguistically, adolescents' superior metalinguistic ability allows them to reflect on language as object, as seen in examples of adolescents' peer interaction in this book. In terms of peer relations, they are more adept at reading emotional and social cues and have greater social skills and self-regulation. Yet, psychosocial and personality factors also threaten this potential and may reduce willingness to engage with others (especially those they do not identify with) or to take risks in their language use.

Age and Peer Interaction Attributes

This chapter has reflected on the relevance of key characteristics of different age spans for interaction between L2 peers. The types of activities that younger and older school students engage in during peer interaction, and how these might support or limit L2 learning, vary with each age span. It is also important to acknowledge that age is one of many factors that impact on the potential benefit of peer interaction and is likely to have a mediating effect. This chapter emphasizes the need for research that looks at the distinctiveness of peer interaction among children and adolescents at different age spans, in order to better inform pedagogical choices concerning peer interaction.

For younger children, peer interactions provide a unique context for language use, one in which participants are relatively symmetrical in status, perspective, and cognitive ability. Social goals of affiliation and reciprocity underlie and shape their interactions. This has linguistic benefits in terms of language play, mimicry, and use of formulaic sequences, provided the child is willing to engage with others. In make-believe play in particular, children mimic adults, other children, and popular fictional characters, including their language and paralinguistic features (Makin et al., 1995). This provides opportunities to practice new forms, different registers, and speech acts. The emotional salience of L2 use during pretend play and language play is also a key element of peer interaction at this age. However, for younger children, peer interaction, particularly in an L2, can be difficult to sustain and often requires adult assistance on task management, reciprocity, resolution of social conflicts, and sustained on-task behavior.

Middle childhood shares many of the characteristics of early childhood in terms of the importance of peers, but this age span is marked by further development and consolidation of cognitive and linguistic abilities. Independent peer interaction in language classrooms becomes more sustainable, as learners are increasingly able to engage in reciprocal interaction and to listen and respond recursively to one another. Children at this age are steadily advancing in their oral and written literacy. Together with growing attentional resources, this affects the potential use of a wide variety of tasks. Focus on form, reflection on language use, and exploratory talk can characterize carefully prepared peer interaction for this age.

Finally, peer interaction in adolescence offers a great potential for L2 learning, due to the learners' advanced cognitive, social, and linguistic abilities at this age. However, psychological, social, and emotional factors can mediate this potential and reduce opportunities for L2 use and experimentation among peers.

Conclusion

In this chapter, we have reflected how developmental characteristics associated with age might contribute to children's engagement with language and with one another. It is clear that at each age there are facilitating and debilitating factors that may promote or hinder the potential of peer interaction for learning, and we have noted the importance of careful planning and training. To understand the potential contribution of L2 peer interaction in language classrooms, we need to take into account how cognitive, affective, and social developmental factors might impact on L2 learning for younger and older children and for adolescents, in contrast to adult learners (Muñoz, 2007; Paradis, 2007; Philp et al., 2008). For younger children, peer interaction may be as significant for social aspects of development as for language development. For young adolescents, the company of peers is also vitally important, but for different reasons. Peer interaction can be highly motivating or deeply demotivating for language learning, as we saw in the previous chapter. Clearly, in research on peer interaction, as with other aspects of instructed language learning, we need to explore the nature, role, and outcomes of this interaction among learners at different age spans. There is relatively little research to date on child L2 learners in upper primary and secondary schools, particularly in foreign language settings.

In terms of pedagogy, it is important to recognize the complexity of decisions that teachers make when setting up contexts for peer interaction and during the monitoring of this interaction. In the first section of this book, we explored a number of different ways in which peer interaction might be realized in the classroom and how it might contribute to learning. Understanding the characteristics of learners at different ages helps us to gain a greater sense of what is achievable through peer interaction and how it is best achieved. For example, younger children require greater scaffolding and direction by the teacher, including assistance with task and behavioral management when engaged on more challenging tasks.

Knowing this allows teachers to prepare against threats to effective peer interaction in the choices they make regarding task goals, grouping, time, and preparation. At this age, informal contexts of pretend play and games provide fruitful contexts for L2 use and development and can promote positive peer relationships in the classroom. In contrast, other types of tasks, and ways of managing peer interaction, will be more suitable to the cognitive abilities and interests of older children. These will be different again for adolescents. With a clear understanding of the goals of interaction and the needs of the learners as they take on particular tasks together, effective peer interaction that promotes processes of language learning is more likely.

SECTION III

The Purpose and Mode of Peer Interaction

8

COMMUNICATIVE TASKS AND PEER INTERACTION

Introduction

Peer interaction in a classroom setting can occur in a number of ways—it can occur before or after lessons in the form of small talk, it can occur during teacher talk or individual work (usually spontaneously and off topic), or it can be structured and brought into the lesson as peer and group work activities, which is the format most commonly investigated. Often when learners are engaged in second language (L2) peer interaction as part of a planned classroom activity, they are completing L2 tasks. In this chapter, we will briefly examine what a task is, before discussing how differences in task design may influence how learners engage in peer interaction in a language classroom. In particular, the concept of task complexity and its influence on language production and learning will be explored.

Tasks and Interaction

Generally considered to be a subset of class activities, tasks require holistic language use. Fill in the blank, sentence completion, and other controlled activities preselect specific language that learners need to use. On the other hand, tasks require learners to independently make use of their language resources in order to achieve a specific goal. Although there are various definitions of tasks, the core concepts used by researchers of tasks are captured by Samuda and Bygate's (2008) recent delineation:

> A task is a holistic activity which engages language use in order to achieve some non-linguistic outcome while meeting a linguistic challenge, with the

overall aim of promoting language learning, through process or product or both. (p. 69)

Tasks form the core methodology of one language teaching approach, task-based language teaching. In a task-based course, tasks rather than skills, forms, or vocabulary sets are the basic syllabus unit (Ellis, 2003). In such a course, the emphasis is on meaningful, holistic language practice, in which learners need to listen, read, speak, or write in order to reach a specific goal. The rationale for task-based language teaching is drawn from theories of language acquisition that emphasize the central role of meaningful language use allied with opportunities to notice how these meanings are encoded through form (e.g., Skehan, 1996, 1998). From this perspective, opportunities for communicative use and noticing form, meaning, and function relationships provide the conditions under which communicative competence in an L2 can most effectively be developed (Willis & Willis, 2007). Other theories that emphasize the social nature of language learning have also been cited in support of using tasks in language teaching (e.g., Nassaji & Swain, 2000; Storch, 1999).

Tasks are used to provide learners with opportunities to experience authentic language use within a classroom setting. Not all tasks require oral interaction—many are based on individuals working on their own, using language to achieve a goal or create a product. For example, a task may require learners to read a biology text to fill information into a chart comparing two species, or to listen to a description of a room and use that to draw a blueprint, or to write a story based on a series of pictures. However, many tasks require learners to communicate with one another in pairs or groups. Such conversational tasks will be our focus in this chapter.

How Do Different Tasks Influence Interaction?

As discussed in Chapter 3, a few empirical studies have demonstrated a link between engagement in conversational tasks with a peer and L2 learning (e.g., Adams, 2007). Fotos (1994), for example, investigated whether engagement in a particular type of conversational task (a consciousness-raising task where learners speak communicatively about a grammar-related problem) led to similar amounts of learning as traditional grammar instruction. She found equal rates of learning between the two types of instruction, indicating that learning grammar in a student-centered, task-based framework can be just as effective as teacher-fronted instruction. Moreover, during the task-based instruction, learners practiced communication skills and negotiated for meaning, enhancing the value of the instruction.

Some linguistic forms may be learned more easily in interaction than others (e.g., Jeon, 2007). As noted in Chapter 6, learning from interaction may also be linked to social factors related to individual assignment of peers in dyads or groups (e.g., Ross-Feldman, 2007). A substantial body of research also suggests that the learning potential of peer interaction tasks may be related to the nature of the task itself. Fotos (1994) also suggests that this possibility may have influenced her results, noting that amounts of negotiation of meaning varied substantially between tasks, leading to variability in learning rates. She found, for example, that more negotiation was triggered in a task with a closed outcome (there is only one correct solution) and which involved split information (each learner had some of the information needed to arrive at the correct solution). This set of task characteristics may have impacted the way learners engaged in the task and the resultant learning opportunities. In this and many other task-focused studies, negotiation of meaning or other collaborative discussion of language form is assumed to lead to learning. It should be noted, as we discussed in Chapters 2 and 3, that this may not always be the case.

Early task-based research studies documented how different characteristics of tasks impacted on peer interaction and learning. This body of studies has focused on the incidence of interactional modifications like negotiation of meaning and focus on form in peer interactions with a variety of tasks. For example, required two-way information exchange tasks promote more engagement in negotiation of meaning than one-way tasks or tasks where information exchange is optional (Pica, Kanagy, & Falodun, 1993). Convergent tasks (in which all learners in a group must agree on a single outcome) may promote more interactional modifications than divergent outcome tasks (Duff, 1986). In a recent study, Gass, Mackey, and Ross-Feldman (2005) examined the communication produced by 74 first language (L1) English learners of Spanish on three different tasks, two of which required information exchange between participants and one in which information exchange was optional. Half of the learners completed these tasks in a classroom setting, the other half in a laboratory setting in order to determine the role that setting might play on the incidence of interactional modifications. The study was conducted in response to earlier critiques of interaction studies positing that learning opportunities were artifacts of the laboratory context of many L2 studies, rather than a product of interaction as found in the classroom (e.g., Foster, 1998).

Gass et al. (2005) examined the incidence of negotiation of meaning, language-related episodes (LREs), and recasts, finding that more focus on form occurred in the two required information exchange tasks than the optional information exchange task. The researchers point out that their data contradicts views that extended, meaningful discussions of language form and meaning are unlikely to occur as peers work together in the classroom. They note that transcripts from their study provided many examples of rich, protracted discussions of language. These discussions included interwoven explicit discussions of language (LREs), statements of misunderstanding (negotiation of meaning), and interactional feedback. Learners used peer interaction as a means of testing out their ideas about language, as in Example 8.1. The example begins with the learners comparing the number of people in their pictures. Learner 1 then tries to ask her interlocutor about the number of birds but uses the Spanish word for "pair" instead. Based on the conversational context, Learner 2 assumes she means "couples" and tries to clarify. This begins a sequence of exchanges including negotiation moves, explicit discussion of language, and finally feedback as the learners resolve the meanings of both *parejas* ("pairs") and *pájaros* ("birds").

Example 8.1

Learner 1: ¿Cuántas personas tienes?

  [How many people do you have?]

Learner 2: (counting) Trece.

  [Thirteen.]

Learner 1: ¿Trece? Tengo uh diecisiete ... ¿Cuántos parejas?

  [Thirteen? I have uh seventeen ... How many pairs?]

Learner 2: ¿Parejas de amores?   ← clarification request

  [Pairs of lovers?]

Learner 1: ¿Qué es parejas?   ← LRE

  [What is "parejas"?]

Learner 2: Pairs.

Learner 1: Oh

Learner 2: No tiene el merry-go-round.

  [It doesn't have the merry-go-round.]

Learner 1: Hmm. ¿Cómo se dice bird?   ← LRE

  [How do you say bird?]

Learner 2: Pájaro

  [Bird]

Learner 1: Oh! That's what I was trying to say. ¿Cuántos pájaros?

  [How many birds?]

Learner 2: Uhm cinco. ¿Cuántos tienes?

  [Uhm, five. How many do you have?]

Learner 1: Tengo nueve, tengo más parejos, ¿parejos? ¿parejas?

  [I have nine, I have nine more (trouble with pronunciation of "birds")]

Learner 2: Paájaros   ← Recast

  [Birds (correct pronunciation)]

(Gass et al., 2005, pp. 598–599)

The authors pointed out that extended discussion of form and meaning in their study did not seem at all related to the setting of the interaction, with similar uses of interactional modification in both the classroom and the laboratory. Rather, the tasks impacted the way that learners engaged in interactional modifications in communication, with more learner discussion of form and meaning consistently found in tasks that require information exchange.

This finding of the centrality of tasks in shaping communication is echoed by Yilmaz's (2011) study of task effects on online communication. Her study contrasted two tasks: a jigsaw story task, in which learners are each given a different set of pictures to describe to their interlocutor with the goal of collaboratively sequencing the pictures into a narrative and writing the narrative; and a dictogloss task, in which learners listen to a story and then collaboratively reconstruct the text. Learners were linked to their partners via networked computers and asked to complete each of the tasks. Yilmaz found that the dictogloss task promoted more LREs, and also that LREs were more likely to be correctly resolved in the dictogloss task. The dictogloss procedure, which involves listening, note taking, and reconstruction, may have promoted more focus on form as learners heard and remembered different aspects of language use in the original text and attempted to reconstruct the text from their divergent notes. Of course, listening to the text first may also have oriented learners to focus on form. This highlights the difficulty of determining how tasks influence interaction—tasks differ in multiple ways, each of which may impact on how learners engage in communication.

Cognition and Task Design

Task types may also differ according to the cognitive demands the task places on the learner. Most often, researchers have evaluated the effect of cognitive demands on learner production (e.g., Gilabert, Baron, & Llanes, 2009; Nuevo, 2006; Robinson, 2001). Learner production is often quantified in terms of the fluency (e.g., number of pauses, length of unbroken speech), accuracy (e.g., error rates), and complexity (e.g., syntactic complexity such as embeddings or lexical complexity such as lexical density). Foster and Skehan (1996) examined these aspects of production for university-level English as a second language (ESL) students over three different task types. They noted that one of the three tasks, labeled a "personal task," in which each partner described a route from the university to their own home, differed in cognitive demands from the other two tasks (a narrative task that required learners to sequence pictures and a decision-making task based on determining prison sentences for hypothetical criminals). The personal task involved very familiar information that the learner had likely discussed in English before, whereas the other two did not. This personal task led to more fluent, but less syntactically complex production. These findings suggest that differences in cognitive load may have impacted on the way that learners produce language when working together on a task, a possibility that Yilmaz (2011) also explored.

The recognition that different types of tasks lead to differences in language production and focus on form puts into focus a central concern with teaching based on a task-based syllabus—sequencing. If tasks are the basis for forming the syllabus, the question for teachers and course designers is how to order tasks to maximize learning benefits. Knowing that different task characteristics influence language use and attention to form in tasks, it is likely that both the selection of appropriate tasks and the sequencing of the tasks may impact on learning outcomes. One early attempt to provide a set of principles was set out by Brown, Anderson, Shillcock, and Yule (1984). They proposed a model of task difficulty based on both design and interpersonal features such as participant relationships, suggesting that a static task (e.g., description) would be easier than a dynamic task (e.g., narration), which in turn would be simpler than an abstract task (e.g., opinion exchange). Within each of these categories, tasks can also be made more difficult in a number of ways, such as adding more elements to the task.

Skehan (1996) introduced a cognitive perspective on determining task complexity, pointing out that the challenge for learners in tasks is to simultaneously attend to the accuracy, complexity, and fluency of their production, a challenge that, coupled with limited L2 proficiency, may overload learner cognitive resources. His limited attentional capacity model is based on the assumption that learners selectively apply attentional resources to aspects of language production most important to the task. For example, in a performance, fluency may be selected over accuracy and complexity. Schmidt envisions teachers manipulating attentional focus over a series of tasks to promote learning. In this framework, learning would occur when learners first focus on complexity (which requires restructuring of knowledge and the emergence of more complex grammatical and lexical forms). When new forms have emerged, learners should then engage in tasks that promote a focus on accuracy (which pushes them to refine control of new structures). Finally, learners should engage in tasks that require them to attend to fluency (allowing them to eliminate disfluencies and process the language forms more efficiently).

Skehan (1998) proposes a three-criteria system for determining task complexity and sequencing tasks, including code complexity (language demands), cognitive complexity (processing demands), and communicative stress (including factors such as modality, time pressure, and number of participants). The purpose of this classification system is to allow teachers to build task-based lessons that lead the learner to focus on form and meaning appropriately for learning. For example, according to this schema, if a teacher lowers cognitive complexity for the during-task stage, the learners won't focus solely on conveying meaning through lexis but instead will have attentional resources to attend to linguistic code. In the posttask phase, teachers can push learners to produce language more fluently, allowing them extra opportunities to use forms focused on earlier.

Robinson's (2005, 2007b) cognition hypothesis has become the basis for many recent studies on task complexity. Similar to Skehan's work, the theory is based on the premise that manipulating task features can influence how learners allocate attentional resources, resulting in different outcomes for language production. However, the theories differ substantially in terms of how this may happen. Drawing on research from cognitive linguistics and cognitive psychology, Robinson proposes a dual approach to understanding cognitive complexity and language production. Most significantly, he draws a distinction between difficulty and complexity. The latter is considered here as an artifact of learner perception, with an influence on how learners approach the task. Task complexity, on the other hand, deals with the intrinsic, cognitive complexity of task features. Difficulty, therefore, is variant, depending in part on individual learner experiences; whereas task complexity is set, determined at the level of task design. Robinson also proposes a dual typology for task complexity, dividing these factors into resource-directing and resource-dispersing factors. A final set of factors, task condition, deals with the interactional setting of communicative tasks, including factors related to the participation demands (such as open or closed solutions) and factors related to the participants in the interaction (such as matched or mixed proficiency). These three groupings of factors—task complexity, task condition, and task difficulty—form the backbone of the model Robinson (2007a) labels the "triadic componential framework."

The prediction is that increasing task complexity along resource-directing factors increases demand on attention and working memory in a way that pushes learners to direct attention to specific aspects of linguistic code. For example, explaining a route on a map with more elements as opposed to a map with fewer elements is predicted to push the leaner to focus on his or her language choices, perhaps in particular on prepositions, because greater precision is needed to complete the task. Robinson suggests that the result in interactive tasks should be language production that is less fluent, less complex, but more accurate. On the other hand, increasing task complexity along resource-dispersing factors increases demands on learners' cognitive resources without directing them to aspects of form. For example, performing a task with no prior opportunity to plan the task would be more complex, but in a way that does not direct resources to any specific aspects of linguistic code. As such, the result is predicted to be a decrease in all three traits of L2 production (i.e., complexity, accuracy, and fluency) in interactive tasks. Robinson considers that because resource-directing complexity points learners toward aspects of linguistic code, it can be manipulated in task design to promote language development. On the other hand, resource-dispersing factors allow learners to focus on their linguistic performance under conditions increasingly authentic to real-world language use. It should also be noted that in both the case of resource-directing and resource-dispersing factors, Robinson predicts that increasing task complexity in interactive tasks will increase the number of interactional modifications in which learners engage.

Following the cognitive models proposed by Skehan and Robinson, a substantial body of research has investigated how cognitive demands of tasks may influence language production, which is used as a gauge for how these demands may impact on learning opportunities in the task. A large proportion of this research has been directed at language production in monologic, rather than interactive, tasks. However, a growing focus is placed on examining these researchers' claims about language use in peer interactive tasks, like those commonly found in communicative classrooms. These studies examine language use typically in terms of the fluency, accuracy, and complexity of production or in terms of the incidence of interactional modifications that may signal learner attention to form. We will first discuss the effects of resource-directing factors, and then of resource-dispersing factors, on peer language use in tasks.

Resource-Directing Factors, Task Design, and Peer Language Use

Research on resource-directing factors in interactional settings has most often manipulated reasoning demands, few versus many elements, and here-and-now versus there-and-then to determine the role of complexity in learner output. Most research has focused on whether changes in the complexity of a task, as predicted by the cognition hypothesis, lead to greater incidence of interactional modifications, including negotiation of meaning moves, feedback, and LREs, as well as modified output.

There is evidence of a connection between more complex tasks and more interactional modifications. For example, in a study by Robinson (2001), both resource-directing and resource-dispersing factors were manipulated. The findings showed that learners produced more confirmation checks and clarification checks when engaged in the more complex task, supporting the claims of the cognition hypothesis. Similar findings are reported in Robinson (2007b), in which only resource-directing factors were manipulated. These studies support the claim that engagement in more cognitively complex tasks promotes the use of interactional modifications. These findings also provide initial support for the notion of designing task-based courses based on task complexity; learners who engage in progressively more complex tasks will receive continued opportunities to negotiate for meaning, giving them opportunities to make connections between language form and meaning and consolidate prior learning through interaction.

However, further findings have indicated that the relationship between cognitive complexity of tasks and occurrence of interactional modifications may not be as simple as Robinson's findings suggest. For example, Nuevo (2006) found no differences in the incidence of negotiation of meaning moves between learners engaged in the low- and high-complexity versions of decision-making tasks made more and less complex along resource-directing factors. For her 96 adult ESL learners, the only significant findings were for the incidence of comprehension checks (where the speaker checks that the interlocutor has understood what he or she said). Counter to cognition hypothesis predictions, this interactional modification occurred more frequently in the low-complexity than high-complexity tasks. A similar pattern was found for the provision of feedback and the use of feedback; learners engaged in low-complexity tasks produced more recasts and were more likely to adopt the recast to modify their production than learners engaged in high-complexity tasks. Additionally, learners who interacted to complete low-complexity tasks were more likely to use metalinguistic terms to discuss language use and fulfill the task. There was no evidence to indicate that increasing task complexity on resource-directing factors would lead to greater use of interactional modifications; rather, interaction on a less cognitively complex task led to learners engaging more often in discussions of linguistic form, corrective feedback, and attempts to clarify problems of miscommunication. That is, they engaged in functions of language production that promote learning.

The relationship between cognitive complexity and language production in peer interactions may also differ across complexity factors. Gilabert et al. (2009) examined negotiation of meaning moves, LREs, and recasts produced by learners engaged in simple and complex versions of three different task types: a narrative task, a map task, and a decision-making task. They found strong evidence that increasing task complexity increased the use of interactional modification, but only for the narrative task (which was made complex through changing the time frame of the narration) and the map task (which was made complex through adding additional elements). For the decision-making task (which was made complex through increasing reasoning demands), there was little evidence that increasing task complexity increased the use of interactional modifications in peer interaction. This raises the possibility that different tasks and different types of task complexity may not impact on learner engagement in interaction in the same way. Coupled with findings from Nuevo (2006), these results suggest that, for interactive tasks, the characterization of resource-directing factors may be oversimplified. Effects of increasing task complexity may not be uniform.

Finally, it is also possible that the impact of task complexity on peer interaction may not hold consistent for learners at different levels of proficiency. For example, Kim (2009) focused on the amount and type of LREs that occurred during picture narration tasks made more complex through manipulating resource-directing factors. Kim found that the relationship between task complexity and discussion of form differed for learners of different proficiency levels. Low-proficiency learners produced more LREs when engaged in the low-complexity narration task, whereas high-proficiency learners produced more LREs in the high-complexity narration tasks. (We further discuss the role of language proficiency in Chapter 5.) Similar to Gilabert et al.'s (2009) results, the findings also differed by task and complexity factor. The same learners, who produced more LREs on the low-complexity version of the narration task, produced more LREs on the high-complexity version of the picture difference task. Again, these findings suggest that applying the ideas of the cognition hypothesis to sequencing tasks for learners in the classroom may not be as simple as initially thought. Although the categorization of features as resource-directing is theoretically neat, in practice there are differences in the way these factors impact on learning opportunities in peer interaction as well as in the way that they interact with issues related to the task type and characteristics of learners engaged in the interaction. These findings recall a familiar theme in this book, namely, that relationships among factors in peer interactions may not be straightforward. Rather, a complex interplay of factors needs to be considered. We should not expect blanket effects in peer interaction, as discussed previously in Chapter 6.

Relatively few studies have looked at the effects of resource-directing variables on the accuracy, fluency, and complexity of language production in peer tasks (as opposed to interactional modifications). These studies also raise questions for the cognition hypothesis. For example, Michel, Kuiken, and Vedder (2007) examined whether the number of elements (a resource-directing variable) impacted on the production of learners working in either monologic or peer interaction tasks. For monologic tasks, the results generally supported the prediction of the cognition hypothesis that increased task complexity would lead to an increase in the accuracy and complexity of production, although the effect for complexity was very small. However, the results for the peer interaction tasks did not support the cognition hypothesis. For these tasks, greater cognitive complexity did not result in greater accuracy. Overall, engagement in peer interaction tasks led to more accurate and fluent—but not more complex—output.

This interaction between task condition (monologic vs. peer interaction) and task complexity (few or many elements) highlights a concern with the application of the cognition hypothesis to interactive tasks. Interaction promotes language use and learning differently than individual production. For example, monologic tasks involve only self-repair, whereas in interactive tasks learners can engage in discussions of form, assist one another's production, and can give and receive feedback. Likewise, learner factors like willingness to communicate and anxiety that impact on individual production are also at play (as discussed in more depth in Chapter 6). In peer interaction, these factors as well as the social dynamic between partners can influence how the communication unfolds. Predictions about the impact of task complexity on peer interaction may need to take these differences into account. Michel et al. (2007) note that similar concerns have been raised for both Skehan's and Robinson's models of task complexity in monologic tasks.

Resource-Dispersing Factors, Task Design, and Peer Language Use

There is also a growing body of research on the effect of resource-dispersing factors on language use in peer interactions. As noted earlier, Robinson's (2001) study included both resource-dispersing and resource-directing factors. His findings showed that increasing task complexity led to significantly more lexically varied speech than the simple task. However, no effects were found for structural complexity and accuracy. Robinson attributes the results on structural complexity to the increased use of comprehension checks and clarification requests in the complex task, which resulted in brief responses with low structural complexity.

One of the variables examined by Robinson (2001), pretask planning, has been the focus of a number of studies of task complexity in peer interaction tasks. For example, Philp, Oliver, and Mackey (2006) examined the role of planning time on the language use of 42 child ESL learners (ages 5–12) working in dyads. The dyads were either given no planning time, two minutes of planning time, or five minutes of planning time, in which they were instructed to simply look at the task pictures and plan what they would say to their partners. There were no effects of planning time on either the fluency or the accuracy of language production. Having five minutes of prior planning led to greater complexity in production; however, this relationship was affected by the age of the learners. Learners in the younger dyads (5–7) actually produced more complex language with no planning time. Philp et al. suggest that the older learners may have used the planning time to consider exact utterances they would use, which may have pushed them to use more complex syntax, as in Example 8. 2.

Example 8.2

A: How many boys you see jumping?

B: Jumping or skipping?

A: Jumping

B: I can see seven boys jumping. How many girls do you see jumping?

A: Two girls (later turn)

B: How many girls do you see are flying?

A: Two girls. How many boys do you see playing football?

B: Three boys. How many girls do you see when they kick XX?

(Philp et al., 2006, p. 562)

Learner A begins this sequence with a complex question. The researchers point out that both learners continue to use this syntax, a process that McDonough and Mackey (2006) refer to as priming. In this case, the use of planning time to consider how to phrase questions may have helped both learners stretch their linguistic resources. For younger learners, the planning time did not seem to affect the complexity of their production. However, not having time to plan led to extended negotiation sequences, as in Example 8.3, where learners try to figure out how to do the task. In these cases, turns discussing task management were more complex than turns where learners simply did the task.

Example 8.3

A: Now you question me

B: Where to put the lizard

A: What

B: Where to put the lizard

A: No you need to tell me put the

B: Lizard in the right

A: No because the lizard I got it you need to do tell me what you can see tell me put the put the bear in the left

B: Where to put the bear on the left

A: Bear put the the giraffe on the right

B: What the hell can't do it we're not to do it it's hard

A: Because you don't know where in the left

B: Left

A: But you don't know because on left there's three box so you don't know where the box which box

(Philp et al., 2006, pp. 559–560)

Although there were more utterances with errors (utterances that can be corrected) when learners were given more planning time, the provision of feedback decreased as planning time increased. It's likely that the learners used planning time to determine their own language use in the interaction; they were less focused on their interlocutor's language use and, therefore, less likely to provide feedback. Philp et al. point out that several of the learners tried to simply recite all the utterances they had practiced in describing their picture, with little regard for their interlocutor's comprehension or response. Engaging in planning prior to the task also led to the learners talking less overall, similar to Foster's (1998) findings. Increasing planning time led to fewer instances of negotiation of meaning and feedback moves, which may have shortened the task. When learners had no planning time, they engaged in long, often complicated negotiation sequences, as seen in Example 8.3.

Such findings suggest that the age of the learner, the requirements of the task, and the amount of planning time are factors that interact to influence how learners engage in task-based peer interaction. Similarly, the type of planning time could impact on the interaction. The 28 adolescent dyads in Mochizuki and Ortega's (2008) study, for example, received either no pretask planning time, unguided planning time, or guided planning time in the form of a worksheet on relative clauses. Guided planning was related to the production of more relative clauses, which were more likely to be grammatically correct. This focus on relative clauses did not seem to draw attention from other aspects of production, as the global accuracy and complexity of the language produced by this group was similar to that of the other two groups. These findings are not positive for planning time in general, but for guided planning time, suggesting that guidance during planning time might maximize the benefits for later production. This highlights the point made previously that the connection between task factors and production may be more complex than initially envisioned.

The way that learners were instructed to plan can also influence task performance, through impacting on the way the learners engaged in discussions of form. Park (2010) separated out the effects of planning time and the effects of the instructions given for the task, trying to determine whether learner attention could be turned to questions of grammar rather than vocabulary as they worked on picture-based storytelling tasks in English as a Foreign Language (EFL) classrooms. In addition to planning time, some groups received specific instructions asking them to focus on grammar during the task performance. Although the learners overall prioritized vocabulary over grammar, learners who received specific instructions to focus on grammar did so more than those who received general instructions. Instructions, rather than planning time, influenced learner behavior. This suggests that findings about guided planning time may reflect the effect of instructions that call on learners to focus on aspects of linguistic form more than the effect of having time to plan. As these studies demonstrate, planning time itself is a complicated variable, with different lengths of time, different amounts of guidance, and different instructions leading to different outcomes for pretask planning and interaction. These findings are reflected in the limited body of research on other resource-dispersing variables as well.

For example, Hardy and Moore (2004) examined the effects of two further resource-dispersing factors, structural task support and prior knowledge of content. Their findings supported the cognition hypothesis predictions for structural support, but not for prior knowledge. Adams and Nik's (in press) findings for prior knowledge also ran contrary to the predictions of the cognition hypothesis that learners who engaged in the more complex task (in this case, without prior knowledge) would produce less accurate and less complex language than those engaged in a less complex task (with prior knowledge). Rather, the learners without prior knowledge produced more accurate and more complex language than those who had prior knowledge about the topic.

Similar to the discussion of pretask planning, these findings suggest that prior knowledge as a variable may be too complex to reduce to a +/− description. Adams and Nik note that prior knowledge in some studies, like Hardy and Moore's (2004) study, was operationalized as specific knowledge of the task content, which learners receive as a pretask treatment. In other studies, however, prior knowledge represented the cumulative information gained over years of study and interest. It is not surprising then that these might have a different impact on how learners engage in tasks. When learners with prior scholastic or professional knowledge are asked to discuss content with which they were very familiar, they may be more likely to be comfortable and engaged in the discussion. This ease and enthusiasm may lead them to focus more on the content they discuss than the linguistic form they use to discuss it. In contrast, learners without this sort of background are less likely to be as absorbed by the task. It may then be more natural for them to do the minimum required to complete the task, but this may also have freed cognitive resources to focus on form.

Indeed, in a posttask interview for Adams and Nik (in press), learners commented that lack of prior knowledge led them to limit the scope of the discussion, as in the subsequent excerpt.

Example 8.4

Me and my other teammates are not familiar with the software. I think the content is more suitable for the electrical engineering students because they should be familiar with electronic circuits. That is why our conversation was dependent on the information we had on the task instruction. We don't have much knowledge on the software in order to give extra information during the discussion.

(Adams & Nik, in press)

This participant's comment suggests that, had they been more comfortable with the topic, they might have developed the content of the discussion further, drawing on their own knowledge to develop the discourse. Being less focused on the content may have made it easier for them to focus on form.

For both pretask planning and prior knowledge, simple categorizations of task complexity factors may fail to capture the ways that task design can influence production and learning. And, like the research discussed on resource-directing factors previously, the findings on the role of resource-dispersing factors have not always conformed to the predictions of the cognition hypothesis. Rather, the cognition hypothesis has proved to be a useful starting point for examining the intricate ways in which complexity factors interact with one another and with factors related to the learner and the setting. For this research to be useful to classroom teachers, there is a need to go beyond binary classifications of tasks to consideration of how different constellations of task factors take particular form in actual classrooms and how task effects on language production are mediated by contextual, setting, and participant variables.

One study to do this is Philp, Walter, and Basturkmen's (2010) qualitative analysis of task-based interactions and posttask interviews to describe the interplay of personal and contextual factors that underpin learner engagement in focus on form in peer interactions. Some of the relevant factors are attitude to error and error correction, attitude to interlocutor, and orientation to task, all of which can mediate (despite task design) whether or not learners will engage in discussions of form during the task. The contribution of this line of research is that it demonstrates that the effects of task-based engagement on language production and learning cannot solely be circumscribed by discussion of cognition but also relate to the social unit formed by a pair or group of learners engaged in the tasks. For task models to capture these effects, both individual variables and group dynamics need to be included.

Tasks, Instruction, and Learning

The research discussed so far in this chapter is largely motivated by the understanding that learners may be able to use language in certain ways in task-based interactions to make these interactions more beneficial for learning. Task complexity research is partially based on the belief that teachers can design and implement tasks in ways that push learners to stretch their linguistic resources, notice gaps in their language knowledge, and practice syntactic and lexical forms that they are just beginning to master. Another body of research focuses on how teachers can mold the classroom experience to help learners use tasks in ways that are productive for learning. Teachers can influence the ways that learners engage in tasks through strategic grouping of participants (Storch, 2002), assigning task roles according to proficiency task roles (Yule & Macdonald, 1990), prior instruction or modeling of interactional strategies (e.g., Kim & McDonough, 2011), post-task feedback (e.g., Gibbons, 2003), and prior training in interpersonal skills (e.g., Dörnyei & Murphey, 2003).

For example, teachers can use prior interactional instruction to impact on how learners engage in interactions. Similar to research on task complexity, studies in this area are focused on determining how to help learners engage in peer interactions in ways that may be beneficial for learning. Rather than manipulating aspects of the task design, this research asks whether it is possible to promote positive interactional patterns by teaching students how to engage in interaction. This is similar to the question posed by Park (2010) on how teacher instructions might orient learners to language production in interactive tasks.

Kim and McDonough (2011) used a model as pretask instruction to encourage Korean EFL learners to engage in focus on form during three tasks. Half of the learners viewed a model video of students engaging in discussions of form while carrying out similar tasks. The researchers examined task transcripts for LREs, finding that learners who had received pretask modeling produced greater quantities of LREs during their interactions. Their LREs were also more likely to result in a correct resolution than those of learners who had not watched the modeling. They additionally found that learners who had viewed the pretask modeling videos were more likely to develop collaborative dynamics than those who had not. Collaborative pair dynamics were defined based on Storch's (2002) discussion of pair dynamics (also discussed in Chapters 5 and 6). Kim and McDonough's findings provide a clear indication that pretask instruction may allow teachers to help students develop positive peer interaction strategies in the classroom.

One unexpected positive finding was increased use of the L2 to discuss form by the learners who had viewed models. The learners in the modeling group were able to base their use of interactional modifications on the examples provided in the videos, using them as patterns to allow them to engage in LREs without resorting to their L1, as in Example 8. 5.

Example 8.5

1 Learner 1: What is disadvantage?

2 Learner 2: Disadvantage is . . . ChangDukGong is closed on Mondays and closed . . . very fast?

3 Learner 1: What you say? ← Clarification request

4 Learner 2: really?

5 Learner 1: no no . . . early ← Explicit correction

6 Learner 2: yes . . . very very . . . early . . .

(Kim & McDonough, 2011, p. 195)

Both the clarification request and the explicit correction in this excerpt were very similar to those modeled in the video. In contrast, learners who had not viewed the videos were more likely to resort to their L1 to resolve miscommunication and discuss usage, as in Example 8.6.

Example 8.6

1 Learner 1: 단점? 단점이 뭐야?

[disadvantage? What is disadvantage?]

2 Learner 2: disadvantage 는 Monday closed.

3 Learner 1: 그럼 좋은 점은?

[Then, what is advantage?]

4 Learner 2: 좋은 점 . . . 뭐지?

[advantage . . . What can that be?]

5 Learner 1: tradition. Korean tradition 이라고 해

[tradition. Say "Korean tradition"]

6 Learner 2: Korean tradition 뭐라고?

[Korean tradition what?]

(Kim & McDonough, 2011, p. 195)

Models are only one means of providing pretask interactional training. Fujii, Obata, Takahashi, and Tanabe (2008) provided instructional sessions to allow learners to practice negotiation of meaning moves prior to engaging in interaction. Their participants took part in an instructional session during which negotiation of meaning was defined and they read and viewed examples of negotiation of meaning. As part of the exercise, they also attempted to complete a task without negotiation, to help them see how it could facilitate communication. The instruction helped learners to increase both the amount of negotiation of meaning they engaged in and their repertoire of negotiation moves. Although most of the learners indicated that they felt the training prepared them to use negotiation moves in peer communication, others noted that they might need more time to be able to apply the training. The researchers suggest that teachers might include several training opportunities to help learners feel confident engaging in negotiation of meaning during tasks. It should be noted that this study was very small scale, so these findings may not apply to other learners.

The effects of pretask modeling or teaching of interactional strategies on peer interactions provide evidence of the complementary roles of peer and teacher-led interaction in classrooms. Although most research on tasks and peer interaction have focused on the effects of task design, in classroom settings, the ways that teachers frame tasks, prepare students for peer interaction, and provide posttask feedback and debriefing also influence the outcomes of peer interaction.

Conclusion

Research on task types and task complexity highlight the difficulty of characterizing the value of peer interactions for L2 learning. It is striking that even well-developed, theoretically motivated, and highly detailed models of task design and implementation have so far not been successful in capturing how learners engage in and benefit from learning during peer interactions. This illustrates the complexity of peer communication tasks compared to monologic and receptive language tasks. As more than one learner is involved, additional factors related to proficiency, individual differences, and social dynamics come into play (these factors are also discussed in more depth in Chapters 5 and 6). It may simply not be possible to predict interactive patterns of language use based solely on task design and implementation. Rather than pushing for specific language use outcomes through task design, teachers may find it more effective to help learners understand how they can get the most from task-based interaction for language learning. However, it should be remembered that this is only one solution that has been shown to work for certain learners in specific settings with particular tasks and learning goals. As we have said repeatedly in this book, the variety of factors that come into play in peer interaction should render simple solutions suspect. Task complexity researchers have often considered peer interaction as one variable in determining how learners will interact. We would contend instead that this obscures the variety of ways that individual learners, tasks, and outcomes converge in any learning setting.

9

COMPUTER-MEDIATED COMMUNICATION

Introduction

The previous chapter focused on how the tasks in which learners are engaged in-fluence their language use and learning opportunities. One aspect of the task that shapes learner discourse is the modality, which will be explored in this chapter and the next. In this chapter, we focus on communication in virtual environments. In-creasingly common both in and out of the classroom, information communication technology offers a host of different opportunities for learning beyond those found in face-to-face communication. In this chapter, we focus primarily on text-based communication, the most common form of computer-mediated communication (CMC). The discussion will focus on how these interactions differ from those in face-to-face communication and how those differences impact on learning.

CMC in Learning Contexts

Developments in information and communication technologies have had a pro-found impact on how we communicate now, and this has had effects in education (see Kern, Ware, & Warschauer, 2004, for a comprehensive analysis of this topic). In 1998, Warschauer argued that to be proficient in a second language (L2), a person must have the ability "to read, write and communicate in an electronic environ-ment" (p. 757), and this has certainly become more true over time. This coupling of communication and technology has begun to take hold in L2 learning con-texts, with teachers becoming aware both of the need for learners to be proficient L2 communicators in computer-mediated contexts and of the potential benefits of CMC for L2 learning. Although some researchers have noted reservations, a growing body of research indicates that CMC as a medium of communication has positive effects for language learners (see Sauro, 2011, for a full overview). Partly this is motivated by the recognition that CMC technology can virtually increase the space available for communication and collaboration. CMC can take place with the person seated at the computer next to you or with someone on the other side of world, whether between native speakers and learners or among learner peers (cf. Blake, 2007; Chapelle, 2004).

CMC is generally considered as "communication that takes place between human beings via the instrumentality of computers" (Herring, 1996, p. 1). CMC can occur in text, audio, or video modes, with many CMC tools including multiple modes of communication. Having these modes available simultaneously may help diversify the practical applications of using computers in the learning processes, while making learning more comprehensive (Beyth-Marom, Saporta, & Caspi, 2005; Chang, 2007; Lamy & Hampel, 2007).

CMC occurs in two modes: asynchronous (ACMC) and synchronous (SCMC). ACMC, such as e-mail, online discussion forums, podcasts, and wikis, involves delayed interaction, which can allow time to compose and edit thoughts before posting to the public (Kim, Anderson, Nguyen-Jahiel, & Archodidou, 2007; Shang, 2007). In contrast, SCMC, such as text chat or video chat, occurs in real time, requiring all interlocutors to be online at the same time (Ramsay, 2003). This makes it better suited to discussing specific questions or problems that require a prompt answer and makes it more like face-to-face communication than ACMC, which more closely approximates writing.

In 1997, Chapelle called on researchers of information technology communication and language learning to draw on theories from L2 acquisition, in particular the interactionist approach (e.g., Gass & Mackey, 2006), to allow for theory-based comparisons of the effectiveness of CMC in promoting language learning. For interaction-based research, the central question is whether CMC offers opportunities for the kind of meaningful interactions that facilitate L2 learning and development in face-to-face settings. A body of research has emerged in response to this challenge, with overall mixed findings for the benefits of interaction via CMC. While much of this research has focused on interactions between native speakers and language learning, as in two-way virtual pen pal programs, quite a number of studies have focused on interaction among language-learning peers. CMC-based peer interaction offers advantages to language teaching, in that it can easily be implemented in large classes and allows for teacher monitoring of multiple interactions, rather than just spot-checking. CMC-based interactions also may encourage more reticent students to participate, evening out participation among groups. However, the quality of CMC-based interactions in terms of language practice has been called into question. In this chapter, we focus on synchronous peer interactions, as the bulk of CMC-based peer interaction studies have taken place in this medium. However, we briefly review existing work on ACMC here as well. More research on peer composition in ACMC is included in Chapter 10.

Peer Communication in SCMC

Although SCMC also occurs in video and audio formats, bandwidth restrictions and platform stability have left text chat as the most common, reliable, and affordable means of SCMC in educational settings (González, 2003). Text chat is often referenced as a hybrid of speech and writing (Herring, 1996; Yates, 1996). Like spoken language, text chat requires rapid, spontaneous exchange of information in real time. On the other hand, like writing, the end product of a text chat is a relatively permanent record of the discourse. Text chat incorporates writing devices like punctuation to express meaning, yet also has unique characteristics that make it unlike speech or writing. For example, although the discourse unfolds in real time, there is a disassociation of production and transmission of language, whereas in speech these occur simultaneously. Thus, each turn in a text chat discourse is fully formed before it is visible to other interlocutors. This allows for several discourse effects; for example, multiple interlocutors can produce messages at the same time, often leading to separation of adjacency pairs within the discourse record. As mentioned previously, text chat results in a written transcript. During the interaction, participants in the discourse can scroll backward and forward through the chat, which may decrease the memory load imposed by two-way communication (Chun & Payne, 2004). Other features of text chat include simplified register and syntax, abbreviations, and the use of symbols to express emotions (Smith, 2003b).

Researchers have acknowledged the use of text chat as an effective medium for L2 learning and practice (Ortega, 2009; Smith, 2004). It is employed for practicing language learning in various ways, including developing intercultural understanding (Belz & Müller-Hartmann, 2003; Ware & Kramsch, 2005), conducting collaborative tasks (Newlands, Anderson, & Mullin, 2003), and promoting autonomous learning (Emde, Schneider, & Kötter, 2001). CMC can be particularly beneficial for foreign language learners, as it opens up access to interaction with native speakers in other countries (Blake, 2005; Lee, 2004).

Research on peer L2 interactions in text chat has fairly consistently shown evidence of learning benefits. For example, Sotillo (2005) found that peer dyads spent more time chatting than native speaker–learner dyads, and that their interactions resulted in more error correction episodes (70% of the correction episodes in the data), illustrating that peer dyads can be a positive site for attention to language in the context of meaning. We consider here further research on the incidence of interactional features in text chat, attention to form and noticing in text chat, characteristics of learner language production in text chat, participation patterns in text chat, and the discourse of text chat.

Interaction, Focus-on-Form, and Text Chat

Several studies have examined negotiation of meaning through interactional modifications and focus on form in text chat. These studies have generally shown that learners focus on form in the context of meaning, using a range of strategies to resolve miscommunication (Blake, 2000; Cheon, 2003; Lai & Zhao, 2006; Sotillo, 2000). Smith (2003b), for example, found that learners were able to use collaborative discourse to communicate despite lexical difficulties, occasionally aided by chat conventions like emoticons and punctuation (illustrated in Example 9.1) to indicate uncertainty. He noted that "learners elicit modified input from one another, are pushed to modify their own linguistic output, and receive important feedback on their TL [target language] use, thus potentially focusing their attention on their problematic utterances" (p. 39). Overall, research on interaction and focus on form in text chat has suggested that features of text chat, including the visual representations of language and the permanence of chat transcript, present advantages over face-to-face communication in terms of L2 practice.

For example, the visual nature of text CMC may allow learners to better manage negotiation sequences. Pellettieri (2000) hypothesized that negotiation sequences in her study were promoted by the visual nature of text chat, which permitted the learners to review their writing and deliberate before posting messages. This is more difficult in face-to-face communication. Easing the cognitive burden of interactional processes like modifying output may widen the range of interactional strategies learners can use, which may result in greater use of the L2. For example, Nik and Adams (2009) found that learners made use of the text chat features, such as punctuation and emoticons, to signal confusion as well as eventual comprehension, helping prevent communication derailment, as in the subsequent example.

Example 9.1

1 Learner 1:   that's why the company did not accept u to work with them

2 Learner 2:   is that true . . .?

3 Learner 2:   :((

4 Learner 3:   wait2 . . . u talking with who [Learner 1]

(Nik & Adams, 2009, p. 148)

The learners use text abbreviations ("u" for "you") to simplify the discourse, and punctuation to indicate emotional responses. Learner 2 uses elliptical markers, for example, to indicate uncertainty when asking for clarification. The use of typographical symbols simplifies the discussion. Learners tended to use chat strategies rather than the first language (L1) to manage communication, which the researchers point out is unusual for peer interaction in a foreign language environment. Analysis of learner comments suggested that the permanence of the chat transcript and the ability of the teacher to monitor chats from the instructor workstation pushed the learners to use interactional strategies rather than to fall back to the L1. This highlights the importance of the teacher's role in CMC peer interactions. Even though the teacher may not be actively participating in the interaction, the teacher's virtual presence may push learners to attend to language in different ways.

L2 learners make use of strategies in text chat relating to the unique features of the mode. For example, when miscommunications occur, they turn back to the transcript, scrolling back through it and reviewing prior messages to pick up the thread of the discussion (Kitade, 2000). Aside from the opportunity to reprocess the talk, this also allows learners time to consider and understand the interaction. The visual nature of the discourse then is a factor that helps learners to continue to interact. This demonstrates the unique advantages text chat has for promoting collaborative learning beyond that found in classrooms.

Beyond promoting comprehension, visual support provided by text can push learners to try out communication moves they don't use normally. Kung's (2004) analysis of chat transcripts indicated that learners produce various interactional features and may even take on expert roles during the interaction, trying out discourse moves modeled by their teachers in class discussions by providing explanations and examples to each other. The learners in Kung's (2004) study also noted that communicating in a visual medium was satisfying, as they felt that they were able to try out target language forms and initiate different interactional features that they may not have had the opportunity to do in a face-to-face classroom setting. Peterson (2009) similarly found that learners used interactional features beyond those they used in face-to-face communication. Like those in Kung's study, his participants seemed to experiment with a teacherlike role in the discourse, providing feedback using strategies similar to those found in regular classrooms. In Example 9.2, the learners are engaged in a task in which they need to select the most appropriate apartment from a selection for a hypothetical renter. When Learner 4 is confused about the task procedure, Learner 3 provides him with a description of the instructions and then uses both text and emoticons to evaluate his attempt to complete the task.

Example 9.2

1 Learner 3: Ok, let's go to sign the contract!

2 Learner 4: what shoud [*sic*] I do next?

3 Learner 3: "we must summarize the result of our conversations and write it in the Moo for check"

4 Learner 3: "Are you still there?"

5 Learner 4: "OK, Let's summarize! Our preferances [*sic*] are Pets are OK, No smoking, No shared bedroom, rent is paid by starbuck's uncle Bill (4o5), Quiet neighborhood, Located in quiet country, 30 minutes from city center, and modern new house. Are there any errors?"

6 Learner 3: "Yes, that's it. (^_^)g"

(Peterson, 2009, p. 310)

Peterson notes that the learners did not take on similar roles in face-to-face communication. He asserted that learners used text chat strategies to communicate ideas they could not easily discuss orally, suggesting that because the text chat environment allowed the students an opportunity to try out these strategies, it enabled them to consistently use the L2 throughout the interaction.

In summary, research consistently shows that text CMC is a positive site for promoting the use of interactional features that have been associated with language learning. Indeed, it may be more positive than these studies have shown because they rely primarily on the chat transcript to document the use of interaction strategies. However, more modifications occur in this communication than the transcripts return (Smith, 2008). Learner contributions to a conversation only post to the chat transcript when the learner has finished composing them (this is the disjoint between production and transmission noted earlier). This means that any focus on form carried out during the typing and revision of the contribution is not represented on the chat transcript. Smith (2008) found that close to 90% of self-repair occurred while learners were composing the messages, prior to hitting the "enter" key and transmitting them, and was therefore invisible in the chat transcripts.

Overall then, more interactional features are used in text SCMC, and they may be used in different ways than they are in face-to-face communication. This medium also seems to influence the way learners focus on linguistic form during the interactions. For example, learners may be more likely to engage in explicit negotiation of meaning in the online text chat than in face-to-face discussion. The text chat running transcript allows learners to more precisely indicate where miscommunication occurs, for example, using cut-and-paste functions to reproduce turns that caused miscommunication to focus attention on them (Lai & Zhao, 2006). Nik, Adams, and Newton (2012) found that, counter to research findings in face-to-face interaction (see Chapter 3), learners engaged in more grammatical than lexical focus on form during text chat. The researchers also suggest that the visual format of text chat may make it easier for learners to focus on less perceptually salient forms like grammatical morphemes.

Very little research to date has directly measured learning gains associated with text chat peer interactions. One study that has done this is de la Fuente's (2002, 2003) examination of vocabulary learning through interactions by L2 learners of Spanish. Analysis of chat transcripts indicated that learners in both modalities focused explicitly on the vocabulary items, although in different ways. Both groups demonstrated learning of vocabulary from treatment to posttest on all measures. The text chat group gained as much vocabulary knowledge as the face-to-face group, as measured by written tests. However, the face-to-face group outperformed the text chat group on oral measures. The researcher suggests that it may have been more difficult for the text chat group to associate written and phonological forms for novel words. This may point to the need for CMC interaction to be complemented by face-to-face interactions for oral work (and vice versa). However, the findings do still demonstrate learning in the text SCMC medium. Shekary and Tahririan's (2006) study also demonstrated learning gains from form-focused episodes in text chat.

Attention, Noticing, and Text Chat

As noted previously, learners in text chat engage in form-focused episodes and resolve communication difficulties using a variety of strategies. During these episodes, learners may orient their attention to form in the context of meaning, which has been hypothesized to be a driving factor in language learning (cf. Schmidt, 2001). Indeed, researchers of peer interaction in face-to-face contexts (e.g., Williams, 2005) have argued that the ephemeral nature of oral communication can make noticing difficult for L2 learners. The written modality of text SCMC creates a more permanent record of the communication as it unfolds, affording learners opportunities to review the discourse. Several researchers have suggested that this may enhance opportunities to attend to language during communication (Fiori, 2005; Sauro, 2009; Sotillo, 2005). Additionally, the written interaction in text chat may make the language more salient (Chapelle, 2001). As Meskill (2005) points out, "Computer screens can serve to anchor attention to forms" (p. 48). As such, communication via text chat may be a particularly good site for noticing during interaction.

The frequent modification of output found in her study of learners engaged in text chat was evidence that the learners noticed negotiation signals and recognized them as feedback (Pellettieri, 2000). Because this noticing can be prompted by either an interlocutor's feedback turn or by review of one's own contributions to the chat transcript, noticing in text SCMC may be somewhat broader than what we see in face-to-face communication. For example, Lai and Zhao (2006) asked learners to review recorded negotiation of meaning sequences and feedback episodes and report what they had thought at the time of the interaction. They found that learners were more likely to report noticing of their errors and noticing of their interlocutor's negotiation signals in text SCMC. Their learners reported that being able to review the transcript prompted noticing, as illustrated in the subsequent examples.

Example 9.3

> If uh, face-to-face, uh, I couldn't review my words, so in online chat, I review after I type.
>
> (Lai & Zhao, 2006, p. 112)

Example 9.4

> [In] online chat, I can trace the conversation on the display, so first I made a [lot of] mistake[s]. But I [was] conscious [that] I have a lot of mistake[s], so I try to improve my sentence.

> (Lai & Zhao, 2006, p. 112)

Lai and Zhao's findings corroborate Blake's (2005) suggestion that learners had ample opportunity to focus on form and reflect on their language production while interacting via text SCMC. Because these opportunities are related to the visual display of text SCMC, they may have different effects for learning than instances of noticing in face-to-face communication.

Although these studies demonstrate that text SCMC may be conducive to promoting noticing, which in turn can facilitate L2 learning, language learners may face difficulty decoding or encoding messages. This is because of the demands of maintaining the rapid information exchange (Iwasaki & Oliver, 2003), which may limit their ability to attend to linguistic form. Additionally, the overlaps and delays in turn taking in text chat can cause noncontingency of error turns and feedback turns, which may impact on noticing in online interactions. Measuring noticing in text chat, as opposed to face-to-face communication, may also require shifts in our research methods. For example, Smith (2005) has argued that subsequent production, rather than the production of modified output, may be a better indicator of noticing of form in text chat. Because the unfolding communication can be seen on the screen, learners are able to focus on and notice forms without explicitly demonstrating that they have noticed or even understood the messages. However, by adopting forms discussed earlier in later production, they implicitly indicate that they have attended to corrections or other interactional modifications, as in the following example:

Example 9.5

1 O: i have a banjo

2 C: what's is it?

3 O: i is a kind of guitar

4 C: really?

5 O: traditionnal [*sic*] guitar

6 O: yes . . . do you like it?

   ~14 lines of text~

21 C: so i mean that i wanna exchange the banjo to bongos

> (Smith, 2005, p. 47)

In the discussion, O provides input on an unknown lexical item to C. Although C does not overtly indicate comprehension, he makes use of the item several turns later, suggesting that he had noticed and understood the definition.

With some exceptions, the studies reviewed so far indicate that peer interactions in text chat promote focus on form episodes, which give learners opportunities to attend to linguistic form while communicating meaning, notice new forms, and through this further their language development. When learners' attention to language production is increased, the production of accurate and complex production is also likely to increase. The following section focuses on language production in text chat.

Production and Peer Text Chat

Examination of language production in the context of text chat helps us consider whether this context provides opportunities for learners to practice their use of language and to focus on producing well-formed, sophisticated language. Thus, it concerns whether text chat allows learners to stretch their linguistic resources. From a theoretical standpoint, text chat has some advantages over face-to-face communication in terms of promoting production for language practice. Discussing communication in face-to-face settings, Skehan (1998) points out that our limited capacity to process language in real time may hamper our ability to attend to language production. Text chat slows the process of communication; text SCMC provides the interlocutors with "more processing time while reading and typing messages" (Smith, 2003a, p. 39). Indeed, Beauvois (1998) has characterized text chat as "conversation in slow motion" (p. 198). Because typing is slower than speaking, the flow of information is slowed down in text chat, allowing extra time for both receptive and productive processing. Along with the visual record of chat that allows for review, this reduced rate of communication may promote greater monitoring (González, 2003; Warschauer, 1996) and may impact the accuracy and complexity of language production. In terms of accuracy, Böhlke (2003) found that learners produced targetlike structures at a similar rate in both face-to-face and text chat modes.

Regardless, there are questions about whether text chat conditions can promote a focus on accuracy in language production. Text chat discourse is characterized by simplified registers, short turns, and use of abbreviations and text speak, and learners accustomed to communication in text chat may not perceive a need to monitor for accuracy (Kern, 1995). Communication conventions in text chat common to both native speakers and L2 learners (e.g., omissions of the "be" verb and misuse of singular/plural) may push learners toward incorporating nontargetlike forms into their subsequent production (Cheon, 2003). Kung (2004) also found large numbers of spelling, grammar, and lexis errors in the language produced in text chat in his study. In posttask interviews, the learners claimed that the medium of text chat contributed to lowering the accuracy of their production. Specifically, they noted that the need to produce rapid online text to remain visible in the interaction pushed them to increase their production rate at the expense of accuracy.

Teachers simply setting explicit expectations for grammatical language use in text chat may not be enough to push learners to produce more accurate language (Lee, 2002). However, emerging research on task conditions in text chat settings indicates that learner attention to form may be shaped with carefully designed tasks and instruction (de la Fuente, 2003). For example, Fiori's (2005) work suggests that instructional interventions that raise consciousness of form can heighten attention to accuracy in text chat language production. This study compared the accuracy of learner language produced by two groups of learners: one that engaged in consciousness-raising activities prior to a meaning-focused chat and one that engaged in chats without prior instruction. Analysis of the chat transcripts indicated that the group without prior instruction did not self-correct many grammatical errors, particularly local errors that did not impede comprehension. The posttest results revealed significant differences between the groups' abilities to produce grammatical sentences. Although Fiori noted the importance of the consciousness-raising activities for these learners, she also pointed out that the effectiveness of the instruction method may have been heightened by the use of text chat, which enabled the learners to review the messages as often as they wanted.

Nik's (2010) study also found that pretask consciousness-raising activities for selected forms increased both the global accuracy of language production in peer text chat as well as the accurate use of the selected forms compared to the production of groups who did not engage in pretask language-focused activities. In the study, learners received explicit instruction as well as practice in the use of modal verbs and auxiliaries in controlled production activities. In a poststudy debriefing interview, learners who had engaged in the pretask language focus felt that it made them more aware of the need to monitor their production for accuracy. Similar to Fiori's findings, learners felt that the intervention pushed them to attend to form, and the visual nature of the text chat medium of communication made it easier for them to do so. On the other hand, learners who did not participate in the pretask consciousness-raising activities noted that they had recognized that they and their teammates were producing grammatically inaccurate language. However, they had not chosen to monitor their language as they had perceived the task as primarily a meaning exchange activity. They framed their understanding of the task within the conventions of text SCMC, where accuracy is not a focus. One learner noted,

Example 9.6

Although both Asha and Na do not use correct grammar, everyone understands what is going on. So, I don't think I need to talk about the error or correct it.

(Nik, 2010, p. 138)

Nik's study also examined a further instructional variable, the degree of task structure, on the accuracy of language production. Some learners were given a task sheet to help them organize the communication in the task and arrive at a consensus solution. The learners in this group produced more accurate language than those who were given less structured task instructions. One learner from this study noted,

Example 9.7

> Usually, when I chat with my friends it is very difficult to organise our conversation. Everybody wants to talk at the same time. Sometimes, you forgot the previous topic of discussion. However, when we have sheet B I can see that everyone knows whose turn should be next. We can wait until the person finishes his/her explanation. So, it is easier for us to track our conversation and we can pay attention to our language, especially our grammar.

(Nik, 2010, p. 124)

In contrast, learners who completed the task under the less structured condition pointed out that in the confusion of trying to organize information from different team members, they did not feel that they could also focus on the accuracy of their production. In a follow-up study, Adams and Nik (in press), examined the role of prior knowledge in CMC peer communication (see also Chapter 8). They found that learners who did not have prior knowledge of the task topic produced more accurate language than those who did have prior knowledge, again indicating that task conditions impact on language use in text chat. These studies provide evidence that text chat can be a positive context for accuracy-focused language practice, if the interaction is framed through instruction to promote this. This suggests that although text chat may be commonly used for quick communication without focus on linguistic accuracy, this need not be the case in instructional settings.

Beyond monitoring for accuracy, language production offers learners opportunities to stretch their linguistic resources by attempting to increase the structural and lexical complexity of their production. Another important question is whether text chat can promote a focus on complexity in production. Similar to questions of accuracy discussed previously, some researchers have argued that the conventions of text chat, particularly the simplified register and frequent use of ellipses and abbreviations, render text chat a poor site for promoting complex production (Lund, 2006). For example, Kung (2004) reported that his learners produced chat transcripts primarily composed of subclausal units, an indication of less complex production. The learners pointed out in interviews that this was a natural effect of adapting their typing speed to meet the demands of text chat, which pushed them to use simplifications.

However, other studies show evidence of complex learner language production in text SCMC. Learners in Warschauer's (1996) study, for example, produced lexically more varied and syntactically more complex language (measured through coordinating clauses) in online text chat than in face-to-face interactions. Sauro and Smith (2010) suggest that the disassociation between production and transmission in text chat may promote greater complexity. They found that when learners took the opportunity to review and modify their production prior to transmission, they produced more syntactically complex (measured through embedded clauses) and lexically diverse language.

Like accuracy of production, instructional interventions have also been shown to affect the complexity of production in L2 peer text chats. Of the studies of accuracy in peer SCMC discussed previously, both Nik (2010) and Fiori (2005) also included measures of complexity. Fiori (2005) found that learners who engaged in pretask consciousness-raising activities produced significantly more syntactically complex language than learners in a comparison group. However, Nik (2010) found that pretask language activities led to lower lexical complexity. It is likely that differences between the two pretask interventions account for this difference. In Fiori's study, the learners engaged in pretask focus on selected forms with no time restriction and were allowed to discuss and prepare for the task. In Nik's study, the learners had less time to engage in focus on form prior to the task.

There has been a tendency among researchers to dismiss the possibility of complex and accurate language production in text SCMC because of the conventional style of communication in this medium. However, the research reviewed here indicates that this may be a hasty conclusion. Rather, these findings suggest quite a complex picture of the uses and potential benefits of peer text chat. On the one hand, the spontaneous nature of chat has led to an expectation that communicators have a higher tolerance for greater inaccuracy and lower complexity in production. On the other hand, distinctive elements of chat such as longer production time and the ability to review past production in the emerging transcript provide opportunities for learners to monitor their production, suggesting the potential for greater attention to form leading to greater accuracy and complexity. It may be that instructional interventions are able to reconcile this tension, pushing learners to make use of those aspects of the technology that encourage monitoring of production. Such interventions help learners reframe text SCMC as an opportunity to focus on the complexity and accuracy of their production. Given favorable instructional circumstances, the unique characteristics of text chat may make it a positive site for language practice. This highlights the important role of the teacher in shaping peer interaction, through the larger classroom instructional practices.

Factors Affecting Participation in Text Chat

Text chat may be a particularly good site for production practice because learners participate more in this medium, and their turns are more equally distributed. Chun (1994) points out that the beginning German learners in his study needed support in L2 oral discussions, including help on what to discuss, how to begin the conversation, and how to interact with their group. In contrast, when using the L2 in text chat, learners seemed more enthusiastic and did not require support to initiate discussions, respond to others, and request clarification. Sullivan and Pratt (1996) compared learner participation in face-to-face and text chat discussions. They found that only 50% of the students participated in the oral class discussion, as opposed to 100% participation in the computer-assisted classroom environment. Similar findings were reported by Warschauer (1996) and Kern (1995). Text chat may allow for "unfettered self-expression, increased student initiative and responsiveness, generation of multiple perspectives on an issue, voicing of differences, and status equalization" (Kern, 1995, p. 470). Nik (2010) and Adams and Nik (in press) both found nearly perfectly even distribution of production in text chat. Regardless of instructional conditions, learners in groups all contributed evenly to the chat discourse.

Why would text chat promote increased participation and even distribution of participation? Many researchers believe that the slower pace of text chat makes it less stressful (Beauvois & Eledge, 1995), as it allows learners time to think and organize ideas before sharing them with their peers. This may particularly be the case for more introverted learners and those with lower communicative proficiency (Coniam & Wong, 2004). Learners in Cheon's (2003) study reported feeling more relaxed expressing themselves in the L2 via text chat as no one could see their faces if they made mistakes. Other learners have reported a preference to contribute to discussions in text chat because they felt invisible. This anonymity might reduce social barriers to interaction, motivating learners to practice language (Freiermuth & Jarrel, 2006). This may suggest that interactive competence could be developed through interaction via text chat.

A number of studies, however, have not found advantages to text chat in terms of anxiety. For example, Lee (2004) and Arnold (2007) did not demonstrate any effect of reduced anxiety or communication apprehension in text chat and other text-based CMC. Baralt and Gurzynski-Weiss (2011) measured stated anxiety following face-to-face and text chat tasks for a group of L2 Spanish learners. Their study did not indicate that anxiety was affected by completing tasks in text chat. Lower anxiety may not be the reason for increased communication in text chat. Another related explanation is that learners are more willing to communicate in text SCMC. Learners in a study by Freiermuth and Jarrel (2006) noted in questionnaires that they were more comfortable communicating by text chat and therefore were more willing to engage in communication. Anxiety plays a role in willingness to communicate along with factors including perceptions of competence and desire to communicate with an interlocutor (cf. Macintyre, Clément, Dörnyei, & Noels, 1998). It's possible, for example, that learner perceptions of their linguistic competence are higher in SCMC because of the slower pace compared to oral communication.

Discourse of Peer Text Chat Interaction

Peer interaction in text chat has also been examined from the perspective of discourse analysis. Within an L2 classroom context, the use of peer text chat can promote a very different type of discourse from traditional institutionally asymmetric teacher-controlled classroom discourse (González-Lloret, 2009). The inclusion of text chat affords learners opportunities to use authentic language in real interaction, and conversation analysis can substantiate how this unfolds. In one study to take this approach, Shin (2006) examined the text chat communication of a group of English as a second language students, focusing on the way they jointly constructed activities through interactional patterns and norms, mediated by the CMC environment. His participants co-constructed interactional patterns and norms, creating a group socialization experience. The online community formed gradually and became a social space for learners to share and construct identities as academics. Shin points out that this gradual transformation from classroom practice to social space highlights the fluidity of CMC as a learning space that can be formed and reformed through learner dialogic engagement.

Although different text-CMC technologies are often undifferentiated in the research, differences among them can shape learner experiences and learner discourse. Smith, Alvarez-Torres, and Zhao (2003), for example, focused on two different text-SCMC tools, one a traditional text chat client and the other a multiple object orientation program (MOO), in which each interlocutor is represented on-screen by an avatar that can be moved among virtual rooms, with communication represented in speech balloons next to the avatars. Discourse in the tasks was more interpersonal in the MOO client and more task focused in the chat client. Additionally, in the MOO client, the greater use of graphics and rich backgrounds may have drawn focus from the core elements of the task to peripheral elements. This suggests that research findings on language, discourse, and learning in text CMC are not neutral to the specific technology chosen; rather, differences in the technology used may impact the social and linguistic experience.

Indeed, the role of the technology in shaping the interactional experience becomes clear as we broaden our focus beyond text SCMC. We will next focus on delayed peer L2 interaction via ACMC, examining the unique ways ACMC technologies promote learning opportunities.

Peer Interaction in ACMC

Both modes of CMC have the potential to promote language learning because both "amplify opportunities for students to pay attention to linguistic form as well as providing a less stressful environment" (Mackey & Gass, 2005, p. 63). ACMC has the added advantage of providing more time and space for reading, reflecting, and writing, as well as for revising and posting. Each of these behaviors is unusual in SCMC interaction (Garrison, Anderson, & Archer, 2000; Smith, 2004), where interactions have more of a sense of immediacy. Extra time can promote a level of syntactic complexity in ACMC discourse (e.g., nominalizations, subordinate and complement clauses, use of passive voice, and heavy noun phrases) that is not commonly found in SCMC (Osman & Herring, 2007), but it can also create a sense of social distance.

Although ACMC does not occur in real time, it still allows for interaction among learners (e.g., Herring, 2004) as well as negotiation of meaning (Bober & Dennen, 2001). For example, Kessler (2009) found students creating an L2 wiki as part of their course focused most of their revisions on collaboratively correcting errors in form, indicating that they used the wiki writing and revision process as a means of focusing on linguistic accuracy. However, he noted that students were reticent to edit errors that did not impede communication, despite instructions for them to focus on accuracy. This is supported by Li's (2000) findings that the nature of different e-mail tasks influenced the way learners attended to accuracy and complexity in their communication. In particular, in tasks with more interaction with other interlocutors, the learner production was more syntactically and lexically complex. The learners also used more complex sentence constructions and a wider range of vocabulary on tasks where they were allowed to select their own topic. This demonstrates a similar point to that discussed on promoting accuracy and complexity in text SCMC. Even though one mode or another may be more likely to promote attention to linguistic form, task design and instructional interventions that help learners frame the communication as an opportunity to focus on language may be necessary to focus learner attention on form.

Like SCMC, peer interaction in ACMC has benefits that extend beyond focus on form and shaping attention in language practice. A further benefit of ACMC is that it helps students develop greater autonomy in managing the development of their written discourse (Lai, 2005), which may affect the quality of their critical thinking (Buraphaeja & Dawson, 2008). While evaluating a technology-supported learning curriculum, Hawkes (2006) found that the CMC learners were more likely to engage in interactions involving critical reflection processes, particularly focusing on key components of sense making including sharing, exploring, and analyzing. Hawkes suggested that the increase in critical thinking processes may occur in ACMC because it allows for interactivity and promotes audience awareness between discourse participants like face-to-face communication does, but without the pressure of real-time communication. Cheng (2010) found that discussion forums allowed learners to engage in two-way scaffolding, which helped learners to orient themselves to writing tasks, allowed them to rehearse writing and negotiate the revision process, and supported their developing understanding of academic writing conventions, including using citations to support their argumentation.

Different ACMC technologies have been shown to support learners' reading and writing processes, helping them to become less teacher dependent and more collaborative as they engage in CMC-based project-oriented research and write for a real audience. For example, Kern (1996) examined e-mail exchanges, whereas Warschauer (1997) looked at learner work published on the Internet for specific audiences. Both researchers found that the public nature of ACMC as well as the immediacy of the audience helped learners create more reader-centered production. They suggest that including ACMC components in writing programs, for example, can allow learners to write for and connect to a real audience, increasing the authenticity of the communication.

Beyond Text in CMC

Because text forms of CMC are most common, it has been the focus of this chapter, and indeed of research on peer interaction in CMC. However, both SCMC and ACMC take place in oral and mixed modal forms (e.g., video chat, podcasts, and online gaming). Research on other contexts such as Second Life (Peterson, 2010a) and Massively Multiplayer Online Roleplaying Games (Peterson, 2010b) show how peer interaction in L2 contexts may move increasingly beyond the chat room. The gaming context is particularly interesting, as it is a large and more and more common context for communication that any learner with an Internet connection can access.

This context usually blends options for text-based and audio-based chat and provides a rich visual context that supports comprehension. Because gaming is generally considered a leisure (rather than business or educational) activity, many learners already engage in games socially. Rankin, Gold, and Gooch (2006) found that learners increased the complexity of their language production while they played and became gradually more comfortable with the range of vocabulary presented in the games. However, these findings were more marked with higher proficiency than lower proficiency learners. The authors caution that the contextual support offered by games must be carefully matched to the learner proficiency, especially because games move quickly in real time, so learners have little time for processing. Although these findings demonstrate promise for other forms of CMC in educational settings, Peterson (2010b) notes that more research on language use beyond text chat is clearly needed.

Conclusion

Research on peer interaction in CMC suggests that there is great potential for learning in ways that complement learning opportunities in face-to-face interaction. But whether this potential is realized depends on a complex group of factors, including the specific technology used, the tasks and materials, the learner orientations to the interaction and to technology use, and the way the communicative tasks are embedded in the larger classroom framework. Although the body of research that examines peer interaction in CMC is large and growing, investigating these factors and all their combinations is daunting. All the while, technology, and opportunities it affords for communication and connection, evolves in ways we have not yet predicted. What we do know is that CMC offers some distinct advantages for peer communication in comparison to face-to-face communication, primarily because the lower speed, the visual nature of the interaction, and the semipermanent record of the communication combine to make forms more salient and to make monitoring of and reflection on language use more possible. Although CMC may push learners to focus on language production and forge new form-meaning connections, simply sitting learners at keyboards will not guarantee such an outcome. Careful attention to task design and implementation are necessary to optimize the potential of CMC in promoting language learning through peer interaction. This further emphasizes a point discussed in Chapter 8, namely, that regardless of modality of communication, the way that teachers structure the larger learning context plays a strong role in how peer interactions are carried out and whether these interactions will be beneficial for language development.

10

PEER WRITING AND READING

Introduction

Second language (L2) learning theories based on learning through oral communication have often been cited as the impetus behind integrating peer interaction into the language classroom. Because of this close connection, research on peer interaction in language learning has focused primarily on oral conversational tasks. However, as we noted in the previous chapter, peer interaction occurs in a number of contexts in language classrooms beyond basic conversation practice. Learners may also work in pairs or groups in language classrooms pooling linguistic resources to solve a grammatical consciousness-raising task (cf. Ellis, 2003). They may talk together as they co-construct a written text (cf. Swain & Lapkin, 2002), discussing both content and expression of meaning through linguistic form. In these cases, learners assist one another in articulating shared meanings and in constructing grammatical structures, allowing for learning beyond oral communication proficiencies. Indeed, several researchers (e.g., Adams, 2003; Storch, 2011) have argued that peer interaction involving the creation or use of written texts may be a particularly beneficial site for language learning because the text serves to anchor forms and make them visual. This makes language production less ephemeral, thereby decreasing the memory load associated with discussing language use in the context of communicating meaning.

In this chapter, we focus on the contribution of peer writing (including collaborative writing and peer review) to language learning and, in the final section, also examine the role of peer reading in L2 development.

L2 Writing

Writing in any language is a complex undertaking. Writing involves the integration of multiple bodies of knowledge, including content knowledge about the ideas for the text, systemic knowledge of the language, process knowledge of how to carry out the writing task, genre knowledge of the purpose of the genre and how to achieve that, and contextual knowledge of the audience's cultural preferences (Hyland, 2010). It is clear then that writing is particularly challenging for L2 learners, who not only have incomplete or nonautomatic knowledge of the linguistic system but also less familiarity with the cultural context of the writing and how different genres are realized in that context.

Writing instructors for both first language (L1) and L2 have long recognized that engaging in the writing process is necessary in order to learn to write (for overview, see Nation, 2009). More recently, however, there has been a growing awareness of the role of engagement in writing in improving learning. This perspective on writing is often labeled "writing to learn" as opposed to "learning to write." These dual perspectives are complementary, building understanding that as students learn to write, they are also engaged in learning content, genre, and language. The cognitive premise of writing to learn is that engaging in writing develops thought "at the point of utterance" (Britton, 1980, p. 68).

Researchers of writing in an L1 have tended to focus on how writing promotes learning across curricular areas, in Hyland's terms, in creating content knowledge. L2 researchers, on the other hand, have additionally focused on the effect of writing in promoting language knowledge. Manchón (2011) distinguishes these orientations as writing to learn content and writing to learn language. Writing might be a particularly appropriate means of language learning: Engaging in writing with a communicative orientation helps learners to make connections between language forms and their meanings, and to control and refine their L2 knowledge structures (Cummings, 1990). Based on a comprehensive review of writing to learn studies, Manchón (2011) concludes that writing fosters linguistic processing that may promote learning; however, the way learner attention is directed to linguistic form may depend on learner variables as well as the type of writing task in which they engage.

Peer interaction is realized in L2 writing contexts in a number of ways, including giving peer feedback and engaging in cooperative revision tasks. One particular form of learner interaction in writing is found in collaborative writing, a process during which learners co-construct a text. We will focus first on collaborative writing, with a particular focus on language-learning opportunities that arise when language learners co-construct a text, and then consider peer review and online peer writing as language-learning contexts.

L2 Collaborative Writing

Although collaborative writing is common in higher education assessment and professional contexts, it has rarely been investigated in L2 learning contexts (Storch, 2011). Bremner (2010), for example, pointed out that collaborative dialogue was only mentioned in general terms in a set of commonly used commercial English as a Foreign Language (EFL) business communication textbooks, and that of the rare cases when collaborative writing tasks were employed, they did not reflect uses of co-constructed writing the learners would encounter in the workplace. However, there has been a recent rise in attention to collaborative writing, which Storch credits to Swain's (1995) work on the output hypothesis. Although most output research has focused on the role of spoken output in learning, an emerging body of research suggests that writing may be a better context than speaking for promoting learning through output. In one longitudinal study, Weissberg (2000) examined the language development of five adult English as a second language (ESL) learners who engaged in speaking in class, journal writing, and academic writing. He found that new syntactic forms were more likely to emerge in written than spoken production. Because writing does not demand online processing, learners are more likely both to receive and to notice and process feedback on written than on spoken production (Harklau, 2002).

Research on collaborative writing is also informed by a sociocultural approach, which applies Vygotskian theory to classroom learning. As noted in Chapters 2 and 3, sociocultural theory is based on the premise that learning is inherently social, that higher order cognitive functions emerge as the result of interpersonal interactions (Vygotsky, 1978). Weissberg speculates that the effectiveness of writing for language learning may be optimized through collaborative writing, as it requires learners both to speak and to write, and in the process to play multiple roles (e.g., as peer tutors, coauthors, or sounding boards), as they engage in collaborative dialogue. (See Chapter 2 for further discussion of collaborative dialogue.)

A body of research indicates that collaborative writing may have positive effects for learning. For example, Wigglesworth and Storch (2009) compared the writing of ESL learners working individually or in pairs to create an argumentative text. The findings indicated that, although working with a peer did not influence the fluency or syntactic complexity of the writing, learners in pairs produced more grammatically accurate writing. This echoes findings by Storch (1999) and Glendinning and Howard (2003), who each found that learners produced more accurate texts when writing collaboratively than when writing individually. The researchers also examined the discourse produced by learners in pairs as they coauthored their text. By categorizing turns according to focus, they found that over a third of the turns in the discourse were devoted to discussing language form, as in the example.

Example 10.1

121 Matt: More and more countries are putting emphas . . . putting a high emphasis on

122   education system

123 Emily: ah ha, on education system . . . ah can can can . . . countries are putting a high

124		emphasis on their education system, is it?
125	Matt:	Mmmm
126	Emily:	Ay? And remember Miss Lena said like "their" cannot be used . . .
127	Matt:	Oh yeah . . . more and more countries are putting a high emphasis on the
128		education system

(Wigglesworth & Storch, 2009, p. 458)

Emily drew her interlocutor's attention to a missing determiner as they constructed their writing. They discussed the form over several turns, reminding each other of prior instruction. Episodes like this were the second most common type of turn, following turns focusing on content. The learners' ability to work together and pool their resources to express content through linguistic form may have led to more accurate writing in the peer condition. These findings echo those of Fernandez Dobao's (2001) study of individual, pair, and group writing among Galician learners of English. She also found advantages for collaborative writing in terms of accuracy. This study additionally compared episodes where learners attended to linguistic form between the pairs and groups, finding that the groups discussed issues of form more often, and these were more successfully resolved. Researchers conclude that discussing form in the context of creating a written text may help learners to use new and more accurate language forms. These findings suggest that when writing is used to learn language, it may make sense to use collaborative writing.

Similarly, there are advantages for collaborative writing in terms of grammatical accuracy. Learners in Storch's (2005) study also were interviewed about their perceptions of collaborative writing. Students did note potential drawbacks of collaborative writing, including concerns about their own and their partner's language ability. They also felt that critiquing a peer's ideas and language use would be face-threatening. (We noted in Chapter 3 similar concerns expressed for peer oral interactions.) However, the overwhelming response was positive, with learners noting that collaborative writing allowed them to pool resources to generate content ideas and focus on form. Learners noted that it is easier to correct a peer's language use than to self-correct, and that peer language was also a source of learning. For example, one learner noted:

Example 10.2

I just watch vocabulary or . . . what vocabulary he was using, he used and . . . Well if he used the vocabulary which I didn't know, I tried to use it for next time.

(Storch, 2005, p. 167)

In a similar study, Malmqvist (2005) found that texts produced between peers tended to be longer and to include more subordination than texts produced by individual learners. She also found that learners focused together on language use across a range of grammatical and lexical forms, and that the majority of these episodes were resolved in a manner that pushed the learners to use targetlike German (although there was wide variation among the groups on this). Although the quantitative findings of these two studies indicate an advantage for peer writing in terms of the linguistic product, qualitative analysis indicates that collaborative writing allows learners to focus attention both on content and language learning through writing.

Although the studies discussed so far have demonstrated learning advantages to collaborative as opposed to individual writing, a second body of work has emerged that explores Cumming's (1990) claims about advantages of writing as a context to learn language. These studies contrast collaborative speaking and collaborative writing tasks to determine whether the written modality influences opportunities to learn language through peer interaction. Adams (2006) compared the language produced by 44 ESL learners engaged in both parts of two-phase tasks. For example, one of the tasks required learners to first discuss a series of pictures to sequence a story and then to collaboratively write the story. Indications that the learners were attending to form included discussions of language issues, self-corrections, and use of targeted forms. These were used to determine whether learners were more likely to notice and process linguistic information while completing the task during the speaking or writing phases. The results showed that learners focused on language form significantly more often during the writing than the speaking phase. Adams noted that when the learners spoke together, they seemed most concerned with communicating ideas for understanding, but not to question use of form. On the other hand, when learners began to write, they seemed to split their attention between the meanings they wanted to convey and their accuracy in encoding those meanings linguistically. Adams speculated that the permanence of the written record, and the learner's knowledge that a researcher would review it, may have oriented their attention to form. These findings are very similar to those of Niu (2009), who contrasted collaborative speaking and collaborative writing sessions of L1 Chinese EFL students. In this study, learners discussed vocabulary, grammar, and discourse issues almost three times as often when engaged in peer writing tasks as in peer speaking tasks.

Writing may not only affect how much learners attend to form, it may also shape how learners attend to form. Adams and Ross-Feldman (2008) compared the way that learners focused on language during collaborative speaking and collaborative writing sections of a task. Looking at data from an earlier study (Adams, 2003), they noted that the way learners initiated and responded to negotiation signals differed when learners were speaking only or when they were also engaged in writing. The following data illustrate these differences. In Example 10.3, the learners are engaged in speaking only, working together to describe and understand a set of pictures.

Example 10.3

1 Learner 1: Y la mujer continua estar durmiendo.

   [And the woman continues to be asleep]

2 Learner 2: Sí en la

   [Yes in the]

3 Learner 1: or continua dormiendo dormir?

   [or continues sleeping sleep?]

4 Learner 2: En en la pintura seis . . .

   [In in the picture six . . .]

(Adams & Ross-Feldman, 2008, p. 247)

Learner 1 clearly signals uncertainty in her expression and tries overtly to begin a discussion of grammatical form. Learner 2, however, ignores the signal and continues the discussion. For this pair of learners, during the speaking section there was not a single discussion of form that ended in a correct resolution. On the other hand, when they began to use the pictures to collaboratively write a narrative, their patterns for addressing issues of form shifted sharply, as evidenced in Example 10.4.

Example 10.4

1 Learner 1:   Su cabeza está lejos de

   [Her head is far from]

2 Learner 2:   uh

3 Learner 1:   Que es? (points to picture) OK?

   [What is it?]

4 Learner 2:   la uh pio de la cama

   [the uh "pio" of the bed]

5 Learner 1:   Los pies

   [The feet]

6 Learner 2:   Pie de la cama

   [Foot of the bed]

7 Learner 1:   Están on su, que es pillow?

   [They are on his, what is pillow?]

8 Learner 2:   No sé la palabra. No para rápido.

   [I don't know the word. Not for fast]

9 Learner 1:   Están en el primer parte de la cama
                   [They are on the first part of the bed]

10 Learner 2:   Oh la cabeza de la cama.
                   [Oh, the head of the bed]

11 Learner 1:   OK Oh en la cabeza de la cama
                   [OK, oh on the head of the bed]

(Adams & Ross-Feldman, 2008, p. 248)

In this excerpt, the learners are discussing the same picture that prompted a negotiation signal in Example 10.3. However, when Learner 1 initiates a discussion of vocabulary by pointing to a section of the picture depicting a headboard, Learner 2 joins in. The learners discuss this vocabulary item for several turns, including a short sequence involving correction of *pios* to *pies* (feet). In total, this episode lasts for 11 turns and ends with agreement on their resolution *cabeza de la cama*, which although non-targetlike, approximates the correct term *cabecera de cama*. This episode demonstrates that collaborative writing can promote a focus on accuracy and learning. There is someone to offer a solution, and an opportunity to talk it through. The peer's turn offers a point of contrast to the speaker's original production, pushing them to rethink things. Even if, as here, the resolution is not targetlike, the discussion has drawn focus to it, which may eventually lead to restructuring, either through noticing the targetlike form in teacher input or through directly asking the teacher for help. In this way, collaborative peer writing experiences may complement teacher-learner interactions by making forms salient for future exploration with the teacher.

Adams and Ross-Feldman (2008) designed their study to examine whether these differences in the quality of focus on form were related to the modality of the discourse. They found evidence that learners were more likely to explicitly signal miscommunications and corrections when engaged in writing. They found no evidence that the modality influenced the use of self-repair and, overall, found that self-repair occurred relatively rarely in the data. They speculate that this may be related to the nature of collaboration, that changing modalities may impact collaborative attention to form more than self-repair (which is an individual focus on form) because learner focus in dyadic tasks is oriented to the shared construction of meaning. As Villamil and de Guerrero (1996) suggest, engagement in collaborative writing may offer learners "an opportunity for bilateral, rather than unilateral, participation and learning; in other words, both peers may give and receive help, both peers may teach and learn" (p. 69).

Collaborative writing, as opposed to collaborative speaking, promotes cognitive processes such as hypothesis testing and rule formation (cf. Swain, 2005), which promote learning. Niu (2009), for example, compared discussion of forms in collaborative oral and written tasks. In oral tasks, learners tended to do this in few turns and to choose a resolution without justification. In contrast, when discussing grammar in collaborative written tasks, they expressed opinions about the forms they and their partners suggested and presented rationales for the resolution agreed on. Their discussion provided an insight into how learners use collaborative talk to form and test hypotheses about forms.

Attention to form promoted by collaborative writing is likely to translate to learning gains for L2 students. For example, Kim (2008) measured vocabulary learning gains of 32 L2 Korean learners who worked individually or collaboratively on a dictogloss text reconstruction task. Although learners attended to form in both contexts, there were greater rates of resolution of grammatical issues among the learners who worked collaboratively. Additionally, learners who worked collaboratively gained more lexical knowledge than those who worked individually. Watanabe and Swain (2007) also found evidence that peer collaboration contributed to learning gains. These studies suggest that peer collaboration increases the learning potential of written tasks.

Overall then, research on collaborative writing in peer groups suggests that this is a particularly beneficial site for learning through interaction. Indeed, many of the critiques of peer interaction—that learners do not focus on form very often and that they focus primarily on vocabulary to the exclusion of grammar and discourse—do not seem to apply to peer interaction that takes place through collaborative writing. When learners sit together to write, they more often engage in discussion of form, and their discussion of form is likely to be more meaningful for promoting learning than when they engage in tasks that only require oral communication. They also produce more accurate and often more complex language than when writing individually.

Classroom logistical concerns with respect to peer interaction may also be assuaged by collaborative writing. One common concern of foreign language teachers is that, when set loose for peer interaction, learners will simply use their L1 to quickly finish tasks. However, when learners need to produce a written product of their task in the target language, it is not possible for them to rely solely on their L1. Also, as we discussed in Chapter 5, some L1 use in tasks can be helpful for learning. For example, Swain and Lapkin (1998) found that the use of the L1 by French immersion students engaged in a collaborative writing task was relatively rare. When learners did use their L1, they often did so to more clearly elucidate form-meaning connections, drawing on their L1 resources in a way that allowed them both to express meanings and to process L2 information. Swain and Lapkin argue that the use of the L1 for foreign language learners engaged in collaborative writing may actually promote learning.

L2 Peer Review

Although much of the research on peer interaction and writing has considered collaborative writing, a substantial body also considers peer review on writing. Peer review is a cover term that includes peer editing, peer response, and peer-supported revision. Peer feedback has often been touted as an alternative to teacher feedback in writing, as a means of providing meaningful feedback to learners (e.g., Paulus, 1999). Although common in L1 writing contexts, the value of peer review has been questioned for L2 learners, with concerns raised about their ability to meaningfully respond to peer writing due to limitations in language competence (Nelson & Murphy, 1992). However, recent research suggests that with attention to a range of factors including strategy training and group dynamics, peer review can benefit both givers and receivers in terms of building critical-thinking skills important to writing and metalinguistic analysis important to language learning.

The benefits of peer review for learning to write include promoting audience awareness and pushing learners to critically evaluate their own writing. When peer review is done well, peers provide a second set of eyes, helping learners to identify logical gaps, problems with organization, and other areas that affect effective argumentation in writing (Ferris, 2003). Scholars working in a sociocultural framework have noted that peer review may constitute a type of other-regulation, allowing learners to achieve more than they could individually (de Guerrero & Villamil, 2000). In this section of the chapter, we will focus on peer review, in particular on peer feedback and peer revision. We then turn to research that has incorporated peer interaction into the peer review process.

One of the earliest studies to examine the effectiveness of peer review was conducted by Paulus (1999), among an ESL writing class at a preacademic English program at a North American university. Peer review was a part of the course from the beginning—learners had been instructed on effective techniques in giving feedback and had reviewed and received coaching during a prior peer review session from their instructor. For the study, they individually created drafts of a persuasive essay, which was then read and commented on by a peer in the class. The learners then met together in pairs and discussed their essays and the feedback. Following a second draft, the teacher gave feedback. Teacher feedback was more influential in the drafting process; just over half of the peer feedback comments led to revisions, whereas 87% of the teacher comments did. Paulus notes, however, that the findings still indicate that peer feedback was attended to as often as not, and that the revisions following peer and teacher feedback tended to be meaning focused and global, rather than surface revisions. This suggests that both teacher and peer feedback may impact the quality of the finished writing.

De Guerrero and Villamil (2000) examined peer feedback through a Vygotskian lens, focusing on how one pair of learners working together was able to other-regulate, leading to self-regulation in the final revision. Using a microgenetic analysis (which analyses changes in production turn by turn), they found a wide variety of scaffolding mechanisms unfolding as the learners reviewed an essay together. Beyond simply providing critique, the peer reviewer also fulfilled such functions as helping the writer maintain interest and attention throughout the review, marking discrepancies in the text, modeling writing and revision strategies, and giving explicit grammar explanations during the discourse. De Guerrero and Villamil suggest that because the reviewer (R) recruited interest in the task and made it manageable, he was able to help the writer (W) take greater responsibility for the revision process. In Example 10.5, from early in the task, the writer does not agree with a suggested revision but adopts it anyway in the revision.

Example 10.5

11 R: Some rules in English, I think, I am not sure, when you write, you shouldn't . . .

12 W: Uh hmm . . .

13 R: You shouldn't abbreviate, use contractions . . .

14 W: I know what you mean . . .

15 R: You understand? You shouldn't write I didn't. You should write I did not. You can check in a book and you'll find no contractions.

16 W: Yeah, but if I write it like that, I find it somewhat, I don't know, unnatural.

17 R: That's because one is used to write like that.

(de Guerrero & Villamil, 2000, p. 57)

W contests the revision but ultimately adopts it following R's insistence. After a few such episodes, however, R initiates a discussion of their roles, attempting to recruit the writer's interest in discussing the text collaboratively.

Example 10.6

42 R: I mean, you . . ., I want you to give me your opinion . . .

43 W: no . . .

44 R: I am only revising, only revising, do you understand?

45 W: because . . .

46 R: As I understand it . . . as I understand it. . . . One thing is how I talk and another is how I should talk (laughter).

(de Guerrero & Villamil, 2000, p. 58)

After this redefinition of their roles and the task, de Guerrero and Villamil report a noticeable change in the discussion, with R loosening control, W suggesting changes, and both learners discussing and proposing alternatives. Beyond the discreet points of knowledge gleaned from the experience, they argue that the peer review promoted this writer's ability to self-regulate and his growth as a more autonomous writer and reviser. Although at a very small scale, the study provides a glimpse into the potential of peer interaction for learning to write.

In a larger study (Villamil & de Guerrero, 1996), the researchers looked at scaffolding and revision among a group of 54 participants. Their study validated Donato's (1994) prior finding that in peer interaction, scaffolding can run in either direction, as both readers and writers fluidly changed from expert to novice roles and back as the discourse unfolded. Villamil and de Guerrero point out that the effectiveness of scaffolding for learning seems to be inextricably linked to the social relationships between learners, which also were not static but changed during the interaction (similar findings are discussed in Chapter 6). Some peers maintained a collaborative relationship throughout the revision sessions, but for others the nature of the relationship shifted as writer and readers sought and relinquished control over the writing and revision process.

Most research on peer feedback has examined the effect of peer feedback in terms of whether it prompts revision in subsequent drafts. But this may not accurately capture the effect of peer feedback on language learning in a Chinese EFL classroom. In Zhao's (2010) study, learners wrote a draft of an essay and received teacher written feedback, as well as a teacher-fronted discussion of common errors. Then learners were paired and given the chance to first read, comment on, and discuss each other's essays. Consistent with prior studies, Zhao found that learners were more likely to make revisions based on teacher than peer feedback. However, follow-up stimulated recall interviews and qualitative interviews indicated that many of the revisions based on teacher feedback were made without comprehension of why the feedback was given, with learners passively accepting teacher feedback. Zhao questioned the effectiveness of teacher feedback beyond immediate revision for learning.

For example, one learner ("Jin"), in an essay about parental love, wrote, "Virtually, there is boundless love hidden in fishbone." The teacher indicated vocabulary issues by underlining parts of the sentence and writing comments beneath. "Virtually" was underlined, with the comment "look up," and "hidden in fishbone" was underlined with the comment "meaning?". The learner revised both parts of this sentence but in interviews made it clear that he did not understand all the purposes of the revision, as demonstrated in the subsequent excerpt.

Example 10.7

R: Do you need help with the feedback received in the first paragraph?

Jin: Yes, this one. What's the difference between "virtually" and "actually"? I was suggested by Art [the writing teacher] to look up "virtually." In our meeting, Art suggested actually. But couldn't virtually be used in this way? I've used it in this way for a long time. I used "virtually" and "actually" interchangeably. I feel they have the same meaning. I use them as an alternative to each other to avoid overusing one word. I still feel they are the same.

(Zhao, 2010, p. 9)

Although the learner had revised the vocabulary choice to a more acceptable alternative, he had clearly not understood the feedback, nor understood why the revision was a better choice. Although many more revisions were made in response to teacher than peer feedback, Zhao found that where peer feedback prompted a revision, learners understood the purpose and value of the revision 83% of the time, as compared to only 58% of revisions following teacher feedback. This suggests that although teacher feedback may lead to improvement in an essay, peer feedback is more likely to lead to learning. This may be related to the equivalence between peers, which makes it more likely for feedback to be within a learner's zone of proximal development. As found through interviews, learners actively sought to understand peer feedback. They speculated that using their L1 constructively in the discussion of their writing with their peers may have helped them to understand more fully the feedback they were given. The relationship between peer revision discussion and subsequent writing and revision is complex and depends not just on the feedback given but also on group dynamics (these ideas are discussed more in Chapter 6). Liang (2010) suggests that more research is needed to understand individual and group factors and their impact on the use of peer feedback in revision and learning.

Overall, the research on peer review in L2 writing classrooms is quite positive. Although not at the same rate as teacher comments, peer comments have consistently been shown to lead to revision. Liang's (2010) research suggests that revisions based on peer comments are more likely to represent changes in understanding of language and writing, rather than blind acceptance of feedback. And indeed, even when peer sessions include times when feedback is accepted blindly without question, relationships formed in these interactions are likely to shift as they shape and are shaped by the joint revision process, allowing the writer to take control of the revision process and readers to jointly negotiation task, language, and writing demands.

L2 Peer Writing Online

The final section on peer interaction and writing will focus on the broadening landscape of L2 writing in virtual environments. Although most discussion of technology and interaction is found in Chapter 8, we will discuss here research on the use of collaborative peer writing in online contexts. In particular, the spread of Web 2.0 technologies (the so-called social technologies) has increased contexts for writing, and in particular for writing for an immediate and responsive audience. Blogs and wikis are examples of writing contexts that allow for collaborative creation of texts as well as peer revision over time in response to interactive feedback and commentary. Writing instructors in both L1 and L2 writing contexts have been quick to make use of these technologies to allow learners to write and collaborate in an authentic context that relates clearly to reading and writing in the real world (Arnold, Ducate, & Kost, 2009; Elola & Oskoz, 2010; Kessler, 2009).

Online writing offers benefits not found in traditional writing. Elola and Oskoz (2010) point out that advantages of computer-mediated communication (CMC)–based collaborative writing include "authoring flexibility, content creation, and the generation of new knowledge" (p. 51). These technologies may be particularly beneficial for promoting collaborative writing because of open editing and review structures and because of the possibility of integrating audio and visual applications. Web-based collaborative writing, on wikis for example, has been shown to promote a focus on structure and organization (Kessler, 2009), rather than solely on local issues, because the ability to quickly and easily make substantive changes promotes major revisions.

The differences between online and paper-based collaborative writing are highlighted in Elola and Oskoz's (2010) study of argumentative writing using wikis among learners of Spanish. One advantage to the technology used here, wikis, is that the page history function allowed the researchers insight into the revision process as it unfolded step-by-step, with some learners creating as many as 100 versions of a page as they wrote and revised the wiki. The learners in this study worked individually and collaboratively in building and revising wiki writing over a number of weeks. The researchers found that collaborative wiki writing led to more focus on linguistic accuracy. Indeed, examination across drafts indicated that, although learners working individually tended to leave revisions for grammatical accuracy to the final version of the wiki, learners working collaboratively attended to linguistic form throughout the process, fluidly shifting attention among content, organization, and linguistic accuracy as they worked through each draft, helping them continually generate and refine form-meaning connections.

Kessler (2009) found that although learners co-constructing a wiki most often made revisions and gave feedback directed at content, there was also extensive discussion of form. Learners in Lee's (2010a) study also noted that collaborative writing in wikis helped them make sense of grammatical points in a meaningful context. This adds support to the finding that learners make use of collaborative web-based writing to focus on form in the context of meaning, that like collaborative writing with pen and paper, web-based writing allows for learners to learn to write while also writing to learn language.

A particular advantage to collaboration using wikis was the ability of the learners to build a permanent, visible discourse (within wiki comments) in which issues related to the topic, organization, structure, and use of sources were debated (Elola and Oskoz, 2010). Learner discussions about wikis in synchronous chats sparked revisions in the wikis, a direct relationship that may have been promoted by the ease of co-constructing text in text chat and then copying it into the wiki. This may be simpler to achieve in text-based CMC compared to face-to-face collaboration, where spoken language must be remembered and processed to revise written text.

Learners have also reported highly positive perceptions of using wiki writing in language courses. For example, learners in Lee's (2010a) study noted that working collaboratively on the wikis was both enjoyable and motivating. Students who had previously held negative views about writing indicated that collaborative wiki writing had changed their perceptions of writing. Lee notes that one reason for this was that the technology allowed them to write for a real audience beyond the teacher, which was motivating. This also may have pushed them to consider linguistic issues beyond grammar and lexis, such as sociolinguistic features of appropriateness. The following example from a wiki discussion page illustrates learner engagement with pragmatics of address in the task.

Example 10.8

1 Odjay:	Hey guys. Do you think this "letter" should be written in "tu" form or usted?
2 Sarah03:	I'd say usted because we're talking to someone who we don't know but I'm not sure.
3 Chantel02:	Yeah i would think it would be usted. We don't know him, and he is also a Dr?
4 Eac45:	Yeah, I agree, we don't know him and he is a doctor – a doctor of love hahah – but a doctor none the less.

(Lee, 2010a, p. 267)

Learners also mentioned that the wikis were motivating because they promoted collaborative writing with peers, which they felt pushed them to attend more to the quality of their writing. They did face frustrations, particularly with the asynchronous nature of wiki writing collaboration, which could leave them waiting around for a group member's contributions. Learners, however, felt that wiki writing helped them to be better writers in class. One learner summarized as follows:

Example 10.9

Having the opportunity to use wikis helped me organize and convey my thoughts more quickly during the in-class composition. I was able to gather ideas and come up with a plan, as if there were a mental map to guide my writing.

(Lee, 2010a, p. 266)

The benefits of online collaborative writing are not limited to wikis. Several studies have also examined writing on blogs: whether writing on blogs can promote collaborative writing (Lee, 2010b) and whether they can help learners to engage meaningfully in peer review (e.g., Dippold, 2009). Lee found that advanced language learners engaged in blogging were able to increase their writing fluency as well as their motivation to write, as a result of writing to a larger audience, findings that reflect the benefits of wiki writing reported previously. Lee also noted that her students frequently provided one another with feedback using comments functions on the blogs, a point echoed by Dippold in her study of advanced German learners. In an interesting pattern highlighting the benefits of peer interaction in writing, Lee pointed out that peer feedback on blogs tended to focus on content and prompt further discussion, whereas teacher feedback tended to focus on form and push learners to attend to accuracy. Online communication may promote this format for peer feedback because the peers recognize that they are part of a larger audience developing a discourse in any particular blog. This highlights the unique contribution of peer review to online writing, showcasing the need for both teacher and peer review to promote a balanced approach to language learning and writing development.

For online peer writing, collaborative writing and peer review are most often combined because online writing tools like wikis and blogs have built-in affordances that invite learners to comment, edit, and revise as they write. This interconnectedness of writing and review seems to be related to the nature of CMC itself. Writing online pushes learners to interact with an audience, so it's more natural to interact with a peer as well. CMC seems to present positive developments for peer collaborative writing, naturally and fluidly encouraging greater pair and group engagement throughout the writing process.

Peer Reading

The majority of this chapter has addressed issues related to peer interaction in L2 learning through writing. However, peer interaction also plays a role in L2 reading. Peer-assisted reading instruction, in which learners work in pairs to comprehend texts, changing roles as tutor and tutee as they move through prestructured tasks, has been used broadly in L1 contexts to build reading skills. For example, learners might read a text together. At the end of each paragraph, the learners assigned as tutor can stop the tutee and ask for a summary of the main point of the paragraph. This helps learners work together to recognize main ideas and supporting details from readings. Alternatively, the tutor may read a text, with the tutee reading it after, and then both learners work in partnership to retell the text. Each task is designed to help learners develop strategies to read more efficiently and to more accurately extract meaning from a text (e.g., Nation, 2009).

The theoretical foundation behind peer reading is similar to that discussed previously for collaborative writing—that discussing and comprehending a text with a peer can help a learner develop strategies and the ability to gradually self-regulate more of the reading process (regulation and other aspects of sociocultural theory are discussed in Chapters 2 and 3). A substantial body of research has examined the effect of peer-assisted reading in L1 contexts, particularly with remedial students who struggle with reading requirements of traditional classrooms. An early meta-analysis by Cohen, Kulik, and Kulik (1982) found that learners in peer-assisted programs generally showed significant gains in reading ability, as well as improvements in attitudes toward reading. A more recent meta-analysis by Rohrbeck, Ginsburg-Block, Fantuzzo, and Miller (2003) found a positive, but weak, effect indicating that the peer-assisted reading was more effective in promoting reading outcomes than other reading instructional methods for primary school students.

A small body of research has investigated peer reading in L2 contexts, generally finding positive effects of collaborative learning in L2 reading. Peer-assisted reading has been shown to increase reading comprehension (Ghaith, 2003). It may also promote positive attitudes toward L2 reading (Ushioda, 1996), likely because it provides learners with a social structure whereby members of a group can help each other to achieve their goals.

Although many ESL classrooms can have the effect of isolating learners from opportunities for authentic interaction, peer-assisted reading activities allow learners to explore a range of language functions used beyond the classroom, with the added benefit of practicing and modeling reading strategies. Liaw (1997) examined the way that learners engaged in reading e-books in groups in an ESL primary school classroom. Learners were encouraged to interact with each other as they worked through the books to try to help one another comprehend. Liaw analyzed the discourse functions that occurred as learners supported one another in understanding. She found that although several groups used commands as their primary discourse move, others used language functions that better invited interactivity and collaboration such as questioning, responding, expressing opinions, and expressing emotions in response to the text.

The impact of peer reading may be moderated by the ways learners engage in the interactions. For example, Murphy (2010) found that, although learners who engaged in peer online reading had higher levels of comprehension than individual readers, this effect was moderated by the quality of the feedback. Some learners were better at engaging in interactions that led to comprehension of the text. This relates to claims discussed in Chapter 6 and elsewhere in this book— that it is not merely interaction, but the way that interaction is fostered and tasks are designed, that allows for communication that promotes learning.

This implies, as we have mentioned in Chapters 5 and 6, that the effects of peer interaction are rarely straightforward or consistent even within one class. Hopewell (2011) came to similar conclusions in a study of peer interaction among 49 child learners in ESL classrooms who shared Spanish as a home language. In her study, learners engaged in peer-assisted reading using either both of their languages or only English. Learners who were allowed to use both languages recalled significantly more of the text than learners who could only use English. Hopewell also found that when learners were expressly allowed to use their L1, they did so more often, but also more strategically. For example, learners used their L1 to explain and explore novel English words. Hopewell noted that when Spanish was prohibited, the learners' attempts to clarify word meanings often led to more confusion. She concludes that restricting learners to the use of one language in peer-assisted reading may constrict their ability to apply a full range of strategies for understanding L2 texts and for scaffolding one another into comprehension. Similar to Murphy's study discussed previously, Hopewell's work suggests that teachers cannot assume that the benefits of peer reading will apply equally in any L2 setting. Rather, the complex interplay of learner, task, and setting factors need to be considered.

Although small in scope, the body of research on peer reading in L2 classrooms has overall put the practice in a positive light. Like research on peer writing, there are advantages both for developing reading skills and for developing communication skills. Learners are able to help each other understand better, assist with novel vocabulary, and model reading strategies. At the same time, reading together opens a new channel for communication, allowing learners to engage in spoken language practice and improve their communication skills during what would normally be individual course work.

Conclusion

Research on peer interaction on literacy tasks indicates overall that these contexts may be beneficial both for promoting language learning and for developing literacy skills. When working with a peer, learners tend to understand more of what they read and produce better writing. They have an outlet for focusing on language during this time as well, as the peer can help draw attention to issues of form and coscaffold attempts to produce or understand the L2 better. Beyond this, working with a peer allows for a communication channel that integrates practice on conversational skills with literacy practice. For researchers, these findings on peer engagement in literacy tasks should cast peer interaction in a new light. Many of the shortcomings cited in the oral peer interaction literature (too little focus on form, too much use of the L1, and overreliance on memory resources) are circumvented or minimized when learners engage in peer interactions not just to talk, but to read and write. This highlights too the danger of drawing conclusions for peer interaction as a whole, based on data collected in conversational tasks. Peer interaction is a context for learning, and modality is a factor that changes the nature of that learning. Although outcomes for peer interactions around literacy tasks vary according to task and participants (and grouping of participants), overall the general trends support the conclusion that peer reading and writing tasks may be a strong context for supporting language learning. Peer interaction is more than conversation; its impact is underestimated when the role of modality and medium of communication is not considered. Including reading and writing modalities in communicative tasks changes the nature of communication in ways that promote learning.

11
PEER INTERACTION AS A CONTEXT FOR ASSESSMENT

Introduction

Until recently, speaking assessment by means of public tests (commercially available tests administered by large testing institutions) has predominantly made use of an oral proficiency interview format in which an examiner/interviewer asks questions and converses with a test-taker on a variety of topics. This is the procedure, for example, for the Foreign Service Institute/Interagency Language Roundtable interview (Lowe, 1983) and the ACTFL/ETS Oral Proficiency Interview (American Council on the Teaching of Foreign Languages, 1986). Since the 1980s in the United Kingdom, with the introduction of communicatively oriented teaching methodology and the growing emphasis on ability to use language for more communicative purposes, testing formats have undergone changes. In particular, the use of peer interaction formats serve to establish a closer relationship between testing and teaching, in which pair and group work is a main feature (Saville & Hargreaves, 1999; Taylor, 2000). For the Certificate of Proficiency in English (CPE) and the First Certificate in English (FCE) by the Cambridge Examination Syndicate, the peer interaction format was first introduced as an alternative option to the traditional single test-taker format (Taylor, 2000). In the peer interaction format, two or more test-takers engage in a task together without the involvement of the examiner, except for initial prompting/soliciting to start the conversation at the outset. Certificates in the Use of English as a Foreign Language included a peer interaction format when the Royal Society of Arts Examinations Board developed the test in the early 1980s. Around the same time in Israel, a group oral format was introduced as a part of the matriculation examination (Shohamy, Reves, & Bejarano, 1986), although in this case, the group discussion task was not retained in the Israeli test battery because of logistical objections from school principals (Reves, 1982). Peer interaction formats have also been implemented in university language courses in Finland (Folland & Robertson, 1976), Italy (Lombardo, 1984), and in school settings in Zambia (Hildson, 1991).

Since the early 1990s, peer interaction formats have been increasingly adopted in public tests, such as the Cambridge English for Speakers of Other Languages, the Certificate in Advanced English (Taylor, 2000), the College English Test (CET) in China for non-English major students (He & Dai, 2006), and School Based Assessment in the Hong Kong Certificate of Education Examination (Gan, 2010; Gan, Davidson, & Hamp-Lyons, 2009; Luk, 2010). The peer interaction format was introduced as a standard format instead of an option for the Key English Test, revised Preliminary English Test, and FCE (Taylor, 2000). In addition, this form of assessment has been used for placement purposes (Bonk & Ockey, 2003; Van Moere, 2006) and as an exit test from academic preparation programs (e.g., Brooks, 2009).

With the increasing use of peer interaction in both public and classroom-based tests, a growing number of studies have investigated various aspects of this form of assessment. A peer interaction format is efficient in terms of the cost, time, and resources (Berry, 2007; Bonk & Ockey, 2003; Ockey, 2009; Van Moere, 2006). In this format, two or more test-takers can be assessed at one time (Folland & Robertson, 1976; Ockey, 2009), and interview training is not required (Ockey, 2009).

Recognition that assessment practices should align with the aims and tasks of classroom practice suggests that peer interaction should be an essential component of assessment. Peer interaction provides a format that is closer to the activities learners engage in in the classroom (Saville & Hargreaves, 1999; Taylor, 2000). This can lead to a positive effect in the classroom by encouraging learners to interact with one another, referred to as 'washback' in the literature (Saville & Hargreaves, 1999). Additionally, it encourages teachers to employ communicative activities such as small-group discussions to prepare students for the test (Hilsdon, 1991; Nevo & Shohamy, 1984; Ockey, 2009). More authentic to real-life situations, such formats provide a closer link between the test results and the target language use situation, the desired domain of score interpretation (Bachman & Palmer, 1996), which assists valid interpretation of the score (Ockey, 2009). Egyud and Glover (2001) report that secondary students prefer peer interaction formats over a one-to-one format.

Furthermore, Ross and Berwick (1992) and Young and Milanovic (1992) showed that examiner-candidate discourse could be highly asymmetrical in terms of features of dominance, contingency, and goal orientation. The fixed role relationship between examiner and candidate in a one-to-one test makes it difficult to escape this asymmetry. The paired format, on the other hand, provides the potential for various interaction patterns: candidate-examiner, candidate-candidate, and interaction between the three participants. Research has shown that the peer interaction format is more representative of normal conversation than an interview format and is less asymmetrical (Galaczi, 2008, van Lier, 1989). For this reason, peer interaction formats can avoid the criticisms related to power relationships (Davis, 2009) that are typically associated with an interview format. This means that a peer interaction format is likely to be less intimidating and test-takers are likely to more be relaxed (Folland & Robertson, 1976), which helps them take more control over the direction of the conversation (Fulcher, 1996; Shohamy et al., 1986). This provides test-takers with the opportunity to show their ability to participate in interaction other than as an "interviewee" responding to questions (Ducasse & Brown, 2009), allowing them to demonstrate a wider range of language functions and roles (Skehan, 2001) and also exhibit their conversational management skills (Galaczi, 2008).

This chapter provides an overview of peer interaction assessment, focusing on the strengths and limitations of this format in the assessment of speaking skills and follow-on effects for teaching and learning. In the literature, a number of different terms are used to refer to peer interaction formats of assessment, including "paired oral assessment" (Davis, 2009), "pair work in oral assessment" (Taylor & Wigglesworth, 2009), "learner–learner test" (Underhill, 1987), "student with student (interaction)" (Weir, 1993), "paired communication test" (Lombardo, 1984), "paired interview" (Brooks, 2009), and "peer-to-peer testing/assessment" (Ducasse & Brown, 2009) These terms describe assessment of two learners interacting together. "Group oral" and "group discussion" are often used when more than two test-takers are involved. In this chapter, these terms are used interchangeably to refer to peer interaction assessment formats.

Overview of Research on the Peer Interaction Format

Since the peer interaction format was first introduced as an alternative format to the oral proficiency interview, a large body of research has examined peer interaction in language assessment. The research orientation of earlier studies is similar to second language acquisition studies. That is, the research investigated the potential impact of the format (i.e., paired interview or interviewer-candidate), the number of test-takers in a group, and factors such as proficiency, dominance, gender, familiarity, or personality on language production and score.

On the whole, the results of the studies have shown that use of peer interaction formats has been positive in terms of test-taker feedback and quality of the language produced by test-takers, but the reliability of the test is not always as high as the traditional interviewer–test-taker format. Research findings indicate that individual and sociocultural factors potentially have a mediating effect on test-takers' performance. However, the relationship between these factors and test outcomes is complex, and it is hard to tease out which factor is most influential on the score.

More recent research concerns the nature of the discourse that learners produce in comparison to that of oral interview. For example, research has investigated the validity of the peer interaction assessments by conducting a fine-grained analysis of test discourse employing conversational analysis (CA) method (e.g., Gan, 2010; Nakatsuhara, 2011). Generally, researchers agree that the discourse test-takers produce in a paired interaction format test and an oral interview is different. Some current research focuses on interactional competence rather than individual performance observed in assessment of peer interaction. Like the second language acquisition studies introduced in previous chapters, many of these studies collect data from multiple sources (e.g., test score, discourse analysis of test-taker performance, analysis of verbal protocol of raters collected during assessment, and test-taker/teacher/rater perceptions of peer interaction format) and investigate the issues from multiple perspectives. In the following section, we will be looking at factors that may have mediating effects on paired interview assessment.

Interlocutor Variables

A common concern among teachers, test-takers, and test administrators about the peer interaction format is the extent to which learners are able to demonstrate their ability in the peer interaction format. In an assessment context, this issue becomes more serious than in the context of classroom teaching and learning as it has an impact on fairness and can be a threat to the reliability of the test. As mentioned previously, if learners' performance varies depending on the interlocutor, the test is not reliable, and test users are not able to make a valid inference about the test-taker's ability based on the test performance, as explored subsequently.

Interlocutor Type and Test Format

Taylor (2000) and Brooks (2009) both compared test discourse produced in peer interaction assessment, and the results are positive for employing this type of assessment in both formal and informal settings. Taylor (2000) analyzed the transcribed data drawn from the CPE test in both one-to-one and paired speaking formats in terms of quantity and quality of the test discourse. The results revealed that test-takers produced more language in the paired format than in the one-to-one format as shown in the substantial increase in the number of turns from paired test-takers. Similarly, Brooks (2009) compared the test scores and discourse drawn from eight test-takers' performance on two formats (interview with test administrator and paired interview) of a high-stake exit test from an Academic Preparation Program at a large Canadian university. The results show significant correlations between students' individual test scores and paired test scores, and also between the test scores of students interacting in pairs.

Paired formats elicit a wider range of features of interaction than individual formats (Taylor, 2000; Brooks, 2009). That is, although the discourse of the interview format revealed a more one-sided type speech pattern, in the paired interview, there were more conversation-like features in the peer interaction, including co-constructed speech, features of soliciting elaboration, overlapping speech, reference to partner's ideas, and paraphrasing. That is, more reciprocal, balanced interaction was observed. The two are contrasted in Examples 11.1 and 11.2.

Example 11.1

29   T: So do you, do you mostly use uh the Internet, do you use the email, to keep in touch with

30   A: Mm hm,

31   T: With your friends

32   A: Yeah

33   T: Back

34   A: Mm hm

35   T: Back home in Japan?

36   A: Yeah.

37   T: And do you, do you use these abbreviations and these short forms of words when you talk to your friends in Japan?

38   A: No never.

39   T: Never?

40   A: I've never done.

41   T: Really?

42   A: No.

(Brooks, 2009, p. 355)

In response to the interviewer's two questions (turns 29 and 35), the test-taker answered briefly without providing added content. In contrast, Example 11.2 shows more balanced interaction between the two test-takers in terms of amount of language produced and also features of conversation such as back-channeling (turns 63, 69, and 71), asking a question (turns 75 and 76), co-constructing (turns 65 and 66), and clarifying the previous statement (turn 74).

Example 11.2

62   J: And at the same time you can see news

63   S: Mm hm

64   J: When you want and you can educate yourself

65   S: And do many things together

66   J: Together chatting

67   S: Yeah chatting, email, everything yeah

68   J: Yeah it's much, much, they, it's offer more things?

69   S: Mm hm

70   J: Even uh to go to movies

71   S: Mm hm

72   J: You at the same time you will enjoy to eat uh popcorns *(J laughs; S laughs)* and to see people, like new people and

73   S: But you know it's dark

74   J: Huh?

75   S: How can you see people?

76   J: What do you think, before you get in *(J laughs; S laughs)*? Yeah, yeah . . .

(Brooks, 2009, p. 359)

Test-takers' views on the format of assessment varies. For example, Brooks (2009) reported that one of the test-takers in Example 11.1 expressed her strong preference for the interview format as the interviewer's control of the conversation made the test-taker feel at ease and more secure than when talking with another test-taker. However, another test-taker reported that the peer interaction format was more relaxing than the interview format, which was described as a one-sided conversation (similar to findings of classroom studies reported in Chapters 2 and 3).

Both Taylor (2000) and Brooks (2009) demonstrate clear differences in performance between interview and peer interaction formats. Their qualitative analysis, however, revealed a more complicated picture. The language use observed in the paired interview format was not always reflected in the description presented by the rating scale and, therefore, did not affect the assigned score either. This is one of the many complications of working with peer assessments. Other factors that may influence validity and reliability of these assessments include variety of English, interlocutor proficiency, personality, and interactional style. Sociocultural accounts of test-takers' performances indicate that these factors are inseparable from their agencies, histories, and personality.

Proficiency

One of the biggest concerns in implementing peer interaction formats in both formal and informal assessment is interlocutor proficiency—specifically, whether being paired with higher or lower proficiency interlocutor has any impact on an individual learner's performance. As discussed in Chapter 5, this is a well-researched issue in teaching and learning contexts, and research there reflects a complex picture. In language testing and assessment research, most studies compared test scores or features observed in the test-taker discourse when test-takers were paired with a learner of the same proficiency and when paired with test-takers of a different proficiency. For example, both Iwashita (1996) and Davis

(2009) found that interlocutor proficiency does not affect test scores as seriously as feared by teachers/test-takers, and test-takers' views on peer interaction formats are generally positive. However, these studies mainly focused on performance of individual test-takers but did not consider interaction styles between test-takers.

Nakatsuhara (2006) investigated the conversational styles of 12 dyads between matched-proficiency-level pairs and mixed-proficiency-level pairs, focusing on patterns of interactional contingency, goal orientation, and quantitative dominance. Although more topic ratifications (i.e., topic approval) were observed in the matched dyads than the mixed dyads, advanced test-takers tended to initiate topics more frequently than intermediate test-takers in mixed-proficiency dyads. As for the amount of talk, advanced test-takers tended to dominate the conversation in matched-proficiency dyads, but the difference was not significant. Qualitative analysis revealed some asymmetrical interactional characteristics in mixed-proficiency pairs, but as found in the quantitative analysis, there were more similarities than differences in conversational styles between mixed- and matched-proficiency pairs. In the mixed pairs, in particular, frequent accommodations were observed as shown in Example 11.3. In this example, the advanced test-taker M provides the word "extra" in turn 2, which assisted the intermediate learner N in continuing her speech. Other types of accommodation observed in the mixed pairs include inviting an intermediate test-taker to initiate a topic. Nakatsuhara (2006) argued that this accommodation contributed, not only by assisting the lower proficiency interlocutor in continuing the conversation, but also by enhancing the conversational and collaborative style of the interaction.

Example 11.3

1   N: but .hh think about holiday, expensive car, it's kind of (.), how's it? (.5)

2   N: [Not not

3   M: [Extra, extra [( )

4   N: [Yeh, extra things, yeh:: so: (.) should be lower ranked,
           eh:: compared to family or house. What do you think?

(Nakatsuhara, 2006, p. 18)

Consistent with previous research, Nakatsuhara also found that despite differences in interaction styles between matched- and mixed-proficiency dyads, test-taker proficiency was not a major concern to the reliability of the test. However, similar to Brooks (2009), Nakatsuhara (2006) notes that interactional features such as accommodation were not included in the rating scale. These studies recommend that such interactional features and strategies be included in the rating scale to better reflect this aspect of communicative competence observed in the peer interaction assessment. This exemplifies a growing trend of researchers to recognize the importance of considering the role of interactional competence in assessment.

Personality Trait

In everyday life, we carry out conversations with all sorts of different people and a variety of personalities. We hear words such as *extravert, introvert, talkative, assertive, dominant, shy,* and *quiet* to describe personality traits and conversation style. Some people talk a lot regardless of the situation, but others change their style dramatically according to the interlocutor and situation (e.g., Labov, 1966). Similar to proficiency, teachers and test administrators query the pairing of test-takers according to talkativeness or personality traits and the impact of these individual difference factors on test performance in pair/group oral assessment.

A body of research has investigated how personality traits may affect the quality and quantity of interaction and on test scores. In these studies, personality traits such as extraversion and introversion, talkativeness (dominance), shyness, and assertiveness were measured through the use of self-assessment scores and were coreferenced with test scores and test-taker discourse data. For example, Ockey (2009) compared assertive and nonassertive test-takers' scores for evidence of effects of the levels of assertiveness among their group members. Two hundred and twenty-five Japanese first-year university students majoring in English as a foreign language were assigned to a group based on their assertiveness, as measured by the Japanese version of the Revised NEO Personality Inventory (Shimanoka, Nakazato, Gondo, & Takayama, 2002) and familiarity with each other and their English proficiency, measured by Phone Pass Set-10 (Bernstein & Cheng, 2007). The results show that assertive test-takers received higher scores than expected when assessed with nonassertive test-takers and, conversely, lower scores than expected when assessed with assertive test-takers, but no difference was found for nonassertive test-takers regardless of the personality trait of their interlocutors. Ockey (2009) suggested that raters might have rewarded assertive test-takers' performance positively if they had taken a leading role in discussion for nonassertive test-takers but penalized assertive test-takers when they competed for a leadership role in discussion with another assertive test-taker. Alternatively, assertive test-takers might have changed their performance depending on their interlocutors' assertiveness. Consistent with work in second language acquisition (Dörnyei, 2005), this suggests a complex picture of the role of personality traits in performance. Like other factors such as interlocutor type, proficiency, tasks, personality have mediating effects on test-taker performances.

Nakatsuhara (2011), building on her 2006 study discussed previously, conducted in-depth analyses of co-constructed interaction in a group oral test to examine a possible relationship among four factors: the level of extraversion, as measured by the extraversion and neuroticism scales of the Japanese version of Eysenck Personality Questionnaire (Iwawaki, Eysenck, & Eysenck, 1980); group size; oral proficiency (test score); and conversation styles. The transcribed group oral data collected from 269 test-takers at an upper secondary high school in Japan were analyzed qualitatively and quantitatively. The analysis showed that the degree of extraversion level had more impact on discourse in groups of four than groups of three. This is illustrated in an excerpt from an interaction involving three test-takers with matched-proficiency level, but unmatched personality traits. A produced 60% of the whole interaction of the group, and B and C shared an equal amount for the remaining 40% (i.e., 20% each). What was notable in this excerpt is that regardless of the different extraversion levels, the three test-takers helped each other to accomplish the task. For example, although C, whose extraversion score was twice as high as his partners, makes several attempts to contribute to the conversation, he doesn't manage to provide more than his agreement; it is B who initiates the topic, and A who assists most (line 4, 14, and 16).

Example 11.4

1→B: I think en- enthusiasm for teaching is most important point, because (3.0)

2   uh:: (5.0)

3→C: Uh: I agree.

4   A: Why?

5→C: uh:::: I think enthusiasm is (.) uh::::: (1.0) u(h)h:: huh huh

6→B: *Hai* ((raising a hand)) [Huh

7   A: [Hah hah hah

8   C: [Hah huh huh

9   C: Uh

10   B: Teacher's enthusiasm makes [us our enthusia(h)sm,

11   C: [Uh uh

12   B: so (.5) we study (1.0) very (1.5)

13→C: So ah:[:

14→A: [We can study more work.

15   C: Uh:::

16   A: I think I agree with enthusiasm for teaching. I think enthu- enthusiasm f

17   for teaching is need (.) necessary, because if I (.) I: (.) I don't (.5) if I can't

18   solve the problem, uh: I want to teach (.5) uh I want to: .hh be taught

19   so- taught (.) by him.

(Nakatsuhara, 2011, pp. 494–495)

Although the extraversion level did not seem to matter to the group of three as shown in Example 11.4, Example 11.5 illustrates that in groups of four the test-takers with a lower extraversion level tend to avoid interaction. In this example, test-takers H and I have a much higher extraversion level than test-takers

G and J. The amount of talk the two extraverts produced together was more than 60% of the whole interaction. In contrast, G's and J's contributions totaled 15% and 20% of the total talk, respectively. Nakatsuhara (2011) notes of J's behavior that she kept her head down, focused on a prompt card, and gave a short response in line 3 despite being asked directly for her opinion. After the second attempt, J finally mentioned her preference, but J's statement in line 9 did not make sense. Introverts' avoidance in participation was frequently observed in groups of four as quiet test-takers can avoid talking more easily in a larger group.

Example 11.5

1   H: What do you think? *(making deliberate eye contact with J)*

2   G: Huh huh uh

3→J: Me too.

4   I: huh huh huh

5→H: Camera C?

6→J: huh huh And camera B is good for class too, because (.) uh:: this camera,

7   this camera has auto-focus system and (.) flash.

8   I: Uh huh huh uh

9   J: Uh uh: Each us, uh? (.5) each each of students, each of students surface
         is clea(h)r.

(Nakatsuhara, 2011, p. 497)

In other studies of this issue, research findings are mixed: Both extraverts and introverts scored higher when their interlocutors were more extraverted than introverted (Berry, 2007); talkative test-takers tended to produce more speech (Van Moere & Kobayashi, 2003); and shyness was a significant predictor for the test score (Bonk & Van Moere, 2004). These different findings are partly due to the range of personality trait batteries used in different studies, as well as various contextual factors, including group size and the stake of the test. If a test is a high-stakes test, regardless of the personality trait, test-takers may try hard to display their best performance, but if the test has a lower impact, less talkative students may avoid interaction and remain silent. It seems that there is no conclusive answer on how to deal with effects of personality traits on test-taker performance in peer interaction assessment, but as suggested previously, test administrators and raters need to be mindful of this issue in test administration and ratings.

Validity

As explained in the beginning of this chapter, the introduction of a peer interaction format in both high-stakes and non-high-stakes tests has been motivated partly by the realization of the asymmetrical nature of the oral-proficiency interview format.

It is assumed that more features of normal conversation (i.e., symmetric nature of interaction) can be observed in peer interaction formats than in interview formats, and peer interaction formats can provide test-takers with a better opportunity to display their ability to use language for the purpose of communication in a target language domain (Bachman & Palmer, 1996). A question is whether a variety of peer interaction format tasks are able to elicit test-takers' performance to reflect their communicative language ability. The validity of peer interaction assessment has been investigated from two different angles through analysis of (a) test-taker discourse and their perceptions of the test format, and (b) raters and their focus in their assessment of test-taker performance.

Test-Taker Discourse

An increasing number of studies have used in-depth analysis of test discourse to examine characteristics of interaction (i.e., discourse strategy, topic management, and interaction style) and to identify conversational features (e.g., topic sequence, topic organization, and range of speech function including suggestions, agreement/disagreement, challenging, co-construction, and patterns of interaction) in order to examine the validity of peer interaction formats of assessment. In general, research shows that these features vary according to test-takers' proficiency and task type (e.g., Galaczi, 2008; Gan, 2010; Gan et al., 2009; He & Dai, 2006; Luk, 2010). Research also shows that test-takers' perceptions of this type of assessment format have raised concerns about the validity of pair oral assessment.

He and Dai (2006) examined the type and degree of interaction test-takers engaged in during task performance on CET–Spoken English Test group discussion. The analysis showed that the most frequently elicited interactional feature is "(Dis) agreeing" (49.5%), followed by "Asking for opinions or information" (24.0%). A relatively low percentage of the remaining six features (i.e., "Challenging," "Supporting," "Modifying," "Persuading," "Developing," and "Negotiating meaning") were reported even if test-takers were required to argue with each other or to ask for clarification. The questionnaire survey revealed that although more than half of the test-takers did not report nervousness or difficulty with the group format, more than 60% of the test-takers regarded examiners as the target audience and reported that they did not pay attention to other learners or quality of discussion by asking for clarification or challenging others.

Luk (2010) has found similar results in her investigation of test-taker discourse and perceptions of peer test formats. Using a CA approach, Luk (2010) examined how the students structured their talk through employing or unconsciously displaying a variety of discourse strategies in analyzing performance in peer group interactions for the school-based assessment (SBA) in Hong Kong. Three recurrent themes emerged from the analysis of the discourse: task management frame (engagement in procedural/routine matters), content delivery (engagement in prompt-oriented presentation), and response frame (engagement in responding to peers). The findings also show that the group discussion was conducted in a highly predictable manner, going through routines such as opening, closing, and orderly turn-taking practices as shown in Example 11.6. In the example, the discussion started by Ba's invitation for others' opinions about the topic, and this was followed by C's response (turn 2) and A's comment (turn 3).

Example 11.6

1 Ba: Hey, if we had a chance to choose a character from our book to be our best friend, which one would you choose? Why?

<10 seconds silent> For me, I would choose the character Judy in the book Daddy Long Leg. Because she is very funny and optimistic. If I am the- she is my best friend, she will make me laugh. And when I'm sad, she will comfort me. Also, she always writes letter to Mr Smith, I think she has a good English language. Therefore, she can teach me many vocabularies and I can improve my English.

<Looks at student C> What do you think?

2 C: Oh, I have the same- I read the same book with you. Um, also I think (Judy) is a friend- is friend, she will express her idea directly. Not like people nowadays, they are always fake, in order to get some benefits. Also, (Judy) like playing basketball. Just like me, I have the same interest with her. We can discuss the same topic.

3 A: Yes, I really like this kind of girl.

4 D: Yes, you can play (the volleyball) also. *<Student A nods>*

5 C: What do you think, Janet?

(Luk, 2010, p. 34, format slightly adapted)

Other notable features observed in the test-taker performances include lengthy speech in the beginning of the assessments. When the test-takers expressed their opinion about the topic in an earlier part of the discussion, their turns were generally long and had been prepared prior to the assessment, as found in He and Dai (2006). Also, even though the test-takers collectively followed the conversation routine in terms of turn taking, co-constructing, and opening/closing, they rarely engaged in negotiation for meaning, possibly for face-saving reasons (similar avoidance of peer correction was described in Chapter 3). On the whole, test-takers tried to display their best performance as effective interlocutors to receive high scores. They were not focusing on being an effective communicator in genuine communication. Luk's interview data, seen in Example 11.7, demonstrate that learners were aware of these behaviors.

Example 11.7

> I heard that some classmates after knowing whom they were going to do the group interaction with would get together to discuss who should start, who should follow up, and who should give conclusion, etc. This really makes it look like acting. — Nellie

> Not just SBA, but any other public exams that involve having to discuss with others look like acting. Before I learnt discussion skills in Form 3, I wouldn't be so polite as to say "sorry" or "I am sorry that" when I ban other's views. Now we have to say "sorry" for exams, but in real life, we won't act like this. I feel rather awkward to be over-polite to other participants in the SBA talk as they are all my friends. — Eva

> The way we spoke was totally unnatural when doing SBA. For example, people would say "I agree with you" in a listless manner. It was obvious that people just used this sentence to help themselves start their talk; it was used to fill up the time gap. — Ally

(Luk, 2010, p. 44)

Questionnaire results revealed that the test-takers were highly positive about the group discussion task, considering it a good opportunity to practice English; however, strong negative attitudes toward the group task were expressed in interviews. Luk reported that the test-takers articulated a strong desire to write out a speech for recitation and to deliver their prepared speech as early as possible to reduce anxiety.

The two studies discussed previously show test-takers' interpretation of the discussion task as an "assessment" event rather than communicative interaction with other members. According to He and Dai (2006), the low frequency of interactional features is partly due to test-takers' lack of confidence in their ability to handle the discussion task as communicative interaction and partly due to a lack of interest.

Test-takers in both He and Dai's (2006) and Luk's (2010) studies engaged in long routinized talk (possibly a prepared talk) in the group discussion assessment, as shown in Example 11.6. The test-takers in Luk's study (2010) were also very much aware of strategies they were expected to use to carry out conversation and made a collective effort to ensure an opportunity for everyone to express their opinion as shown subsequently. In Example 11.8, the conversation took place after all members expressed their reasons for choosing to live with Emma. In line 11, C continued Daisy's statement in line 10. This was followed by A's agreement and her comment on Daisy in line 12. Each member adds extra information or makes evaluative comments as in lines 12 and 15. Turns are nicely distributed between each member of the group. Luk (2010) comments that although the content of the conversation is trivial, "the test-takers were able to maintain the impression of interactive exchanges to fill up the remaining talk time" (p. 42).

Example 11.8

10 Daisy: And also can learn the piano ???

11 C: ??? for her to teach you.

12 A: I agree with you. <laughter> Daisy, I think the character you choose have a similar to you. You are also a good listener.

13 Daisy: Thank you. <laughter>

14 B: I really want to make a friend with all of your best friends you suggested.

15 C: I think all of our ideas are good and is really- <laughter>

16 A: Also, Emma- Emma love- do not- is afraid of being bored. I also. So we can play together to have fun. And maybe she can bring me to some ball and to learning dancing.

17 C: To make some new friends, such as boyfriends. <laughter from all>

18 A: Do you want to come with me?

19 B/C: Oh, sure! <laughter from all>

(Luk, 2010, p. 41, format slightly adapted)

Luk (2010) attributes this test-takers' strategy of faithful observance to conversational routines to their lack of opportunities to interact with friends in English outside the English classrooms. Even with good understanding and training in interactional features of English conversation, without much experience in the target language use domain, their attempts to use interactional strategies remain rather artificial, as reflected in Examples 11.6 and 11.8. Luk (2010) argues that given the monolingual environment and lack of use of English outside the classroom, it may not be realistic to expect all students to use interactional strategies typical of the target language domain. This demonstrates a limitation for use of peer interaction in foreign language settings even where peer interaction format assessments have established a closer relationship between testing and teaching,

Peer interaction formats have been implemented widely, based on the assumption that this format would provide more opportunities to enable test-takers to display their skills in conversation-like interaction, but as He and Dai (2006) commented, conversational features do not appear in speaking tests just because test-takers engage in conversation with a partner with equal social power (p. 393). The two studies discussed previously show that neither test-takers nor assessors can ignore differences between interacting for performance and interacting for genuine communication purposes, and this needs to be addressed in both teaching and test preparation.

Rater Orientation

One of the issues in ensuring reliable and valid assessment practice in peer interaction format is that of ratings and rating criteria. In performance assessment such as oral interaction in peer interviews, test-takers' performance is determined through ratings based on descriptions of their performance at each level in the criteria. In other words, "raters and rating are in a crucial mediating position between output and outcomes" (Ducasse & Brown, 2009, p. 422). Therefore, the validity of the test rests on the criteria. As Brown (2005) explains, "In any assessment involving judgment it is the criteria by which the performance is judged which define the construct" (p. 26).

A few studies have examined interactional features of performance ratings by analyzing verbal protocols collected during rater assessment of peer interaction test performances. May (2009) found that the key features of the interaction as perceived by 12 native speaker raters were the way test-takers achieved the task by collaborating, cooperating, and assisting each other rather than through their individual competence. Similarly Ducasse and Brown (2009) identified three main features of interaction: nonverbal interpersonal communication (use of body language and gaze), interactive listening (the test-takers' manner of displaying attention or engagement), and interactional management (the management of the topics and turns). Interpreting the findings, both May (2009) and Ducasse and Brown (2009) pointed out that the interaction aspect of performance in general was not always described in the rating scales used in the studies, and they suggest a scale that reflects the complexities of interactional competence in a paired speaking test in order to assess test-takers' interactional competence.

The two studies discussed previously suggest that what draws raters' attention during assessment of peer interaction test performance is very different from what is being assessed in oral proficiency interviews. These findings clearly not only indicate different characteristics observed in the peer interaction format compared to oral proficiency interviews, but also provide information about the construct of interaction and interactional competence.

Conclusion

This chapter provides an overview of the widely implemented practice of peer assessment in both public and nonpublic tests. Research in this area has mainly concerned potential mediating effects of interlocutor variables on test-taker performance and issues surrounding validity of peer interaction format assessment. As found in peer interaction research reported on in earlier chapters, there are various ways in which interlocutor variables interact and influence characteristics of test-takers' performance, including interaction style and degree of engagement in conversation. However, performance variation does not appear to have a serious impact on test scores. This is partly because interactional features within test-taker discourse and raters' observance of these in the test are not well incorporated in rating scales.

Despite positive feedback from students, teachers, and test users, as well as positive washback, there are a number of challenges for use of peer interaction formats. One involves test-taker perceptions of the purpose of such assessment.

When they consider this to be performance-focused, rather than for genuine conversation, this can lead to rehearsed speech and precrafted turn taking between students. This has implications for the validity of the test as a measure of spontaneous interactional competence. Another challenge concerns learners' limited opportunities to develop interactional competence in foreign language settings. This in turn results in inauthentic styles of interaction. The third and final challenge is to operationalize interactional competence in order to incorporate it in rating scales.

These challenges present different issues that teachers and test developers face in their use of peer interaction in the language classroom and in assessment. Peer interaction format assessments were introduced to establish a closer link between teaching and testing practices in communicative oriented classrooms. This has been achieved to a certain extent considering the wide implementation, positive perceptions, and washback of the practice in classrooms. Factors discussed earlier in this book that have been shown to have mediating effects on the nature of peer interaction such as tasks, interlocutor proficiency, and social relationships in the classroom certainly also influence peer language assessment practices. Because of the complex interplay of factors in peer interaction, far better descriptions of what it means to be interactionally competent in this context are needed in order to improve the validity of peer assessment ratings. As in earlier chapters, we have seen that simply treating the peer interaction as a one-dimensional context may lead us to gloss over the variety of factors that need to be understood about peer interaction. Peer interaction assessment is an example of how ignoring this complexity can have consequences for learners even beyond the classroom.

12

THE CONTRIBUTION OF PEER INTERACTION

In this book, we have brought together research on peer interaction that encompasses a wide range of contexts, varying in setting, participants, purpose, and mode of interaction. We argue that overall this research presents a positive picture. Peers do provide an important context for second language (L2) learning and play a unique and significant role in the process. However, the extent to which this promise is fulfilled varies greatly. As noted in first language (L1) research, peer interaction cannot be assumed always to be beneficial or to have blanket effects (De Lisi & Golbeck, 1999). A myriad of factors mediate the outcomes of peer interaction for L2 learning. This final chapter provides an overview of the potential of peer interaction for L2 learning in different settings. In particular, we highlight three central aspects of peer interaction. The first concerns the complementary nature of peer and teacher-learner interaction. This is something we allude to in other chapters but treat in detail here, as the primary focus of this chapter. Second, there are strengths and limitations to the contribution of peers. We reflect on which aspects of learning are best served by peer interaction and those unlikely to be fostered by peer interaction. Third, we highlight a phenomenon that appears in almost every chapter of the book: *moderation*, that is, the mediating effects of factors such as setting, coparticipation, task, and learner characteristics. In each section, we also discuss implications for pedagogy and future research.

Peer Interaction in Context: Complementary Roles of Teacher and Peer

The great strength of peer interaction lies in its complementarity to teacher-learner interaction. Before we can evaluate the strengths and limitations of peer L2 learners in the learning process, we must first highlight the relevance of the classroom context itself to the potential role that peers may play. This book has necessarily focused uniquely on interaction between L2 learners in classrooms. Yet this somewhat limits our ability to look at one of its true advantages: complementarity with what the teacher does. This is realized in a number of ways: One of these is through the dual roles of the teacher as language expert and the peer as fellow learner, with whom to explore, test, and develop language skills. To explore the symbiotic relationship between these two roles, we will, in the spirit of an epilogue, consider data of peer interaction that spans the wider context of the teaching unit as a whole.

The distinctive roles played by peers and by the teacher work in tandem over time and across contexts, each contributing in the cumulative process of learning, as Batstone and Philp (2013) note. To illustrate this, we draw from a classroom data set collected by Cao (2009) among 11 international students enrolled in a pretertiary English for Academic Purposes (EAP) course. Over several weeks of lessons, the students worked on a project related to health issues, with a central task of carrying out a survey. Over the lessons, students were required to work collaboratively to research an area of interest related to health, produce a survey questionnaire (based on a model text), conduct the survey, analyze the results, and present the results in class. Through the subsequent examples, we trace the recurrence of one form in one of the lessons and see ways in which two learners working together cumulatively gather input and start to manipulate this form in more targetlike ways. What we want to highlight here is the incomplete nature of peer interaction alone—the contribution of the peer interaction is only fully realized in the light of how it is supported by the teacher-learner interaction.

Teachers' Roles in Supporting Peer Interaction

Although not participating directly in peer interaction, the teacher plays a number of crucial roles. One of these roles is in framing the task and providing key language input. For example, in this class, during whole class interaction, the teacher draws the students' attention to the format and language of a model questionnaire: The students are introduced to the language of this genre as a model for writing their own surveys. The students are incidentally exposed repeatedly to the phrases "have you had" and "have you ever (+ verb)" through the model questionnaire (e.g., "have you had a drink containing alcohol in the last year?"), and by the teacher (T), as seen in Example 12.1.

Example 12.1

619 T: Yeah if you ask the question *have you ever decided* it means *have you ever made* a decision, I'm going to quit smoking, OK, but it doesn't mean you did quit smoking it just means one day you woke up and thought I might quit smoking, so you have to think carefully about the grammar

of your question, *have you ever lived* in smoking environment, what does that mean?

(Cao, 2009, unpublished raw data)

The teacher provides valuable input to the students and through a series of questions draws their attention to the meaning of certain phrases that they will need to use later in their own survey writing.

Another role of the teacher is as an ever-present resource, even when group work is the dominant pattern of interaction. As students collaborate to decide on the topic of their survey, and construct the questionnaire together, the teacher monitors their progress. During group interaction, we see the complementary ways that peers and the teacher contribute to the learning process. In Example 12.2, we see the teacher skillfully scaffold the learners' use of the target language. At one point, the teacher momentarily assists in response to a question from one student concerning the phrase "have you ever." The student perfects her use of the phrase, heavily supported by the teacher through completion (line 966), a recast (line 968), explicit correction and elicitation (lines 970, 971), and confirmation (line 973).

Example 12.2

963   S: but can I ask if I want to say did you did you have ever (.) tried or

964   T: Have you ever   ← recast

965   S: Have you ever tried or

966   T: plastic surgery   ← completion

967   S: Yeah

968   T: Have you had   ← recast

969   S: Had OK yeah yeah thank you, have you ever had any any plastic surgeries before OK

970   T: You don't need before so   ← explicit correction

971   T: What's the question have you   ← elicitation

972   S: Have you ever had any plastic surgery

973   T: Have you ever had any plastic surgery   ← confirmation

974   S: That's it OK

(Cao, 2009, unpublished raw data, annotations added)

The Learners' Roles: Exploring, Experimenting, and Questioning

In Chapters 2, 6, 9, and 10, we have emphasized the contribution of peer work as a space for exploring and experimenting with the target language. Left to their own resources, learners inevitably run into difficulties. After the teacher's corrective feedback, the two learners seek to extend the use of the phrase "have you had" but struggle to frame time as a dimension in the question "how many times." One student introduces the use of "did you do," a non-targetlike solution. They puzzle over this for some time, and further verbs are tried out—"did you have" and "have you gone." Thus, peer interaction plays a crucial role in this experimental phase of the learning process, as they move from formulaic language to incorporation within their own interlanguage. It is with peers that learners have the opportunity to try out language on their own, to truly test out the limits of their understanding and ability to use the language gleaned from the teacher's input. It is through this unmonitored interaction with one another that they can puzzle through the language, make a mess, and notice form-meaning connections as well as gaps in their knowledge. Although language difficulty may be only partially or incorrectly resolved during such peer interaction, this experimentation with language production is a step toward their eventual more targetlike use of this form and, crucially, sets the learners up to notice the solution when later presented in teacher-learner interaction.

Complementarity in Roles

This reflects the complementary roles played by peers and teacher. As seen in some oral collaborative tasks, and particularly in collaborative written tasks (see Chapters 2, 9, and 10), it is while working out how to say something that learners may notice a problem and struggle to solve it. It is in this context that the teacher's input is of most obvious use in Example 12.3 (114 turns after Example 12.2). Here, it is after the students negotiate for some time (18 turns) that they enlist the help of the teacher. She recasts with "how many times have you had" and provides further metalinguistic feedback. This expands the learners' understanding of the meaning and use of this grammatical form. What is important for us to notice here is that it is *because* of the peers' interaction with one another that they are now deeply engaged in the problem and its solution; it is trying out the language themselves that leads them to seek help. Earlier struggles in peer interaction lead the two students to actually come to focus on this form and to seek to resolve the problem. Once again, the teacher complements the learning cycle by providing the missing knowledge at the time that they need it—after they appear to have reached the limits of their own resources (lines 21 and 22).

Example 12.3

1088   S: Have you done have you done?

1089   J: Have you gone I think

1090   S: Gone

1091   J: It's not it's not done because done is the one who the doctor done the surgery but you gone

1092   S: Gone gone?

1093   J: You can ask [the teacher]

1094   S: [Teacher], a question, it's here and here, it will be like how many how many times did you do or have you gone

1095   J: How many times have you gone

1096   T: How many times have you had

1097   S: Have you OK

1098   T: Have you had plastic surgery

1099   S: At which age have you had also

1100   T: Yes, have you had present perfect 'cos we're talking about in their lifetime

It is important to remember that peer interaction does not operate in isolation, but in the context of other classroom experiences. In Chapters 3, 5, and 10, we reported teachers' and learners' concerns of insufficient or inappropriate feedback in peer interaction and provided examples. Although alarming if this is the only picture, it is just one side of the story—the teacher also provides feedback and input, which is likely to be of most benefit when coupled with learners' recognition of need as a result of earlier struggles.

Following on from Example 12.3, as the teacher leaves their conversation, J murmurs "which age you had"—a cautionary tale lest we think all is resolved—clearly the students are still evolving in their understanding and interlanguage use of this form and will continue to experiment with it. In fact, a week later, after completing the survey and collecting their sample, the students presented the results in class, and student S summed up by saying "the majority of them didn't had any um plastic surgeries."

What these data reflect is, first, the complementary nature of peer and teacher-learner interaction and, second, the cumulative nature of learning. Through the many different contexts of classroom interaction (peer and teacher-led), students are exposed to relevant input and given multiple opportunities to try out new language and manipulate it within different contexts or for slightly different shifts in meaning. The benefit of peer interaction arises partly as a function of how it is situated within the variety of classroom interactions.

Interactions Across Time, Speaker, Setting, and Modality

Tied to this observation of cumulative learning across varied settings, we have seen, too, through the chapters of this book that peer interaction itself provides different and complementary kinds of learning opportunities according to mode, participant, and purpose (e.g., face-to-face vs. computer-mediated conversation; oral vs. written mediums). This is reflected in a study of an EAP class in Canada for Japanese study abroad students. Duff and Kobayashi (2010) similarly report the temporal and spatial nature of teaching and learning: It occurs across time, and between different con-stellations of speakers, settings, and modality. They describe L2-learning processes in an EAP classroom among Japanese learners of English in Canada as a process of socialization into particular linguistic and cultural practices, and highlight the "itera-tive, longitudinal nature of their language socialization " (p. 91).

The context of the classroom and the teacher in the classroom are both crucial components. The limitations of peer interaction are complemented by the strengths of the teacher-learner interaction and vice versa, as we saw in Chapters 3, 5, and 6. We presented here just one way in which peer interaction is supported by teacher interaction, but of course, there are many other ways—for example, through selection and explanation of appropriate tasks, framing or advance organizers (Samuda & Bygate, 2009), scaffolding (Gibbons, 2002; Duff & Kobayashi, 2010), procedural support and orientation to form (Toth, 2008), precasting and corrective feedback during and after peer interaction (Ellis, 2003), and fostering of effective collaboration (Dörnyei & Murpehy, 2003). In Ohta's (2001) observational study of learners in their first two years of learning Japanese, for example, she concludes that peer interactive tasks were more effective when the teacher provided support where needed.

The Source of Complementarity

Complementarity arises because of the relationships between participants and the roles they play within the particular cultural context of any classroom. This is evi-dent in many reflections on the nature of classroom discourse. Allwright (1998b, p. 125), for example, sees "the key contextual factor" in classroom language learn-ing as "co-presence," that is, the recognition that "classroom language learning and teaching have to take place in the presence of others," and suggests that social pro-cesses impact on learning. The types of interactions that occur between teacher and student(s) will differ from peer interaction, in part because of the asymmetry between participants. Regarding teacher-learner interaction, Allwright (1998b, p. 125) suggests that "the duties and rights of teachers and taught are different."

Teacher-led participatory interaction is typically characterized by centrally managed contributions by students, and this management is generally understood as fitting. As seen in Example 12.4 from a reception class for 6- to 7-year-old new arrivals, students can be "put on the spot" (first line) or stretched in the accuracy of their L2 production (last line).

Example 12.4

T: Are there any questions about his news? Alright. Anna will I get a question from you?

S: Why you go to shopping?

S2: Because my Dad said to go and to to play the chart (. . .)

T: Good now one question. Is there a question?

S: Why you have fitness in your house?

S2: Because so I can be strong feet and strong hands

T: So she can have a strong body

(Mackey, Oliver, & Leeman, 2003, unpublished raw data)

Teacher-learner interaction always holds the possibility that appropriate corrective feedback or assistance is at hand if required. There is a sense that at least one person in the room knows what they are doing, and those who don't can confidently rely on their support. In fact, Allwright (1998b, p. 145) characterizes teachers as those "expected to know what learners are expected not to know." In contrast, peer interaction is characterized by internally managed participation—that is, it is managed by the group members, and this management is contestable. As we discussed in Chapters 2 and 9, this allows for greater experimentation and debate on form, meaning, and use of language.

Peer interaction itself will differ widely in potential opportunities for learning based on the relationships and interactional patterns between the participants. Breen (1985) similarly argues: "How and why learners do what they do will be strongly influenced by their situation, who they are with, and by their perceptions of both" (p. 138). As a number of studies suggest, collaboration between peers may be strongly associated with personality combinations, perceptions of self and other, past histories, and experiences (Kim & McDonough, 2008; Storch, 2002; Watanabe & Swain, 2008). This is evident from discussions of the social dimension to peer interaction, noted in Chapters 5, 6, 7, and 11. Research undertaken from ecological (van Lier, 2000), sociocognitive (Batstone, 2008), sociocultural (Gánem-Guitérrez, 2013), and socialization (Duff & Kobayahsi, 2010) perspectives is well placed to explore the potential of peer interaction in this regard. Such theories that emphasize the dynamic and complex nature of language use and development may be particularly conducive to exploring the intricate nature of peer interaction and the ways it may contribute to, or even inhibit, learning.

Implications for Research and Pedagogy

Complementarity has clear implications for research on instructional L2 learning. It is rare to find research that reflects the interdependent nature of teacher-learner and peer interaction over time. This requires careful longitudinal work that traces the emergent and social nature of learning in language classrooms and more comprehensive data sets that include both teacher-led and peer interaction over many lessons. However, such research can provide useful insights into the ways in which peer interaction contributes to the learning process in classrooms.

A symbiotic view of peer and teacher-learner interaction also has implications for language pedagogy. It suggests that the usefulness of any peer interaction should not be evaluated in *comparison* to teacher-learner interaction as the goals and outcomes are quite different. Nor should it be evaluated purely on the basis of what occurs within any one particular interaction. As we argue above, it is evident that language learning is a process that occurs over time, across related interactions, and among different participants in diverse settings (e.g., whole class, small groups, individual to individual, in different modes, face-to-face, or digitally mediated). These interactions each contribute to the learning trajectories of those in the class, sometimes in complementary ways and at other times in conflicting ways (e.g., Batstone & Philp, 2013; Breen, 1985). Each is colored by previous interactions and experiences, and by what occurs subsequently, not only in peer interaction but also during teacher–small group interaction and teacher-class interaction. This is discussed further in the next section in which we evaluate the particular strengths and limitations of peer interaction.

Scope of Peer Interaction: Strengths and Limitations

A Limited Context for Skilled Feedback and Targetlike Input

An important seam running through this book relates to the finding, in so many different facets of the language-learning process, that some aspects are better served by teacher-led interaction, whereas others are the strength of peer interaction. Language professionals, students, and L2 acquisition researchers alike express concerns over peer interaction in the classroom, including peer assessment, and these apprehensions should not be minimized. They reflect the potential limitations of peer work. This is particularly so of foreign language settings where learners have limited access to target language input. These concerns predominantly relate to the unreliable nature of peers as a context for targetlike input and corrective feedback, or for focusing on grammatical forms in language, in comparison to teacher-learner interaction. This is illustrated subsequently in teachers' (Example 12.5) and learners' (Example 12.6) reports of misgivings about pair and group work.

Example 12.5

Veronica: You do a presentation, you do this inductive grammar stuff, then you give a pair activity and you listen to them and they're using it completely incorrectly.

Suphot: [The learners] weren't really getting into the game or the pair work the way it was really set up, [they] just talk on their own agendas.

(McDonough, 2004, p. 210)

Example 12.6

Piyaporn: [Not helpful because] many of my classmates know very little English.

Wanwisa: Doesn't help much because sometimes they use the wrong grammar.

(McDonough, 2004, p. 221)

As discussed in Chapter 3, research demonstrates that, although peer corrective feedback is possible, consistent targetlike feedback and models of L2 use are clearly the province of the teacher. The limitation of learner input in comparison to teacher input is typically reflected in a lack of confidence in error identification and correction and greater attention to face saving (Philp, Walter, & Basturkmen, 2010). Further, lacking experience, peers are unlikely to be able to provide scaffolding with the skill of a trained teacher. Learner input is characterized by inconsistencies, interlanguage forms, infrequent feedback, and a reduced ability to provide synonyms or to paraphrase or reformulate meanings (e.g., Pica, Lincoln-Porter, Paninos, & Linnell, 1996). It is simply not as rich a source of target language input.

Another concern relates to reticence to use the target language. Code switching is typical in contexts with a shared L1, particularly among lower proficiency learners (Tognini, Philp, & Oliver, 2010), both due to limited L2 competence and peer pressure (Cao, 2009; Tarone & Swain, 1995). In both foreign language and L2 contexts, L2 peers may work in ways that hinder progress, and this includes maintaining L1 use in ways that reduce rather than support opportunities for target language input and use. Having said that, as noted in Chapter 5, it is important to also recognize that L1 use can promote L2 learning (e.g., Antón & DiCamilla, 1998; Swain & Lapkin, 1998).

Task-based interaction among peers can also be socially problematic. For example, peers can act as gatekeepers and generally exclude those who are "different" (Miller, 2003). In Chapters 1 and 6, we noted the potential occurrence of dysfunctional groups, exclusion, and unequal participation, particularly among younger age groups. This suggests the importance of careful management by the teacher, discussed subsequently.

Strengths of Peers: Equivalence and "Having a Go"

Although acknowledging the limitations of peers as partners in the language-learning process, it is just as important to recognize the strengths of peer interactions and to capitalize on these for learning purposes. In contrast to teacher-fronted interaction, peer interaction is a much more egalitarian context for practice and is generally felt to be less stressful than teacher-led interaction, precisely because it will not be carefully monitored: There is no expert present, and correction, if given, can be a matter for debate. The same is true of peer interaction assessment, as seen in Chapter 11. As we discussed in Chapter 6, the social nature of peer interaction strongly influences the potential contribution of peers to learning: Peers provide a "safe" space to try out language, to take risks, to have fun with language, and to experiment and make mistakes without worrying about "being right." These are all important for interlanguage development when they encourage a degree of spontaneity and learner-generated language use (Philp & Tognini, 2010). This potential is reflected in the following statements from high school learners of French and Italian as a foreign language during focus groups.

Example 12.7

S1:   You're a lot more confident [when working with friends]. (*Assent from others in background.*) Like, if you can make a mistake and you . . .

S2:   . . . like you help each other out.

S1:   . . . the teacher knows everything. So if you make a mistake, you feel stupid, but your friends, they understand the same words as you.

(Tognini, 2008, p. 275)

S3:   When you're working with your partner, you don't care about being silly . . . Like *(laughter from the other students)* when you say the wrong thing, or like you try to make up a word of your own that you think is in French and like, you just have fun with your partner. You don't have to be so serious.

(Tognini, 2008, pp. 289–290)

Of course, as we have made clear throughout this book, peer interaction varies greatly—age, situation, task, participants, and goals are among the many factors that mediate the nature of peer interaction in any classroom. These broad generalizations are not intended to characterize every peer interaction but to suggest commonly found differences between peer and teacher-led talk.

Affective Value of Peer Talk

Peer interaction also holds affective value, and this can contribute to the enjoyment of learning with others and motivation to continue. Particular to child learners, it is the emotional salience of children's interaction with peers that marks it as quite different from their interaction with adults in classroom contexts. As we noted in Chapters 5 and 6, the affective and social aspects of peer interaction contribute in unique ways to learning, which are not true of teacher-child interaction. The activities that peers engage in afford a context for spontaneous L2 use, and this serves both linguistic and social goals.

The Role of Task and Mode

Research has suggested ways to manipulate greater opportunities for collaboration and co-construction through task design and choice of mode. In addition, pretask planning helps learners to first plot basic language and content, freeing up attentional resources during active production so that learners can pay attention to one another. Other work suggests ways to optimize effective peer interaction—for example, through promoting a class culture that supports cooperative learning and active listening (e.g., Dörnyei & Malderez, 1997); strategic grouping of participants (Storch, 2002); assigned task roles (Yule & Macdonald, 1990); and intentional training in interpersonal skills (e.g., Dörnyei & Murphey, 2003), including pretask modeling (discussed in Chapter 8). For younger learners, explicit training on co-operation between group members is particularly important (Galton & Williamson, 1992; Johnson, Johnson, Holubec, & Roy, 1984; McCafferty, Jabobs, & DaSilva Iddings, 2006).

Conversely, research has also suggested ways in which we can compensate for some of the potential weaknesses of peer interaction, and this has implications both for pedagogy and for future research. As noted in Chapter 9, the use of computer-mediated communication provides possibilities for peers to interact with one another, yet be monitored unobtrusively and even asynchronously by the teacher so that language issues can be dealt with after peer talk. As discussed in Chapter 8, task-based research has identified ways that task design features can be manipulated to encourage greater equality in participation, higher incidence of targeted forms, or use of particular communication strategies. There are many potential contributions of peer interaction that may be promoted through the ways in which participants are grouped, the roles they are assigned, and how they are oriented to the task itself. These aspects of task management contribute to the potential success or failure of peer tutoring and the potential for learners to benefit from teaching their peers as much as being taught (van Lier, 1996; Watanabe & Swain, 2007). The intricacy of classroom interaction is explored in the final section below.

Moderation

A third feature that strongly emerges from this review of peer interaction is the intricate nature of the language-learning process in instructed settings. There are a myriad of factors (environmental, cognitive, social, and individual) behind the potential success or failure of any interaction, and these factors appear to operate interdependently (Cao, 2009). This is well recognized in theoretical perspectives that emphasize the dynamic, complex, and interdependent nature of learning in instructional contexts. The contribution of peer interaction is heavily influenced by the people involved, the roles that they assume, the task they are performing at the time, and the context of all that has gone before and is going on at the time. Laursen (2010) encapsulates this notion well in a review of research on peer relationships and influences on adolescents:

> Moderation is the new watchword. The impact of peer relationships over individual adjustment may be greater when they are treated as moderators or settings that accelerate or impede outcomes, rather than as predictors that have direct effects on outcomes. (p. 898)

It is important to recognize that the potential of peer interaction for learning is mediated by setting, participants, and tasks but also by the relationships between participants and their prior experiences together. This is reflected throughout the research on peer interaction and L2 learning, but (as yet) rarely intentionally examined. For example, in Chapter 5, we saw that research on the role of proficiency pairings on outcomes of peer interaction suggests that it is relatively unpredictable. The task, the relationship between the participants, and their perception of one another's competence level in the language or knowledge of the topic all color the potential learning opportunities in terms of what is said, what is perceived, and how or whether it is used. Rather than directly influencing the outcomes of interaction, proficiency seems to act as a moderating variable, subtly influencing other related factors.

Perhaps most obvious to date in the research is the way in which social relations between peers mediate processes and outcomes of interaction, as discussed in Chapter 6. These relationships in turn are patterned by their shared histories as much as each individual's prior learning experiences, personality traits, goals, and motivations.

Conclusion

In this book, we have seen that any one theoretical perspective can only provide a partial picture of the benefits and limitations of peer interaction. For example, a sociocultural analysis of collaborative task-based interaction is particularly suited to highlighting the co-constructed nature of their dialogue; it emphasizes the way in which each participant's involvement and input contributes to the whole (e.g., Swain, 2010). In addition, a socialization perspective may help us to recognize the ways in which peer pressure and peer support act to reinforce (or to undermine) L2 use in the classroom (e.g., Cekaite, 2007). Alternatively, drawing on complexity theory, Larsen-Freeman and Cameron (2008) highlight the intricacies of the classroom context and the ways in which participants coadapt to one another's perceived actions and output, in ways that may be supportive or obstructive for language learning.

The research on peer interaction and L2 learning to date is a small beginning compared to the focus on teacher/native speaker interaction with learners in instructional and laboratory settings. It is miniscule when matched against the research on peer interaction in mainstream educational contexts. Practitioners and researchers in applied linguistics should not view peer interaction as a poor consolation for teacher-fronted interaction or as simply an opportunity for learners to have more time to practice. Nor can peer interaction offer what the teacher provides. Rather, the research to date suggests that peers provide a vital context for learning, which complements the role played by the teacher. With regard to pedagogy, this book has highlighted the need to recognize this complementarity in expectations for peer interaction. We have seen differences in outcomes according to mode and purpose and suggested ways these may be manipulated to different ends. We have stressed, too, the mediating role of participant relations and characteristics, such as age and proficiency. Three key strengths of peer interaction stand out as features on which teachers can capitalize. First, peer interaction can provide a context for learners to move from declarative knowledge of the language, and dependence on formulaic language, to productive and more fluent language use. Second, working collaboratively enables learners to experiment and test out new forms for specific meanings. Their struggles may increase their awareness of language form and sensitivity to solutions presented in teacher-learner interactions. Third, peer interaction can heighten the affective benefits of interaction and motivation to learn. When effectively managed and planned, peer interaction plays a unique and significant role in instructed language learning, particularly when supported by the teaching environment.

REFERENCES

Adams, R. (2003). L2 output, reformulation, and noticing: Implications for IL development. *Language Teaching Research, 7*(3), 347–376.

Adams, R. (2006). L2 tasks and orientation to form: A role for modality? *ITL. International Journal of Applied Linguistics, 152,* 7–34.

Adams, R. (2007). Do second language learners benefit from interacting with each other? In A. Mackey (Ed.), *Conversational interaction in second language acquisition: A series of empirical studies* (pp. 29–51). Oxford, United Kingdom: Oxford University Press.

Adams, R., & Nik, N. (in press). Prior knowledge and second language task production in text chat. In L. Ortega & M. Gonzalez-Lloret (Eds.), *Technology and tasks: Exploring technology-mediated TBLT.* Amsterdam, The Netherlands: John Benjamins.

Adams, R., Nuevo, A. M., & Egi, T. (2011). Explicit and implicit feedback, modified output, and SLA: Does explicit and implicit feedback promote learning and earner–learner interactions? *The Modern Language Journal, 95*(1), 42–63.

Adams, R., & Ross-Feldman, L. (2008). Does writing influence learner attention to form? The speaking-writing connection in second language and academic literacy development. In D. Belcher & A. Hirvela (Eds.), *The oral/literate connection: Perspectives on L2 speaking/writing connections* (pp. 243–267). Ann Arbor, MI: University of Michigan Press.

Allwright, D. (1998a). Am I now, have I ever been, and could I ever be—a developer? In M. Engin, J. Harvey, & J. O'Dwyer (Eds.), *Teacher training/teacher development: Integration and diversity* (pp. 138–143). Bilkent, Turkey: Bilkent University School of English Language.

Allwright, D. (1998b). Contextual factors in classroom language learning: An overview. In K. Malmakjaer & J. Williams (Eds.), *Context in learning and language understanding* (pp. 115–134). Cambridge, United Kingdom: Cambridge University Press.

American Council on the Teaching of Foreign Languages. (1986). *ACTFL proficiency guidelines.* Hastings-on-Hudson, NY: Author.

Anderson, J. R. (1983). *The architecture of cognition.* Cambridge, MA: Harvard University Press.

Anderson, J. R. (1992). Automaticity and the ACT* theory. *American Journal of Psychology, 105,* 165–180.

Anderson, J. R. (1996). ACT: A simple theory of complex cognition. *American Psychologist, 51,* 355–365.

Antón, M., & DiCamilla, F. (1998). Socio-cognitive functions of L1 collaborative interaction in the L2 classroom. *The Canadian Modern Language Review, 54*(3), 314–342.

Arnold, N. (2007). Reducing foreign language communication apprehension with computer-mediated communication: A preliminary study. *System, 35*(4), 469–486.

Arnold, N., Ducate, L., & Kost, C. (2009). Collaborative writing in wikis: Insights from culture project in German class. In L. Lomicka & G. Lord (Eds.), *The next generation: Social networking and online collaboration in foreign language learning* (Vol. 5, pp. 115–144). CALICO Monograph Series. San Marcos, TX: Texas State University.

Bachman, L. F., & Palmer, A. S. (1996). *Language testing in practice.* Oxford, United Kingdom: Oxford University Press.

Baralt, M., & Gurzynski-Weiss, L. (2011). Comparing learners' state anxiety during task-based interaction in computer-mediated and face-to-face communication. *Language Teaching Research, 15,* 201–229.

Bardovi-Harlig, K. (2002). A new starting point? Investigating formulaic use and input. *Studies in Second Language Acquisition, 24,* 189–198.

Barnard, R. (2009). Submerged in the mainstream? A case study of an immigrant learner in a New Zealand primary classroom. *Language and Education, 23*(3), 233–248.

Barnes, D. (2008). Exploratory talk for learning. In N. Mercer & S. Hodgkinson (Eds.), *Exploring talk in schools* (pp. 1–16). London, United Kingdom: SAGE Publications.

Barnes, D., & Todd, F. (1977). *Communication and learning in small groups.* London, England: Routledge and Kegan Paul.

Batstone, R. (2008). Issues and options in sociocognition. In Batstone, R. (Ed.) *Sociocognitive perspectives on language use and language learning* (pp. 3–23). Oxford: Oxford University Press.

Batstone, R., & Philp, J. (2013). Classroom interaction and learning across time and space. In K. McDonough & A. Mackey (Eds.), *Second language interaction in diverse educational contexts* (pp. 109–128). Amsterdam, The Netherlands: John Benjamins.

Beauvois, H. M. (1998). Conversations in slow motion: Computer-mediated communication in the foreign language classroom. *The Canadian Modern Language Review, 54*(2), 198–217.

Beauvois, H. M., & Eledge, J. (1995). Personality types and megabytes: Student attitudes toward computer-mediated communication (CMC) in the language classroom. *CALICO Journal, 13*(2–3), 27–45.

Belz, J. A., & Müller-Hartmann, A. (2003). Teachers as intercultural learners: Negotiating German-American telecollaboration along the institutional fault line. *The Modern Language Journal, 87*(1), 71–89.

Berk, L. E. (2006). *Child development* (7th ed.). Boston, MA: Pearson Education.

Berk, L. E. (2013). *Child development* (9th ed.). Boston, MA: Pearson Education.

Berman, R. (2007). Language knowledge and use across adolescence. In E. Hoff & M. Shatz (Eds.), *Blackwell handbook of language development* (pp. 347–367). Malden, MA: Blackwell.

Bernstein, J., & Cheng, J. (2007). Logic and validation of fully automatic spoken English test. In M. Holland & F. P. Fisher (Eds.), *The path of speech technologies in computer assisted language learning: From research toward practice* (pp. 174–194). Florence, KY: Routledge.

Berry, V. (2007). *Personality differences and oral test performance.* Frankfurt, Germany: Peter Lang.

Beyth-Marom, R., Saporta, K., & Caspi, A. (2005). Synchronous vs. asynchronous tutorials: Factors affecting students' preferences and choices. *Journal of Research on Technology in Education, 37*(3), 245–262.

Blake, R. (2000). Computer mediated communication. A window on L2 Spanish interlanguage. *Language Learning & Technology, 4*(1), 120–136.

Blake, R. (2005). Bimodal CMC: The glue of language learning at a distance. *CALICO Journal, 22*(3), 497–511.

Blake, R. (2007). New trends in using technology in the language curriculum. *Annual Review of Applied Linguistics, 27,* 76–97.

Blake, R., & Zyzik, E. (2003). Who's helping whom? Learner/heritage speakers' networked discussions in Spanish. *Applied Linguistics, 24,* 519–544.

Blatchford, P., Kutnik, P., Baines, E., & Galton, M. (2003). Toward a social pedagogy of classroom group-work. *International Journal of Educational Research, 39,* 153–172.

Block, D. (2003). *The social turn in second language acquisition.* Edinburgh, Scotland: Edinburgh University Press.

Blum-Kulka, S., & Snow, C. E. (2009). Introduction: The potential of peer talk. *Discourse Studies, 6,* 291–306.

Bober, M. J., & Dennen, V. P. (2001). Intersubjectivity: Facilitating knowledge construction in online environments. *Educational Media International, 38,* 241–250.

Böhlke, O. (2003). A comparison of student participation levels by group size and language stages during chat room and face-to-face discussions in German. *CALICO Journal, 21*(1), 67–87.

Bohn, O. (1986). Formulas, frame structures and stereotypes in early syntactic development. Some new evidence from L2 acquisition. *Linguistics, 24,* 185–202.

Bonk, W. J., & Ockey, G. J. (2003). A many-facet Rasch analysis of the second language group oral discussion task. *Language Testing, 20,* 89–110.

Bonk, W. J., & Van Moere, A. (2004, March). *L2 group oral testing: The influence of shyness/outgoingness, match of interlocutors' proficiency level, and gender on individual scores.* Paper presented at the Language Testing Research Colloquium, Temecula, California.

Bowles, M. (2011a). Exploring the role of modality: L2-heritage learner interactions in the Spanish language classroom. *The Heritage Language Journal, 8,* 30–65.

Bowles, M. (2011b). Measuring implicit and explicit linguistic knowledge: What can heritage language learners contribute? *Studies in Second Language Acquisition, 33,* 247–271.

Breen, M. (1985). The social context for language learning—a neglected situation? *Studies in Second Language Acquisition, 7,* 135–158.

Bremner, S. (2010). Collaborative writing: Bridging the gap between the textbook and the workplace. *English for Specific Purposes, 29*(2), 121–132.

Britton, J. (1980). Shaping at the point of utterance. In A. Freedman & I. Pringle (Eds.), *Reinventing the rhetorical tradition* (pp. 61–65). Canadian Council of Teachers of English, L&S Books; University of Central Arkansas.

Broner, M., & Tarone, E. (2001). Is it fun? Language play in a fifth-grade Spanish immersion classroom. *The Modern Language Journal, 85,* 363–379.

Brooks, L. (2009). Interacting in pairs in a test of oral proficiency: Co-constructing a better performance. *Language Testing, 26*(3), 341–366.

Brown, A. (2005). *Interviewer variability in oral proficiency interviews.* Frankfurt, Germany: Peter Lang.

Brown, G., Anderson, A., Shillcock, R., & Yule, G. (1984). *Teaching talk: Strategies for production and assessment.* Cambridge, United Kingdom: Cambridge University Press.

Bruton, A., & Samuda, V. (1980). Learner and teacher roles in the treatment of oral error in group work. *RELC Journal, 11,* 49–63.

Buckwalter, P. (2001). Repair sequences in Spanish L2 dyadic discourse: A descriptive study. *The Modern Language Journal, 85*(3), 380–397.

Buraphaeja, V., & Dawson, K. (2008). Content analysis in computer-mediated communication: Analyzing models for assessing critical thinking through the lens of social constructivism. *The American Journal of Distance Education, 22,* 130–145.

Cao, Y. (2009). *Understanding the notion of interdependence, and the dynamics of willingness to communicate* (Unpublished doctoral dissertation). The University of Auckland, Auckland, New Zealand.

Cekaite, A. (2007). A child's development in interactional competence in a Swedish L2 classroom. *The Modern Language Journal, 91*(1), 45–62.

Cekaite, A., & Aronsson, K. (2005). Language play, a collaborative resource in children's L2 learning. *Applied Linguistics, 26,* 169–191.

Chambers, J. K. (1995). *Sociolinguistic theory.* Oxford, United Kingdom: Blackwell.

Chang, L. (2007). The effects of using CALL on advanced Chinese foreign language learners. *CALICO Journal, 24*(2), 331–353.

Chapelle, C. (1997). CALL in the year 2000: Still in search of research paradigms? *Language Learning & Technology, 1*(1), 19–43.

Chapelle, C. (2001). *Computer applications in second language acquisition: Foundations for teaching, testing and research.* Cambridge, United Kingdom: Cambridge University Press.

Chapelle, C. (2004). Technology and second language learning: Expanding methods and agendas. *System, 32,* 593–601.

Chavez, M. (2006). Classroom-language use in teacher-led instruction and teachers' self-perceived roles. *IRAL, 44,* 49–102.

Cheng, R. (2010). Computer-mediated scaffolding in L2 students' academic literacy development. *CALICO Journal, 28*(1), 74–98.

Cheon, H. (2003). The viability of computer mediated communication in the Korean secondary EFL classroom. *Asian EFL Journal, 5*(1), 1–56.

Choi, H. (2011). *Diverse peer interaction in small group work: Analysis of low-proficiency learners' language related episodes, contingent on group member proficiency levels* (Unpublished master of applied linguistics coursework dissertation). Brisbane, Australia: The University of Queensland.

Chun, D. (1994). Using computer networking to facilitate the acquisition of interactive competence. *System, 22*(1), 17–31.

Chun, D. M., & Payne, J. S. (2004). What makes students click: Working memory and look-up behavior. *System, 32,* 481–503.

Cohen, P., Kulik, J. A., & Kulik, C. C. (1982). Educational outcomes of tutoring: A meta-analysis of findings. *American Educational Research Journal, 19,* 237–248.

Collier, V. (1987). *The effect of age on acquisition of a second language in school.* National Clearing House for Bilingual Education. Occasional Papers Winter 1987/1988. Retrieved from http://www.eric.ed.gov/PDFS/ED296580.pdf

Coniam, D., & Wong, R. (2004). Internet relay chat as a tool in the autonomous development of ESL learners' English language ability: An exploratory study. *System, 32*(3), 321–335.

Cook, G. (2000). *Language play, language learning.* Oxford, United Kingdom: Oxford University Press.

Corden, R. (2000). *Literacy and learning through talk.* Buckingham, UK: Open University Press.

Cumming, A. (1990). Metalinguistic and ideational thinking in second language composing. *Written Communication, 7,* 482–511.

Cummins, J. (2000). *Language, power, and pedagogy: Bilingual children in the crossfire.* Bristol, United Kingdom: Multilingual Matters.

Damon, W. (1984). Peer education: The untapped potential. *Journal of Applied Developmental Psychology 5,* 331–343.

Damon, W., & Phelps, E. (1989a). Critical distinctions among three approaches to peer education. *International Journal of Educational Research, 58,* 9–19.

Damon, W., & Phelps, E. (1989b). Critical distinctions among three methods of peer education. *International Journal of Educational Research, 13,* 9–20.

Davis, L. (2009). The influence of interlocutor proficiency in a paired oral assessment. *Language Testing, 26*(3), 367–396.

de Bot, K. (1996). The psycholinguistics of the output hypothesis. *Language Learning, 46*(3), 529–555.

de Guerrero, M. C. M., & Villamil, O. S. (2000). Activating the ZPD: Mutual scaffolding in L2 peer revision. *The Modern Language Journal, 84*(1), 51–68.

DeKeyser, R. (1998). Beyond focus on form: Cognitive perspectives on learning and practicing second language grammar. In C. Doughty & J. Williams (Eds.), *Focus on form in classroom language acquisition* (pp. 42–63). New York, NY: Cambridge University Press.

DeKeyser, R. (2001). Automaticity and automatization. In P. Robinson (Ed.), *Cognition and second language instruction* (pp. 125–151). New York, NY: Cambridge University Press.

DeKeyser, R. (2007). Conclusion: The future of practice. In R. DeKeyser, *Practice in a second language* (pp. 287–304). Cambridge, United Kingdom: Cambridge University Press.

de la Fuente, M. J. (2002). Negotiation and oral acquisition of L2 vocabulary: The roles of input and output in the receptive and productive acquisition of words. *Studies in Second Language Acquisition, 24,* 81–112.

de la Fuente, M. J. (2003). Is SLA Interactionist Theory Relevant to CALL? A Study on the Effects of Computer-Mediated Interaction in L2 Vocabulary Acquisition. *Computer Assisted Language Learning, 16*(1), 47–81.

De Lisi, R., & Golbeck, S. L. (1999). Implication of Piaget's theory for peer-learning. In A. M. O'Donnell & A. King (Eds.), *Cognitive perspectives on peer-learning* (pp. 3–38). Mahwah, NJ: Lawrence Erlbaum Associates.

Dippold, D. (2009). Peer feedback through blogs: Student and teacher perceptions in an advanced German class. *ReCALL, 21*(01), 18.

Donato, R. (1994). Collective scaffolding in second language learning. In J. Lantolf & G. Appel (Eds.), *Vygotskian approaches to second language learning* (pp. 33–56). Norwood, NJ: Ablex.

Dörnyei, Z. (2005). *The psychology of the language learner: Individual differences in second language acquisition.* Mahwah, NJ: Lawrence Erlbaum Associates.

Dörnyei, Z., & Malderez, A. (1997). Group dynamics and foreign language teaching. *System, 25*(1), 1, 65–81.

Dörnyei, Z., & Murphey, T. (2003). *Group dynamics in the language classroom.* Cambridge, United Kingdom: Cambridge University Press.

Ducasse, A. M., & Brown, A. (2009). Assessing paired orals: Raters' orientation to interaction. *Language Testing, 26*(3), 423–443.

Duchesne, S., McMaugh, A., Bochner, S., & Krause, K. (2012). *Educational psychology for learning and teaching.* Melbourne, Australia: Cengage Learning.

Duchesne, S., McMaugh, A., Bochner, S., & Krause, K. (2013). *Educational psychology for learning and teaching* (4th ed.). Melbourne, Australia: Cengage Learning.

Duff, P., & Kobayahsi, M. (2010). The intersection of social, cognitive, and cultural processes in language learning: A second language socialization approach. In R. Batstone (Ed.), *Sociocognitive aspects of second language learning and teaching* (pp. 76–93). Oxford, United Kingdom: Oxford University Press.

Duff, P. A. (1986). Another look at interlanguage talk: Taking task to task. In R. Day (Ed.), *Talking to learners: Conversation in second language acquisition* (pp. 147–181). Rowley, MA: Newbury House.

Dunn, J. (1999). Siblings, friends, and the development of social understanding. In W. A. Collins & B. Laursen (Eds.), *Relationships as social contexts* (pp. 263–279). Mahwah, NJ: Lawrence Erlbaum Associates.

Dunn, J. (2002). Sibling relationships. In P. K. Smith & C. H. Hart (Eds.) *Blackwell handbook of childhood social development* (pp.223–237). Malden, MA: Blackwell.

Dunn, J. (2008). Siblings and socialization. In J. E. Grusec & P. D. Hastings (Eds.), *Handbook of socialization: Theory and research* (pp. 309–327). New York, NY: The Guilford Press.

Eguchi, M., & Eguchi, K. (2006). The limited effect of PBL on EFL learners: A case study of English magazine projects. *Asian EFL Journal, 8*(3), 207–225.

Egyud, G., & Glover, P. (2001). Oral testing in pairs—a secondary school perspective. *English Language Teaching Journal, 55*(1), 70–76.

Ellis, N. C. (1996). Analyzing language sequence in the sequence of language acquisition: Some comments on Major and Ioup. *Studies in Second Language Acquisition, 18,* 361–368.

Ellis, N. C. (2002). Frequency effects in language acquisition: A review with implications for theories of implicit and explicit language acquisition. *Studies in Second Language Acquisition, 24,* 143–188.

Ellis, N. C. (2003). Constructions, chunking and connectionism: The emergence of second language structure. In C. Doughty & M. Long (Eds.), *The handbook of second language acquisition* (pp. 33–68). Oxford, United Kingdom: Blackwell.

Ellis, N. C. (2005). At the interface: Dynamic interactions of explicit and implicit language knowledge. *Studies in Second Language Acquisition, 27,* 305–352.

Ellis, R. (1984). *Classroom second language development.* Oxford, United Kingdom: Pergamon.

Ellis, R. (2003). *Task-based language learning and teaching.* Oxford, United Kingdom: Oxford University Press.

Ellis, R. (2008). *The study of second language acquisition.* Oxford, United Kingdom: Oxford University Press.

Ellis, R. (2012). *Language teaching research and pedagogy.* West Sussex: Wiley-Blackwell.

Ellis, R. Basturkmen, H. & Loewen, S. (2001). Learner Uptake in Communicative ESL Lessons. *Language Learning 51*(2): 281–318.

Elola, I., & Oskoz, A. (2010). Collaborative writing: Fostering foreign language and writing conventions development. *Language Learning & Technology, 14*(3), 51–71.

Emde, S., Schneider, J., & Kötter, M. (2001). Technically speaking: Transforming language learning through virtual learning environment. *The Modern Language Journal, 85*(2), 210–225.

Ervin-Tripp, S. M. (1991). Play in language development. In B. Scales, A. Almy, M. Almy, A. Nicolopoulou, & S. M. Ervin-Tripp (Eds.), *Play and the social context of development in early care and education* (pp. 84–98). New York, NY: Columbia Teachers College.

Ewald, J. (2008). The assumption of participation in small group work: An investigation of L2 teachers' and learners' expectations. *Issues in Applied Linguistics, 16*(2), 151–174.

Fassler, R. (1998). Room for talk: Peer support for getting into English in an ESL kindergarten. *Early Childhood Research Quarterly, 13*(3), 379–409.

Fernandez Dobao, A. M. (2001). Communication strategies in the interlanguage of Galician students of English: The influence of learner- and task-related factors. *Atlantis, 23*(1), 41–62.

Ferris, D. R. (2003). *Response to student writing: Implications for second language students.* Mahwah, NJ: Lawrence Erlbaum Associates.

Fiori, M. L. (2005). The development of grammatical competence through synchronous computer-mediated communication. *CALICO Journal, 22*(3), 567–602.

Folland, D., & Robertson, D. (1976). Towards objectivity in group oral testing. *English Language Teaching Journal, 30*, 156–167.

Foster, P. (1998). A classroom perspective on the negotiation of meaning. *Applied Linguistics, 19*(1), 1–23.

Foster, P., & Ohta, A. (2005). Negotiation for meaning and peer assistance in second language classrooms. *Applied Linguistics, 26*(3), 402–430.

Foster, P., & Skehan, P. (1996). The influence of planning and task type on second language performance. *Studies in Second Language Acquisition, 18*, 299–323.

Fotos, S. (1994). Integrating grammar instruction and communicative language use through grammar consciousness-raising tasks. *TESOL Quarterly, 28*, 323–351.

Freiermuth, M., & Jarrel, D. (2006). Willingness to communicate: Can online chat help? *IRAL: International Journal of Applied Linguistics in Language Teaching, 16*(2), 189–212.

Fujii, A., & Mackey, A. (2009). Interactional feedback in learner-learner interactions in a task-based EFL classroom. *IRAL: International Review of Applied Linguistics in Language Teaching, 47*, 267–301.

Fujii, A., Obata, M., Takahashi, S., & Tanabe, S. (2008). Training learners to negotiate for meaning: An exploratory case study. *Language Research Bulletin, 23*, 1–15.

Fulcher, G. (1996). Testing tasks: Issues in task design and the group oral. *Language Testing, 13*(1), 23–51.

Galaczi, E. (2008). Peer-peer interaction in a speaking test: The case of the First Certificate in English examination. *Language Assessment Quarterly, 5*(2), 89–119.

Galton, M., Hargreaves, L., & Pell, T. (2009). Group work and whole-class teaching with 11- to 14-year-olds compared. *Cambridge Journal of Education, 39*(1), 119–140.

Galton, M., & Williamson, J. (1992). *Group work in the primary classroom.* London, United Kingdom: Routledge.

Gan, Z. (2010). Interaction in group oral assessment: A case study of higher- and lower-scoring students. *Language Testing, 27*(4), 585–602.

Gánem-Guitérrez, G. A. (2013). Sociocultural theory and second language development: Theoretical foundations and insights from research. In M. P. Garcia Mayo, M. J. Gutierrez Mangado, & M. Martinez Adrián (Eds.), *Contemporary approaches to second language acquisition* (pp. 129–152). Amsterdam, The Netherlands: John Benjamins.

García Mayo, M., & Alegria de la Colina, A. (2007). Attention to form across collaborative tasks by low-proficiency learners in an EFL setting. In M. García Mayo (Ed.), *Investigating tasks in formal language learning* (pp. 91–116). Bristol, United Kingdom: Multilingual Matters.

García-Mayo, M. P., & Pica, T. (2000). L2 learner interaction in a foreign language setting: Are learning needs addressed? *IRAL: International Review of Applied Linguistics, 38*(1), 35–58.

Garrett, P., & Shortall, T. (2002). Learners' evaluation of teacher-fronted and student-centred classroom activities. *Language Teaching Research, 6,* 25–57.

Garrison, D. R., Anderson, T., & Archer, W. (2000). Critical thinking in a text based environment: Computer conferencing in higher education. *Internet and Higher Education, 2*(2), 87–105.

Gass, S. (1997). *Input, interaction, and the second language learner.* Mahwah, Lawrence Erlbaum.

Gass, S., & Varonis, E. (1985). Variation in native speaker speech modification to non-native speakers. *Studies in Second Language Acquisition, 7,* 37–57.

Gass, S., & Varonis, E. (1989). Incorporated repairs in nonnative discourse. In M. Eisenstein (Ed.), *The dynamic interlanguage* (pp. 71–86). New York, NY: Platinum Press.

Gass, S., & Varonis, E. (1994). Input, interaction and second language production. *Studies in Second Language Acquisition, 16,* 283–302.

Gass, S., & Mackey, A. (2002). Frequency effects and second language acquisition: A complex picture? *Studies in Second Language Acquisition, 24*(2), 249–260.

Gass, S., & Mackey, A. (2006). Input, interaction, and output: An overview. *AILA Review, 19*(1), 3–17.

Gass, S., Mackey, A., & Ross-Feldman, L. (2005). Task-based interactions in classroom and laboratory settings. *Language Learning, 55*(8), 575–611.

Gatbonton, E., & Segalowitz, N. (1988). Creative automatization: Principles for promoting fluency within a communicative framework *TESOL Quarterly, 22*(3), 473–492.

Ghaith, G. (2003). Effects of the learning together model of cooperative learning on English as a foreign language reading achievement, academic self-esteem, and feelings of school alienation. *Bilingual Research Journal, 27,* 451–474.

Gibbons, P. (1991). *Learning to learn in a second language.* Sydney, Australia: Primary English Teaching Association.

Gibbons, P. (2002). *Scaffolding language, scaffolding learning: Teaching second language learners in the mainstream classroom.* Portsmouth, NH: Heinemann.

Gibbons, P. (2003). Mediating language learning: teacher interactions with ESL students in a content-based classroom, *TESOL Quarterly, 37,* 247–273.

Giddens, A. (1984). *The constitution of society.* Los Angeles, CA: University of California Press.

Gilabert, R., Baron, J., & Llanes, A. (2009). Manipulating cognitive complexity across task types and its impact on learners' interaction during oral performance. *IRAL: International Review of Applied Linguistics in Language Teaching, 47*(3–4), 367–395.

Glendinning, E., & Howard, R. (2003). Lotus ScreenCam as an aid to investigating student writing. *Computer Assisted Language Learning, 16*(1), 31–46.

González, D. (2003). Teaching and learning through chat: A taxonomy of educational chat for EFL/ESL. *Teaching English with Technology, 3*(4). Retrieved from http://www.tewt-journal.org/pastissues2003.htm

González-Lloret, M. (2009). *No me llames de usted, tratame de tu': L2 address behavior development through synchronous computer-mediated communication* (Unpublished doctoral dissertation). Honolulu: University of Hawai'i at Manoa.

Hardy, I. M., & Moore, J. L. (2004). Foreign language students' conversational negotiations in different task environments. *Applied Linguistics, 25,* 340–370.

Harklau, L. (2002). The role of writing in classroom second language acquisition. *Journal of Second Language Writing, 11,* 329–350.

Harklau, L. (2007). The adolescent English language learner: Identities lost and found. In J. Cummins & C. Davison (Eds.), *International handbook of English language teaching* (pp. 559–573). Norwell, MA: Springer.

Harmer, J. (2001). *The practice of second language teaching.* New York, NY: Longman.

Hartup, W. (1983). Peer relations. In E. M. Hetherington (Vol. Ed.) & P. H. Mussen (Gen. Ed.), *Handbook of child psychology: Vol. 4. Socialization, personality and social development* (pp. 103–196). New York, NY: Wiley.

Hartup, W. W. (1989). Social relationships and their developmental significance. *American Psychologist, 44,* 120–126.

Hartup, W. W. (2011). Critical issues and theoretical viewpoints. In K. H. Rubin, W. M. Bukowski & B. Larsen (Eds.), *Handbook of peer interactions, relationships and groups* (pp. 3–19). New York, NY: The Guildford Press.

Hawkes, M. (2006). Linguistic discourse variables as indicators of reflective online interaction. *The American Journal of Distance Education, 20,* 231–244.

He, L., & Dai, Y. (2006). A corpus-based investigation into the validity of the CET-SET group discussion. *Language Testing, 23*(3), 370–401.

Herring, S. (1996). *Computer-mediated communication: Linguistic, social and cross-cultural perspectives.* Amsterdam, The Netherlands: John Benjamins.

Herring, S. C. (2004). Computer-mediated discourse analysis: An approach to researching online behavior. In S. A. Barab, R. Kling, & J. Gray (Eds.), *Designing virtual communities in the service of learning* (pp. 338–376). Cambridge, United Kingdom: Cambridge University Press.

Hildson, J. (1991). The group oral exam: Advantages and limitations. In J. C. Alderson & B. North (Eds.), *Language testing in the 90's: The communicative legacy.* London, United Kingdom: Modern English Publications and the British Council.

Hogan, D., & Tudge, J. (1999). Implications of Vygotsky's theory for peer learning. In S. O'Donnell & A. King (Eds.), *Cognitive perspectives on peer learning* (pp. 39–66). Mahwah, NJ: Lawrence Erlbaum Associates.

Hopewell, S. (2011). Leveraging bilingualism to accelerate English reading comprehension. *International Journal of Bilingual Education and Bilingualism, 14,* 603–620.

Hulstijn, J. (2002). Towards a unified account of the representation, processing and acquisition of second language knowledge. *Second Language Research 18*(3), 193–223.

Hyland, K. (2010). Researching writing. In B. Paltridge & A. Phakiti (Eds.), *Continuum companion to research methods in applied linguistics* (pp. 191–204). London, United Kingdom: Continuum.

Iwasaki, J., & Oliver, R. (2003). Chat-line interaction and negative feedback. *Australian Review of Applied Linguistics, 17,* 60–73.

Iwashita, N. (1993). *Comprehensible output in NNS-NNS interaction in Japanese as a foreign language* (Unpublished master's dissertation). The University of Melbourne, Melbourne, Australia.

Iwashita, N. (1996). The validity of the paired interview format in oral performance assessment. *Melbourne Papers in Language Testing, 5*(2), 51–65.

Iwashita, N. (1999). Tasks and learners' output in nonnative-nonnative interaction. In K. Kanno (Ed.), *Studies on the acquisition of Japanese as a second language* (pp. 31–53). Amsterdam, The Netherlands: John Benjamins.

Iwashita, N. (2001). The effect of learner proficiency on interactional moves and modified output in nonnative-nonnative interaction in Japanese as a foreign language. *System, 29*(2), 267–287.

Iwashita, N. (2011). [Task engagement and its relationship with L2 development.] Unpublished data.

Iwawaki, S., Eysenck, S. B. G., & Eysenck, H. J. (1980). Japanese and English personality structure: A cross-cultural study. *Psychologia, 23,* 195–205.

Izumi, S. (2003). Comprehension and production process in second language learning: In search of the psycholinguistic rationale of the output hypothesis. *Applied Linguistics, 24*(2), 168–196.

Jeon, S. (2007). Interaction-driven L2 Learning: Characterizing linguistic development. In A. Mackey (Ed.), *Conversational interaction in second language acquisition: A series of empirical studies* (pp. 379–403). Oxford, United Kingdom: Oxford University Press.

Jia, G., & Aaronson, D. (2003). A longitudinal study of Chinese children and adolescents learning English in the United States. *Applied Psycholinguistics, 24,* 131–161.

John, O. P. and Srivastava, S. (1999). The big-five trait taxonomy: History, measurement, and theoretical perspectives. In L. A. Pervin & O. P. John (Eds.), *Handbook of personality: Theory and research* (2nd ed.), (pp. 102–139). New York, NY: Guilford Press.

Johnson, D., Johnson, R. T., Holubec, E., & Roy, P. (1984). *Circles of learning.* Alexandria, VA: Association for Supervision and Curriculum Development.

Kern, R. (1995). Restructuring classroom interaction with networked computers: Effects on quantity and characteristics of language production. *The Modern Language Journal, 79*(4), 457–476.

Kern, R. (1996). Computer-mediated communication: Using e-mail exchanges to explore personal histories in two cultures. In M. Warschauer (Ed.), *Telecollaboration in foreign language learning: Proceedings of the Hawaii symposium* (pp. 105–119). Honolulu, HI: University of Hawaii.

Kern, R., Ware, P. D., & Warschauer, M. (2004). Crossing frontiers: New directions in online pedagogy and research. *Annual Review of Applied Linguistics, 24,* 243–260.

Kessler, G. (2009). Student-initiated attention to form in Wiki-based collaborative writing. *Language Learning & Technology, 13*(1), 79–95.

Kibler, A. (2010). Writing through two languages: First language expertise in a language minority classroom. *Journal of Second Language Writing, 19*(3), 121–142.

Kim, I.-H., Anderson, R., Nguyen-Jahiel, K., & Archodidou, A. (2007). Discourse patterns during children's collaborative online discussions. *The Journal of the Learning Sciences, 16*(3), 333–370.

Kim, Y. (2008). The contribution of collaborative and individual tasks to the acquisition of L2 vocabulary. *The Modern Language Journal, 92*(1), 114–130.

Kim, Y. (2009). The effects of task complexity on learner-learner interaction. *System, 37*(2), 254–268.

Kim, Y., & McDonough, K. (2008). The effect of interlocutor proficiency on the collaborative dialogue between Korean as a second language learners. *Language Teaching Research, 12,* 211–234.

Kim, Y., & McDonough, K. (2011). Using pretask modelling to encourage collaborative learning opportunities. *Language Teaching Research, 15*(2), 183–199.

Kitade, K. (2000). L2 learners' discourse and SLA theories in CMC: Collaborative interaction in internet chat. *Computer Assisted Language Learning, 13*(2), 143–166.

Kowal, M., & Swain, M. (1994). Using collaborative language production tasks to promote students' language awareness. *Language Awareness, 3*(1), 73–93.

Krashen, S. (1985). *The input hypothesis.* London, United Kingdom: Longman.

Krashen, S., & Scarcella, R. (1978). On routines and patterns in second language acquisition and performance. *Language Learning, 28,* 283–300.

Kung, S. C. (2004). Synchronous electronic discussions in an EFL reading class. *English Language Teaching Journal, 58*(2), 164–173.

Kutnick, P., Hodgkinson, S., Sebba, J., Humphreys, S., Galton, M., Steward, S., Blatchford, P. & E. Baines. (2006). *Pupil grouping strategies and practices at key stage 2 and 3.* Research Report 796. Nottingham, UK: DfES Publications.

Labov, W. (1966). *The social stratification of English in New York City.* Washington, DC: Center for Applied Linguistics.

Lai, C. (2005). The role of communicative practices and talking with and through the computer. In Y. Zhao (Ed.), *Research in technology and second language learning. Developments and directions* (pp. 249–285). Charlotte, NC: Information Age Publishing.

Lai, C., & Zhao, Y. (2006). Noticing and text-based chat. *Language Learning & Technology, 10*(3), 102–120.

Lamy, M.-L., & Hampel, R. (2007). *Online communication in language learning.* New York, NY: Palgrave Macmillan.

Lantolf, J. P. (2000a). Introduction. In J. P. Lantolf (Ed.), *Sociocultural theory and second language learning* (pp. 1–26). Oxford, United Kingdom: Oxford University Press.

Lantolf, J. P. (2000b). Second language learning as a mediated process. *Language Teaching.* Oxford: Oxford University Press.

Lantolf, J. P., & Appel, G. (1994). The theoretical framework: An introduction to Vygotskian perspectives on second language research. In J. P. Lantolf & G. Appel (Eds.), *Vygotskian approaches to second language learning* (pp. 1–32). Norwood, NJ: Ablex.

Lantolf, J. P., & Thorne, S. (2006). *Sociocultural theory and the genesis of second language development.* Oxford, United Kingdom: Oxford University Press.

Larsen-Freeman, D., & Cameron, L. (2008). *Complex systems and applied linguistics.* Oxford, United Kingdom: Oxford University Press.

Laursen, B. (2010). Capturing the peer context: The paradox of progress. *Journal of Adolescence, 33,* 897–902.

Laursen, B., & Hartup, W. W. (2002). The origins of reciprocity and social exchange in friendships [Special issue: New directions for child and adolescent development]. *Social Exchange in Development, 95,* 27–40.

Lazareton, A., & Davis, L. (2008). A microanalytic perspective on discourse, proficiency, and identity in paired oral assessment. *Language Assessment Quarterly, 5,* 313–335.

Lee, L. (2002). Synchronous online exchanges: A study of modification devices on nonnative discourse interaction. *System, 30,* 275–288.

Lee, L. (2004). Learners' perspectives on networked collaborative interaction with native speakers of Spanish in the US. *Language Learning & Technology, 8*(1), 83–100.

Lee, L. (2008). Focus on form through collaborative scaffolding in expert-to-novice online interaction. *Language Learning & Technology, 12*(3), 53–72.

Lee, L. (2010a). Exploring Wiki-mediated collaborative writing: A case study in an elementary Spanish course. *CALICO Journal, 27*(2), 260–276.

Lee, L. (2010b). Fostering reflective writing and interactive exchange through blogging in an advanced language course. *ReCALL, 22*(2), 212–227.

Leeser, M. J. (2004). Learner proficiency and focus on form during collaborative dialogue. *Language Teaching Research, 8*(1), 55–82.

Levelt, W. J. M. (1989). *Speaking.* Cambridge, MA: Bradford/MIT Press.

Li, D. (1998). It's always more difficult than you plan and imagine: Teachers' perceived difficulties in introducing the communicative approach in South Korea. *TESOL Quarterly, 32,* 677–703.

Liang, M. Y. (2010). Using synchronous online peer response groups in EFL writing: Revision-related discourse. *Language Learning & Technology, 14*(1), 45–64.

Liaw, M. L. (1997). An analysis of ESL children's verbal interaction during computer book reading. *Computers in the Schools, 13*(3–4), 55–73.

Lightbown, P. (1985). Great expectations: Second-language acquisition research and classroom teaching. *Applied Linguistics, 6*(2), 173–189.

Lombardo, L. (1984). Oral testing: Getting a sample of real language. *English Teaching Forum, 22*(1), 2–6.

Long, M. (1981). Input, interaction and second-language acquisition. *Annals of the New York Academy of Sciences, 379,* 259–278.

Long, M. (1983). Native speaker/non-native speaker conversation and the negotiation of comprehensible input. *Applied Linguistics, 4,* 126–141.

Long, M. (1996). The role of the linguistic environment in second language acquisition. In W. C. Ritchie & T. K. Bhatia (Eds.), *Handbook of second language acquisition* (pp. 413–468). New York, NY: Academic Press.

Long, M., & Porter, P. (1985). Group work, interlanguage talk, and second language acquisition. *TESOL Quarterly, 19,* 207–228.

Long, M. (2007). *Problems in SLA.* Mahwah, NJ: Lawrence Erlbaum Associates.

Lourenço, O. (2012). Piaget and Vygotsky: Many resemblances, and a crucial difference. *New Ideas in Psychology, 30*(3), 281–295.

Lowe, P. (1983). The ILR oral interview: Origins, applications, pitfalls, and implications. *Die Unterrichtspraxis, 16,* 230–244.

Luk, J. (2010). Talking to score: Impression management in L2 oral assessment and the co-construction of a test discourse genre. *Language Assessment Quarterly, 7*(1), 25–53.

Lund, A. (2006). The multiple contexts of online language teaching. *Language Teaching Research, 10*(2), 181–204.

Lynch, A. E. (2008). The linguistic similarities of Spanish heritage and second language learners. *Foreign Language Annals, 41,* 252–281.

Lyster, R., & Ranta, L. (1997). Corrective feedback and learner uptake. *Studies in Second Language Acquisition, 19*(1), 37–66.

Macintyre, P. D., Clément, R., Dörnyei, Z., & Noels, K. A. (1998). Conceptualizing willingness to communicate in a L2: A situational model of L2 confidence and affiliation. *The Modern Language Journal, 82*(4), 545–562.

Mackey, A. (2007). Introduction: The role of conversational interaction in second language acquisition. In A. Mackey (Ed.), *Conversational interaction in second language acquisition* (pp. 1–26). Oxford, United Kingdom: Oxford University Press.

Mackey, A. (2012). *Input, interaction and corrective feedback in L2 classrooms.* Oxford, United Kingdom: Oxford University Press.

Mackey, A., Al-Khalil, M., Atanassova, G., Hama, M., Logan-Terry, A., & Nakatsukasa, K. (2007). Teachers' intentions and learners' perceptions about corrective feedback in the L2 classroom. *Innovations in Language Learning and Teaching, 1*(1), 129–152.

Mackey, A. & Gass, S. (2005). *Second language research: Methodology and design.* New Jersey: Lawrence Erlbaum Associates.

Mackey, A., & Goo, J. M. (2007). Interaction research in SLA: A meta-analysis and research synthesis. In A. Mackey (Ed.), *Conversational interaction in second language acquisition* (pp. 379–452). New York, NY: Oxford University Press.

Mackey, A., Oliver, R., & Leeman, J. (2003). Interactional input and the incorporation of feedback: An exploration of NS-NNS and NNS-NNS adult and child dyads. *Language Learning, 53*(1), 35–66.

Makin, L., Campbell, J., & Jones Diaz, C. (1995). *One childhood, many languages.* Sydney, Australia: Harper Educational.

Malmqvist, A. (2005). How does group discussion in reconstruction tasks affect written language output? *Language Awareness, 14*(2–3), 128–141.

Manchón, R. M. (2011). Writing to learn the language: Issues in theory and research. In R. M. Manchón (Ed.), *Learning-to-write and writing-to-learn in an additional language* (pp. 61–82). Amsterdam, The Netherlands: John Benjamins.

May, L. (2009). Co-constructed interaction in a paired speaking test: The rater's perspective. *Language Testing, 26*(3), 397–421.

McCafferty, S., Jacobs, G., & DaSilva Iddings, A. (2006). *Cooperative learning and second language teaching.* Cambridge, United Kingdom: Cambridge University Press.

McDonough, K. (2004). Learner-learner interaction during pair and small group activities in a Thai EFL context. *System, 32*(2), 207–224.

McDonough, K., & Mackey, A. (2006). Responses to recasts: Repetitions, primed production and linguistic development. *The Modern Language Journal, 56*(4), 693–720.

McLaughlin, B. (1990). Restructuring. *Applied Linguistics, 11,* 113–128.

McLaughlin, B., & Heredia, R. (1996). Information processing approaches to the study of second language acquisition. In W. Ritchie & T. K. Bhatia (Eds.), *Handbook of language acquisition* (pp. 213–228). New York, NY: Academic Press.

Mercer, N. (1996). The quality of talk in children's collaborative activity in the classroom. *Learning and Instruction, 6*(4), 359–377.

Mercer, N. (2000). *Words and minds: How we use language to think together.* London, United Kingdom: Routledge.

Meskill, C. (2005). Triadic scaffolds: Tools for teaching English language learners with computers. *Language Learning & Technology, 9,* 46–59.

Michel, M., Kuiken, F., & Vedder, I. (2007). The influence of complexity in monologic versus dialogic tasks in Dutch L2. *IRAL: International Review of Applied Linguistics in Language Teaching, 45,* 241–259.

Miller, J. (2000). Language use, identity and social interaction: Migrant students in Australia. *Research on Language and Social Interaction, 33,* 69–100.

Miller, J. (2003). *Audible difference: ESL and social identity in schools.* Bristol, United Kingdom: Multilingual Matters.

Miller, P. H., Kessel, F. S., & Flavell, J. H. (1970). Thinking about people thinking about people thinking about. . .: A study of social cognitive development. *Child Development, 41,* 613–623.

Ministry of Education. (2008). *Making language and learning work 2.* Ministry of Education, Produced and published by Cognition Consulting, Team Solutions and Visual Learning, Wellington, New Zealand.

Mochizuki, N., & Ortega, L. (2008). Balancing communication and grammar in beginning-level foreign language classrooms: A study of guided planning and relativization. *Language Teaching Research, 12*(1), 11–37.

Montrul, S. (2008). *Incomplete acquisition in bilingualism: Re-examining the age factor.* Amsterdam, The Netherlands: John Benjamins.

Muñoz, C. (2003). Variation in oral skills development and age of onset. In M. P. Garcia Mayo & M. L. Garcia Lecumberri (Eds.), *Age and the acquisition of English as a foreign language: Theoretical issues and fieldwork* (pp. 161–181). Clevedon, Avon, United Kingdom: Multilingual Matters.

Muñoz, C. (2007). Age-related differences and second language learning practice. In R. DeKeyser (Ed.), *Practice in a second language* (pp. 229–255). Cambridge, United Kingdom: Cambridge University Press.

Muranoi, H. (2007). Output practice in the L2 classroom. In R. DeKeyser (Ed.), *Practice in a second language* (pp. 51–84). New York, NY: Cambridge University Press.

Murphy, P. (2010). Web-based collaborative reading exercises for learners in remote locations: The effects of computer-mediated feedback and interaction via computer-mediated communication. *ReCALL, 22*(02), 112–134.

Myles, F., Hooper, J., & Mitchell, R. (1998). Rote or rule? Exploring the role of formulaic language in classroom foreign language learning. *Language Learning, 48,* 323–363.

Myles, F., Mitchell, R., & Hooper, J. (1999). Interrogative chunks in French L2: A basis for creative construction. *Studies in Second Language Acquisition, 21*(1), 49–80.

Nakatsuhara, F. (2006). The impact of proficiency level on conversational styles in paired speaking tests. *Cambridge ESOL Research Notes, 25,* 15–20.

Nakatsuhara, F. (2011). Effects of test-taker characteristics and the number of participants in group oral tests. *Language Testing, 28*(4), 483–508.

Nassaji, H., & Swain, M. (2000). A Vygotskian perspective on corrective feedback in L2: The effect of random versus negotiated help on the learning of English articles. *Language Awareness, 9*(1), 34–51.

Nation, I. S. P. (2009). *Teaching ESL/EFL reading and writing.* New York, NY: Routledge, Taylor & Francis.

Nation, I. S. P., & Newton, J. (2009). *Teaching ESL/EFL listening and speaking.* London, United Kingdom: Taylor & Francis.

Nattinger, J., & DeCarrico, J. (1992). *Lexical phrases and language teaching.* Oxford, United Kingdom: Oxford University Press.

Nelson, G. L., & Murphy, J. M. (1992). An L2 writing group: Talk and social dimension. *Journal of Second Language Writing, 1,* 171–193.

Nevo, D., & Shohamy, E. (1984). *Applying the joint committee's evaluation standards for the assessment of alternative testing methods.* Paper presented at the Annual Meeting of the American Educational Research Association, New Orleans, LA.

Newlands, A., Anderson, A. H., & Mullin, J. (2003). Adapting communicative strategies to computer-mediated communication: An analysis of task performance and dialogue structure. *Applied Cognitive Psychology, 17,* 325–348.

Nik, N. (2010). *Examining the language learning potential of a task-based approach to synchronous computer-mediated communication* (Unpublished doctoral dissertation). Victoria University of Wellington, Wellington, New Zealand.

Nik, N., & Adams, R. (2009). TBLT and SCMC: How do students use communication strategies? *Asian Journal of English Language Teaching, 19,* 135–158.

Nik, N., Adams, R., & Newton, J. (2012). Writing to learn via text-SCMC: Task implementation and focus on form. *Journal of Second Language Writing, 21,* 23–39.

Niu, R. (2009). Effect of task-inherent production modes on EFL learners' focus on form. *Language Awareness, 18,* 384–402.

Norton, B. (2000). *Identity and language learning.* Harlow, United Kingdom: Pearson.

Norton, B., & Toohey, K. (2001). Identity, language learning and social change. *Language Teaching, 44*(4), 412–446.

Nuevo, A. M. (2006). *Task complexity and interaction: L2 learning opportunities and development* (Unpublished doctoral dissertation). Georgetown University, Washington, D.C.

Nunan, D. (1999). *Second language teaching and learning.* Boston, MA: Heinle & Heinle.

Ockey, G. (2009). The effects of group members' personalities on a test taker's L2 group oral discussion test scores. *Language Testing, 26*(2), 161–186.

O'Donnell, A. M. (2006). The role of peers and group learning. In P. Alexander & P. Winne (Eds.), *Handbook of educational psychology* (2nd ed., pp. 781–802). Mahwah, NJ: Lawrence Erlbaum Associates.

Ogden, L. (2000). Collaborative tasks, collaborative children: An analysis of reciprocity during peer interaction at key stage 1. *British Educational Research Journal, 26*(2), 211–216.

Oh, J. S., Jun, S.-A., Knightly, L. M., & Au, T. (2003). Holding on to childhood language memory. *Cognition, 86*(3), B53–B64.

Ohta, A. S. (2000a). Rethinking interaction in SLA: Developmentally appropriate assistance in the zone of proximal development and the acquisition of L2 grammar. In J. P. Lantolf

(Ed.), *Sociocultural theory and second language learning* (pp. 51–78). Oxford, United Kingdom: Oxford University Press.

Ohta, A. S. (2000b). Rethinking recasts: A learner-centered examination of corrective feedback in the Japanese language classroom. In J. K. Hall & L. S. Verplaetse (Eds.), *Second and foreign language learning through classroom interaction* (pp. 47–72). Mahwah, NJ: Lawrence Erlbaum Associates.

Ohta, A. S. (2001). *Second language acquisition processes in the classroom: Learning Japanese.* Mahwah, NJ: Lawrence Erlbaum Associates.

Oliver, R. (1995). Negative feedback in child NS/NNS conversation. *Studies in Second Language Acquisition, 18*(4), 459–481.

Oliver, R., Philp, J., & Duchesne, S. (2012). *Children's engagement in task based interaction: Does age make a difference?* Unpublished manuscript, Curtin University, Perth, Australia.

Oliver, R., Philp, J., & Mackey, A. (2008). The impact of teacher input, guidance and feedback on ESL children's task-based interactions. In J. Philp, A. Mackey, & R. Oliver (Eds.), *Second language acquisition and the younger learner* (pp. 131–148). Amsterdam, The Netherlands: John Benjamins.

Ortega, L. (2007). Meaningful L2 practice in foreign language classrooms: A cognitive-interactionist SLA perspective. In R. DeKeyser, *Practice in a second language* (pp. 180–207). Cambridge, United Kingdom: Cambridge University Press.

Ortega, L. (2009). Interaction and attention to form in L2 text-based computer-mediated communication. In A. Mackey & C. Polio (Eds.), *Multiple perspectives on interaction in second language acquisition: Second language research in honor of Susan M. Gass.* New York, NY: Taylor & Francis.

Osman, G., & Herring, S. C. (2007). Interaction, facilitation, and deep learning in cross-cultural chat: A case study. *Internet and Higher Education, 10,* 125–141.

Paradis, J. (2007). Second language acquisition in childhood. In E. Hoff & M. Shatz (Eds.), *Blackwell handbook of language development* (pp. 387–406). Malden, MA: Blackwell.

Park, S. (2010). The influence of pretask instructions and pretask planning on focus on form during Korean EFL task-based interaction. *Language Teaching Research, 14*(1), 9–26.

Paulus, T. M. (1999). The effect of peer and teacher feedback on student writing. *Journal of Second Language Writing, 8,* 265–289.

Pavlenko, A. (2002). Postcultural approaches to the study of social factors in second language learning and use. In V. Cook (Ed.), *Portraits of the L2 user* (pp. 275–302). Clevedon, Avon, United Kingdom: Multilingual Matters.

Pawley, A., & Syder, F. (1983). Two puzzles for linguistic theory: Native-like selection and native-like fluency. In J. C. Richards & R. Schmidt (Eds.), *Language and communication* (pp. 191–227). London, United Kingdom: Longman.

Pellegrini, A., & Blatchford, P. (2000). *The child at school: Interactions with peers and teachers.* London, United Kingdom: Arnold; New York, NY: Oxford University Press.

Pellettieri, J. (2000). Negotiation in cyberspace: The role of chatting in the development of grammatical competence. In M. Warschauer & R. Kern (Eds.), *Network-based language teaching: Concepts and practice* (pp. 59–86). Cambridge, United Kingdom: Cambridge University Press.

Peng, J. (2007). Willingness to communicate in the Chinese EFL classroom: A cultural perspective. In J. Liu (Ed.), *English language teaching in China: New approaches, perspectives and standards* (pp. 250–269). London, United Kingdom: Continuum.

Peregoy, S., & Boyle, O. (1999). Multiple embedded scaffolds: Support for English speakers in a two-way Spanish immersion kindergarten. *Bilingual Research Journal, 23*(2/3), 135–146.

Perera, N. (2001). The role of prefabricated language in young children's second language acquisition. *Bilingual Research Journal 25*: 327–356.

Peterson, M. (2009). Learner interaction in synchronous CMC: a sociocultural perspective. *Computer Assisted Language Learning, 22*(4), 303–321.

Peterson, M. (2010a). Task-based language teaching in network-based CALL: An analysis of research on learner interaction in synchronous CMC. In M. Thomas & H. Reinders (Eds.), *Task-based language learning and teaching with technology* (pp. 41–62). London: Continuum.

Peterson, M. (2010b). Massively multiplayer online role-playing games as arenas for second language learning. *Computer Assisted Language Learning, 23*(5), 429–439.

Philp, J. (1993). [Formulaic sequences in language production of a 6 year old L2 learner.] Unpublished data.

Philp, J. (2012). The noticing hypothesis. In P. Robinson (Ed.), *Routledge encyclopedia of SLA* (pp. 464–467). New York, NY: Routledge.

Philp, J., & Duchesne, S. (2008). When the gate opens: The interaction between social and linguistic goals in child second language development. In J. Philp, R. Oliver, & A. Mackey (Eds.), *Second language acquisition and the younger learner* (pp. 83–103). Amsterdam, The Netherlands: John Benjamins.

Philp, J., & Iwashita, N. (2013). Talking, tuning in and noticing: Exploring the benefits of output in task-based peer interaction. *Language Awareness*. Retrieved at http://www.tandfonline.com/doi/abs/10.1080/09658416.2012.758128

Philp, J., & Mackey, A. (2010). Interaction research: What can socially informed approaches offer to cognitivists (and vice versa)? In R. Batstone (Ed.), *Sociocognitive perspectives on language use and language learning* (pp. 210–228). Oxford, United Kingdom: Oxford University Press.

Philp, J., Mackey, A., & Oliver, R. (2008). Child's play? Second language acquisition and the younger learner in context. In J. Philp, R. Oliver, & A. Mackey (Eds.), *Second language acquisition and the younger learner* (pp. 131–147). Amsterdam, The Netherlands: John Benjamins.

Philp, J., Oliver, R., & Mackey, A. (2006). The impact of planning time on children's task-based interactions. *System, 34*(4), 547–565.

Philp, J., & Tognini, R. (2010). Language acquisition in foreign language contexts and the differential benefits of interaction. *International Review of Applied Linguistics, 47*, 245–266.

Philp, J., Walter, S., & Basturkmen, H. (2010). Peer interaction in the foreign language classroom: What factors foster a focus on form? *Language Awareness, 19*(4), 261–279.

Pica, T. (1992, July). *Second language learning through interaction and the negotiation of conditions, processes, and outcomes*. Paper presented at the First Pacific Second Language Research Forum, Sydney, Australia.

Pica, T. (1994). Research on negotiation: What does it reveal about second-language learning condition, processes, and outcomes? *Language Learning, 44*(3), 493–527.

Pica, T. (2013). From input, output and comprehension to negotiation, evidence and attention: An overview of theory and research on learner interaction and SLA. In M. P. García Mayo, M. J. Gutierrez Mangado, & M. Martínez Adrián (Eds.), *Contemporary approaches to second language acquisition* (pp. 49–70). Amsterdam, The Netherlands: John Benjamins.

Pica, T., & Doughty, C. (1985a). Input and interaction in the communicative language classroom: A comparison of teacher-fronted and group activities. In S. Gass & C. Madden (Eds.), *Input in second language acquisition* (pp. 115–132). Lowley, MA: Newbury House.

Pica, T., & Doughty, C. (1985b). The role of group work in classroom second language acquisition. *Studies in Second Language Acquisition, 7*, 233–248.

Pica, T., Kanagy, R., & Falodun, J. (1993). Choosing and using communication tasks for second language instruction. In G. Crookes & S. Gass (Eds.), *Tasks and language learning: Integrating theory and practice* (pp. 9–34). Clevedon, Avon, United Kingdom: Multilingual Matters.

Pica, T., Lincoln-Porter, F., Paninos, D., & Linnell, J. D. (1996). Language learners' interaction: How does it address the input, output, and feedback needs of L2 learners? *TESOL Quarterly, 30*(1), 59–84.

Porter, P. A. (1986). How learners talk to each other: Input and interaction in task-centered discussions. In R. R. Day (Ed.), *Talking to learn: Conversation in second language acquisition* (pp. 200–222). Rowley, MA: Newbury House.

Ramsay, G. (2003). "Virtual" learning communities beyond the classroom: Perceptions of tertiary Chinese language and non-language learners. *Australian Review of Applied Linguistics Series S, 17,* 3–24.

Rankin, Y., Gold, R., & Gooch, B. (2006). 3D role-playing games as language learning tools. In E. Gröller & L. Szirmay-Kalos (Eds.), *Proceedings of EuroGraphics 2006* 25, 3. New York: ACM.

Reves, T. (1982). The group oral examination: A field experiment. *World Language English, 1*(4), 259–262.

Robinson, P. (2001). Task complexity, task difficulty, and task production: Exploring interactions in a componential framework. *Applied Linguistics, 22,* 27–57.

Robinson, P. (2005). Cognitive complexity and task sequencing: Studies in a componential framework for second language task design. *IRAL: International Review of Applied Linguistics in Language Teaching 43*(1), 1–33.

Robinson, P. (2007a). Criteria for classifying and sequencing pedagogic tasks. In M. P. Garcia-Mayo (Ed.), *Investigating tasks in formal language learning* (pp. 7–26). Clevedon, Avon, United Kingdom: Multilingual Matters.

Robinson, P. (2007b). Task complexity, theory of mind, and intentional reasoning: Effects on L2 speech production, interaction, uptake and perceptions of task difficulty. *IRAL: International Review of Applied Linguistics in Language Teaching, 45,* 193–213.

Rohrbeck, C. A., Ginsburg-Block, M. D., Fantuzzo, J. W., & Miller, T. R. (2003). Peer-assisted learning interventions with elementary school students: A meta-analytic review. *Journal of Educational Psychology, 95,* 240–257.

Ross, S., & Berwick, R. (1992). The discourse of accommodation in oral proficiency interviews. *Studies in Second Language Acquisition, 14*(2), 159–176.

Ross-Feldman, L. (2007). Interaction in the L2 classroom: Does gender influence learning opportunities? In A. Mackey (Ed.), *Conversational interaction in second language acquisition: A collection of empirical studies* (pp. 53–77). Oxford, United Kingdom: Oxford University Press.

Salomon, G., & Globerson, T. (1989). When teams do not function the way they ought to. *The Journal of Educational Research, 13*(1), 89–100.

Samuda, V., & Bygate, M. (2008). *Tasks in second language learning.* New York, NY: Palgrave/Macmillan.

Samuda, V., & Bygate, M. (2009). Creating pressure in task pedagogy: The joint roles of field, purpose, and engagement within the interaction approach. In A. Mackey & C. Polio (Eds.), *Multiple perspectives on interaction* (pp. 90–116). New York, NY: Routledge.

Sato, M. (2007). Social relationships in conversational interaction: Comparison of learner-learner and learner-NS dyads. *JALT Journal, 29*(2), 183–208.

Sato, M., & Lyster, R. (2007). Modified output of Japanese ELF learners: Variable effects of interlocutor versus feedback types. In A. Mackey (Ed.), *Conversational interaction in second language acquisition* (pp. 123–142). Oxford, United Kingdom: Oxford University Press.

Sauro, S. (2009). Computer-mediated corrective feedback and the development of L2 grammar. *Language Learning & Technology, 13*(1), 96–120.

Sauro, S. (2011). SCMC for SLA: A research synthesis. *CALICO Journal, 28,* 369–391.

Sauro, S., & Smith, B. (2010). Investigating L2 performance in text chat. *Applied Linguistics, 31*(4), 554–577.

Saville, N., & Hargreaves, P. (1999). Assessing speaking in the revised FCE. *English Language Teaching Journal, 53*(1), 42–51.

Schegloff, E. A., Jefferson, G., & Sacks, H. (1977). The preference for self-correction in the organisation of repair in conversation. *Language, 53,* 361–382.

Schmidt, R. (1992). Psychological mechanisms underlying second language fluency. *Studies in Second Language Acquisition, 14*(3), 357–385.

Schmidt, R. (1995). Consciousness and foreign language learning: A tutorial on the role of attention and awareness in learning. In R. Schmidt (Ed.), *Attention and awareness in foreign language learning* (pp. 1–64). Honolulu, HI: Second Language Teaching & Curriculum Center, University of Hawai'i at Manoa.

Schmidt, R. (2001). Attention. In P. Robinson (Ed.), *Cognition and second language instruction* (pp. 3–32). New York, NY: Cambridge University Press.

Schmidt, R., & Frota, S. N. (1986). Developing basic conversational ability in a second language: A case study of an adult learner of Portuguese. In R. Day (Ed.), *Talking to learn: Conversation in second language acquisition* (pp. 237–326). Rowley, MA: Newbury House.

Segalowitz, N. (2000). Automaticity and attentional skill in fluent performance. In H. Riggenbach (Ed.), *Perspectives on fluency* (pp. 200–219). Ann Arbor, MI: University of Michigan Press.

Segalowitz, N. (2003). Automaticity and second language acquisition. In C. Doughty & M. Long (Eds.), *The handbook of second language acquisition* (pp. 382–408). Oxford, United Kingdom: Blackwell.

Segalowitz, N. (2010). *The cognitive bases of second language fluency.* New York: Routledge.

Sfard, A. (1998). On two metaphors for learning and the dangers of choosing just one. *Educational Researchers, 27,* 4–13.

Shang, H.-F. (2007). An exploratory study of e-mail application on FL writing performance. *Computer Assisted Language Learning, 20*(1), 79–96.

Shehadeh, A. (2001). Self and other-initiated modified output during task-based interaction. *TESOL Quarterly, 35,* 433–457.

Shekary, M., & Tahririan, M. H. (2006). Negotiation of meaning and noticing in text-based online chat. *The Modern Language Journal, 90*(4), 557–573.

Shimanoka, Y., Nakazato, K., Gondo, Y., & Takayama, M. (2002). *NEO-PI-R NEO-FFI manual.* Tokyo, Japan: Tokyo Shinri.

Shin, D. S. (2006). ESL students' computer-mediated communication practices: Context configuration. *Language Learning & Technology, 10*(3), 65–84.

Shohamy, E., Reves, T., & Bejarano, T. (1986). Introducing a new comprehensive test of oral proficiency. *English Language Teaching Journal, 40,* 212–220.

Sinclair, J. (1991). *Corpus, concordance, collocation.* Oxford, United Kingdom: Oxford University Press.

Skehan, P. (1996). A framework for the implementation of task-based instruction. *Applied Linguistics, 17,* 38–62.

Skehan, P. (1998). *A cognitive approach to language learning.* Oxford, United Kingdom: Oxford University Press.

Skehan, P. (2001). Tasks and language performance assessment. In M. Bygate, P. Skehan, & M. Swain (Eds.), *Researching pedagogic tasks, second language learning, teaching and testing* (pp. 167–185). Harlow, UK: Longman.

Smith, B. (2003a). Computer-mediated negotiated interaction: An expanded model. *The Modern Language Journal, 87,* 38–57.

Smith, B. (2003b). The use of communication strategies in computer-mediated communication. *System, 31,* 29–53.

Smith, B. (2004). Computer-mediated negotiated interaction and lexical acquisition. *Studies in Second Language Acquisition, 26,* 365–398.

Smith, B. (2005). The relationship between negotiated interaction, learner uptake, and lexical acquisition in task-based computer-mediated communication. *TESOL Quarterly, 39*(1), 33–58.

Smith, B. (2008). Methodological hurdles in captures CMC data: The case of the missing self-repair. *Language Learning & Technology, 12*(1), 85–103.

Smith, B., Alvarez-Torres, M. J., & Zhao, Y. (2003). Features of CMC technologies and their impact on language learners' online interaction. *Computers in Human Behavior, 19,* 703–729.

Sotillo, M. S. (2000). Discourse functions and syntactic complexity in synchronous and asynchronous communication. *Language Learning & Technology, 4*(1), 82–119.

Sotillo, M. S. (2005). Corrective feedback via instant messenger learning activities in NS-NNS and NNS-NNS dyads. *CALICO Journal, 22,* 467–496.

Soto, C., John, O., Gosling, S., & Potter, J. (2011). Age differences in personality traits from 10 to 65: Big five domains and facets in a large cross-sectional sample. *Journal of Personality and Social Psychology, 100*(2), 330–348.

Storch, N. (1999). Are two heads better than one? Pair work and grammatical accuracy. *System, 27,* 363–374.

Storch, N. (2002). Patterns of interaction in ESL pair work. *Language Learning, 52*(1), 119–158.

Storch, N. (2005). Collaborative writing: Product, process, and students' reflections. *Journal of Second Language Writing, 14*(3), 153–173.

Storch, N. (2008). Metatalk in a pair work activity: Level of engagement and implications for language development. *Language Awareness, 17,* 95–114.

Storch, N. (2011). Collaborative writing in L2 contexts: Processes, outcomes, and future directions. *Annual Review of Applied Linguistics, 31*(3), 275–288.

Storch, N., & Wigglesworth, G. (2003). Is there a role for the use of the L1 in an L2 setting? *TESOL Quarterly, 37,* 760–770.

Strong, M. (1983). Social styles and the second language acquisition of Spanish-speaking kindergartners. *TESOL Quarterly, 17,* 241–258.

Sullivan, N., & Pratt, E. (1996). A comparative study of two ESL writing environments: A computer-assisted classroom and a traditional oral classroom. *System 29*(4), 491–501.

Sullivan, P. (2000). Language play and communicative language teaching in Vietnamese classroom. In J. Lantolf (Ed.), *Sociocultural theory and second language learning* (pp. 115–131). Oxford, United Kingdom: Oxford University Press.

Swain, M. (1985). Communicative competence: Some roles of comprehensible input and comprehensible output in its development. In S. Gass & C. Madden (Eds.), *Input in second language acquisition* (pp. 235–253). Rowley, MA: Newbury House.

Swain, M. (1995). Three functions of output in second language learning. In G. Cook & B. Seidhofer (Eds.), *For H. G. Widdowson: Principles and practice in the study of language: A festschrift on the occasion of his 60th birthday* (pp. 125–144). Oxford, United Kingdom: Oxford University Press.

Swain, M. (1998). Focus on form through conscious reflection. In C. Doughty & J. Williams (Eds.), *Focus on form in classroom second language acquisition* (pp. 64–82). Cambridge, United Kingdom: Cambridge University Press.

Swain, M. (2000). The output hypothesis and beyond: Mediating acquisition through collaborative dialogue. In J. P. Lantolf (Ed.), *Sociocultural theory and second language learning* (pp. 97–114). Oxford, United Kingdom: Oxford University Press.

Swain, M. (2005). The output hypothesis: Theory and research. In E. Hinkel (Ed.), *Handbook of research in second language teaching and learning* (pp. 471–483). Mahwah, NJ: Lawrence Erlbaum Associates.

Swain, M. (2010). Talking-it-through: Language as a source of learning. In R. Batstone (Ed.), *Sociocognitive perspectives on language use and language learning* (pp. 112–130). Oxford, United Kingdom: Oxford University Press.

Swain, M., Brooks, L., & Tocalli-Beller, A. (2002). Peer-peer dialogue as a means of second language learning. *Annual Review of Applied Linguistics, 22,* 171–185.

Swain, M., & Deters, P. (2007). "New" mainstream SLA theory: Expanded and enriched. *The Modern Language Journal, 91,* 820–836.

Swain, M., & Lapkin, S. (1995). Problems in output and the cognitive processes they generate: A step towards second language learning. *Applied Linguistics, 16*(3), 371–391.

Swain, M., & Lapkin, S. (1998). Interaction and second language learning: Two adolescent French immersion students working together. *The Modern Language Journal, 82,* 320–337.

Swain, M., & Lapkin, S. (2002). Talking it through: Two French immersion learners' response to reformulation. *International Journal of Educational Research, 37,* 285–304.

Swain, M., & Suzuki, W. (2008). Interaction, output, and communicative language learning. In B. Spolsky & F. M. Hult (Eds.), *The handbook of educational linguistics* (pp. 557–570). Malden, MA: Blackwell.

Swan, M. (2005). Legislation by hypothesis: The case of task-based instruction. *Applied Linguistics, 26*(3), 376–401.

Szuber, A. (2007). Native Polish-speaking adolescent immigrants' exposure to and use of English. *International Journal of Bilingual Education and Bilingualism, 10*(1), 26–57.

Tarone, E., & Swain, M. (1995). A sociolinguistic perspective on second language use in immersion classrooms. *The Modern Language Journal, 79,* 166–178.

Taylor, L. (2000). Investigating the paired speaking test format. *Cambridge ESOL Research Notes, 2,* 14–15.

Taylor, L., & Wigglesworth, G. (2009). Are two heads better than one? Pair work in L2 assessment contexts. *Language Testing, 26,* 325–339.

Tinker-Sachs, G. (2007). The challenges of adopting and adapting task-based cooperative teaching and learning in an EFL context. In K. v. d. Branden, K. v. Gorp, & M. Verhelst (Eds.), *Tasks in action: Task-based language education from a classroom-based perspective* (pp. 253–264). Newcastle, UK: Cambridge Scholars Press.

Tognini, R. (2008). *Interaction in languages other than English classes in Western Australian primary and secondary schools: Theory, practice and perceptions* (Unpublished, doctoral dissertation). Edith Cowan University, Perth, Australia.

Tognini, R., Philp, J., & Oliver, R. (2010). Rehearsing, conversing, working it out: Second language use in peer interaction. *Australian Review of Applied Linguistics, 33*(3), 28.1–28.25.

Toohey, K. (1998). Breaking them up; taking them away: ESL students in grade one. *TESOL Quarterly, 32,* 61–84.

Toohey, K. (2000). *Learning English at school.* Clevedon, UK: Multilingual Matters.

Topping, K., & Ehly, S. (1998). Introduction to peer assisted learning. In K. Topping & S. Ehly (Eds.), *Peer assisted learning* (pp. 1–24). Mahwah, NJ: Lawrence Erlbaum Associates.

Toth, P. D. (2008). Teacher- and learner-led discourse in task-based grammar instruction: Providing procedural assistance for L2 morphosyntactic development. *Language Learning, 58*(2), 237–283.

Underhill, N. (1987). *Testing spoken language: A handbook of oral testing techniques.* Cambridge, United Kingdom: Cambridge University Press.

Ushioda, E. (1996). *Learner autonomy 5: The role of motivation.* Dublin, Ireland: Authentik.

Valdés, G. (2001). Heritage language students: Profiles and possibilities. In J. Peyton, J. Ranard, & S. McGinnis (Eds.), *Heritage languages in America: Preserving a national resource* (pp. 37–80). McHenry, IL: The Center for Applied Linguistics and Delta Systems.

van Lier, L. (1989). Reeling, writhing, drawling, stretching and fainting in coils: Oral proficiency interviews as conversations. *TESOL Quarterly, 23,* 489–508.

van Lier, L. (1996). *Interaction in the language curriculum: Awareness, autonomy and authenticity.* London, United Kingdom: Longman.

van Lier, L. (1998). The relationship between consciousness, interaction and language learning. *Language Awareness, 7*(2–3), 128–145.

van Lier, L. (2000). From input to affordance: Social-interactive learning from an ecological perspective. In J. Lantolf (ed.) *Sociocultural theory and second language learning,* (pp. 245–260). Oxford: Oxford University Press.

Van Moere, A. (2006). Validity evidence in a university group oral test. *Language Testing, 23,* 411–440.

Van Moere, A., & Kobayashi, M. (2003, July). *Who speaks most in this group? Does that matter?* Paper presented at the annual meeting of the Language Testing and Research Colloquium, Reading, United Kingdom.

Varonis, E. M., & Gass, S. (1985). Non-native/non-native conversations: A model for negotiation of meaning. *Applied Linguistics, 6*(1), 71–90.

Villamil, O. S., & de Guerrero, M. C. M. (1996). Peer revision in the L2 classroom: Social-cognitive activities, mediating strategies, and aspects of social behavior. *Journal of Second Language Writing, 5*(1), 51–75.

Vygotsky, L. S. (1978). *Mind in society: The development of higher psychological processes.* Cambridge, MA: Harvard University Press.

Vygotsky, L. S. (1986). *Thought and language.* Cambridge, MA: MIT Press.

Wajnryb, R. (1990). *Grammar dictation.* Oxford, United Kingdom: Oxford University Press.

Ware, P. D., & Kramsch, C. (2005). Toward an intercultural stance: Teaching German and English through telecollaboration. *The Modern Language Journal, 89*(2), 190–205.

Warschauer, M. (1996). Comparing face-to-face and electronic discussion in the second language classroom. *CALICO Journal, 13*(2), 7–26.

Warschauer, M. (1997). Computer-mediated collaborative learning: Theory and practice. *The Modern Language Journal, 81,* 470–481.

Warschauer, M. (1998). Researching technology in TESOL: Determinist, instrumental, and critical approaches. *TESOL Quarterly, 32,* 757–761.

Watanabe, Y. (2008). Peer-peer interaction between L2 learners of different proficiency levels: Their interactions and reflections. *The Canadian Modern Language Review, 64*(4), 605–635.

Watanabe, Y., & Swain, M. (2007). Effects of proficiency differences and patterns of pair interaction on second language learning: Collaborative dialogue between adult ESL learners. *Language Teaching Research, 11*(2), 121–142.

Watanabe, Y., & Swain, M. (2008). Perception of learner proficiency: Its impact on the interaction between an ESL learner and her higher and lower proficiency partners. *Language Awareness, 17*(2), 115–130.

Weaver, C. (2007). Willingness to communicate: A mediating factor in the interaction between learners and tasks. In K. v. d. Branden & K. v. G. M. Verhest (Eds.), *Tasks in action: Task-based language education from a classroom-based perspective* (pp. 159–194). Newcastle, UK: Cambridge Scholars Press.

Weir, C. (1993). *Understanding and developing language tests.* New York, NY: Prentice Hall.

Weissberg, R. (2000). Developing relationships in the acquisition of English syntax: Writing versus speech. *Learning and Instruction, 10,* 37–53.

White, J. (2008). Speeding up acquisition of *his* and *her.* Explicit L1/L2 contrasts help. In J. Philp, R. Oliver, & A. Mackey (Eds.), *Second language acquisition and the younger learner* (pp. 191–230). Amsterdam, The Netherlands: John Benjamins.

Wigglesworth, G., & Storch, N. (2009). Pair versus individual writing: Effects on fluency, complexity and accuracy. *Language Testing, 26*(3), 445–466.

Willett, J. (1995). Becoming first graders in an L2: An ethnographic study of L2 socialization. *TESOL Quarterly, 29*(3), 473–503.

Williams, J. (1999). Learner-generated attention to form. *Language Learning, 49*(4), 583–625.

Williams, J. (2001). The effectiveness of spontaneous attention to form. *System, 29,* 325–340.

Williams, J. (2005). Form-focused instruction. In E. Hinkel (Ed.), *Handbook of research in second language teaching and learning* (pp. 673–691). Mahwah, NJ: Lawrence Erlbaum Associates.

Willis, D., & Willis, J. (2007). *Doing task-based teaching.* Oxford, United Kingdom: Oxford University Press.

Wong Fillmore, L. (1976). *The second time around: Cognitive and social strategies in second language acquisition* (Unpublished doctoral dissertation). Stanford University, San Francisco, CA.

Wray, A. (2000). Formulaic sequences in second language teaching: Principle and practice. *Applied Linguistics 21*(4), 463–489.

Wray, A. (2002). *Formulaic language and the lexicon.* Cambridge, United Kingdom: Cambridge University Press.

Wray, A., & Perkins, M. (2000). The functions of formulaic language: An integrated model. *Language & Communication, 20*(1), 1–28.

Wray, D. (2010). From learning to teaching. In J. Arthur & T. Cremin (Eds.), *Learning to teach in the primary school* (pp. 53–65). London, United Kingdom: Routledge.

Yates, S. J. (1996). Oral and written linguistic aspects of computer conferencing. In S. Herring (Ed.), *Computer-mediated communication: Linguistic, social and cross-cultural perspectives* (pp. 29–46). Amsterdam, The Netherlands: John Benjamins.

Yilmaz, Y. (2011). Task effects on focus on form in synchronous computer-mediated communication. *The Modern Language Journal, 95*(1), 115–132.

Young, R., & Milanovic, M. (1992). Discourse variation in oral proficiency interviews. *Studies in Second Language Acquisition, 14,* 403–424.

Yule, G., & Macdonald, D. (1990). Resolving referential conflicts in L2 interaction: The effect of proficiency and interactive role. *Language Learning, 40*(4), 539–556.

Zhang, E. Y. (2007). TBLT innovation in primary school English language teaching in mainland China. In K. v. d. Branden, K. v. Grop, & M. Verhelst (Eds.), *Tasks in action: Task-based language education from a classroom-based perspective* (pp. 68–91). Newcastle, UK: Cambridge Scholars Press.

Zhao, H. (2010). Investigating learners' use and understanding of peer and teacher feedback on writing: A comparative study in a Chinese English writing classroom. *Assessing Writing, 15*(1), 3–17.

AUTHOR INDEX

SUBJECT INDEX